MEDIA INDUSTRIES

ANNENBERG/LONGMAN COMMUNICATION BOOKS
George Gerbner and Marsha Siefert, Editors
The Annenberg School of Communications
University of Pennsylvania, Philadelphia

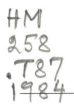

Joseph Turow
Purdue University

MEDIA INDUSTRIES

The Production of News and Entertainment

Longman

New York & London

Excerpts (on page 8) from lyrics of "Let Me Sing and I'm Happy" by Irving Berlin. Copyright 1928, 1929 Irving Berlin. Copyright renewed 1955, 1956 Irving Berlin. Reproduced by permission Irving Berlin Music Corporation.

Portions (on pages 72–76) of "The Role of 'The Audience' in Publishing Children's Books" by Joseph Turow in the *Journal of Popular Culture*, vol. 16. Copyright 1982 the Journal of Popular Culture. Reprinted by permission.

Portions (on pages 85–89) of "Another View of Citizen Feedback to Mass Media" by Joseph Turow in *Public Opinion Quarterly*, vol. 41. Copyright 1978 Public Opinion Quarterly. Reprinted by permission.

Portions (on pages 163–164) of the *Six Gun Mystique* by John Cawelti. Copyright 1975 by Popular Press. Reprinted by permission.

Portions (on pages 168–169) of *The Fiction Factory* by Quentin Reynolds. Copyright 1955 Street and Smith Publications, Inc. Reprinted by permission of Random House, Inc.

Portions (on pages 171–174) of "Casting for Television: The Anatomy of Social Typing" by Joseph Turow in the *Journal of Communications*, vol. 28. Copyright 1978 Journal of Communications. Reprinted by permission.

Portions (on pages 180–182) of "Unconventional Programs on Commercial Television" by Joseph Turow in *Individuals in Mass Media Organizations* edited by James Ettema and D. Charles Whitney. Copyright 1983 Sage Publications. Reprinted by permission.

4/78 / June 85

Media Industries
The Production of News and Entertainment

Longman Inc., 1560 Broadway, New York, N.Y. 10036
Associated companies, branches, and representatives
throughout the world.

Developmental Editor: Gordon T. R. Anderson
Editorial and Design Supervisor: Thomas Bacher
Manufacturing Supervisor: Marion Hess
Production Supervisor: Ferne Y. Kawahara

Library of Congress Cataloging in Publication Data
Turow, Joseph.
    Media industries.

    (Annenberg/Longman communication books)
    Bibliography: p.
    Includes index.
    1. Mass media—Social aspects.   2. Power (Social
sciences)   I. Title.   II. Series.
HM258.T87 1984   302.2′34   83–17519
ISBN 0–582–28359–0

Manufactured in the United States of America
Printing: 9 8 7 6 5 4 3 2 1   Year: 92 91 90 89 88 87 86 85 84

To Judith

Contents

Preface

This book is the product of my attempt, over the past decade and a half, to answer two basic questions: (1) What forces cause continuity and change in mass media material, and (2) to what extent can publics use those forces to bring about the changes in mass media that they want?

The more I learn, the more I realize how complex the answers to these questions are. They are intertwined tightly with the issue of power and control in society. They relate to the broad spectrum of societal resources that define the holders of power and how they use it. And they relate to industrial and organizational processes through which power and control are exercised.

I was an undergraduate at the University of Pennsylvania, majoring in English and dabbling in American Studies, when I began to work systematically on this subject. I carried on the work during my graduate studies at Penn's Annenberg School of Communications, and it continues in the Department of Communication at Purdue University. There have been many people to thank along the way; some of them don't even know they helped me. On the undergraduate level, Benjamin Fisher, Robert Lucid, Neil Leonard, and Garth Jowett planted fascinating ideas about culture and society, and pointed out the joys of systematic research in the area. In graduate school, George Gerbner, Robert Lewis Shayon, Larry Gross, Charles Wright, and William Melody were particularly instrumental in guiding my interests. So were Annenberg students—Doug Goldschmidt,

Steve Rappaport, Godfrey Pinto, Jim Miller, and others. Those were good times. We learned a lot from one another.

Fortunately, the same has been true at Purdue. Being in a friendly atmosphere where people value ideas and exchange them freely has been conducive to research. Money to carry out come of the investigations described in this book was provided by the Purdue Research Foundation. The Federal Communications Commission and (for summer teaching support) UCLA also gave me the wherewithal to carry out certain projects.

Additional thanks go to Marsha Siefert, who edited the manuscript with strong doses of good advice; to three anonymous reviewers, who will see that I adopted a good number of their suggestions; to Sandy Wilson at Purdue who word-processed the manuscript over a number of months; and to Tren Andersen and Tom Bacher who moved the process along efficiently at Longman.

Through it all, my family has always been there, interested, supportive and encouraging. Abraham and Danuta Turow, especially, have combined a strong awareness of the value of education with a deep-rooted humanism. That is the best example a son could have. Judith Turow, my wife, has followed this book and several other projects from beginning to end. Her suggestions, patience, and understanding have been invaluable.

Joseph Turow

One

Mass Media Industries: A Resource Dependence Approach

I wonder if I could have survived my childhood without the escape from it offered by radio. A fat kid, I could play on the same team as Jack Armstrong and still be reassured by the Fat Man that "heavy" guys could be heroes in their own right. A bookworm, I could be smugly satisfied that avid readers such as Ellery Queen, Sherlock Holmes, and I really won out in the end. And, in the midst of poverty, Jack, Doc, and Reggie assured me that the only good thing to do with money was to get rid of it fast so you could get on to something important.

Jim Harmon, in *The Great Radio Heroes*[1]

I must confess, Lone Ranger, that lately I have been having some uneasy feelings about you and what you did to me. You were the creation of a commercialized image, an image that made us both believe that reality was something other than what we experienced.

Richard Quinney, in *The Insurgent Sociologist*[2]

The Lone Ranger. Sherlock Holmes. Ellery Queen. Jack Armstrong (All American Boy). The Fat Man. Jack Packard, Doc Long, and Reggie York of radio's "I Love a Mystery." Names that can jump off the page to ignite memories and fantasies of millions of Americans, and of millions upon millions of people throughout the world. Certainly, some of the names are more famous than others. Sherlock Holmes, The Lone Ranger, and Ellery Queen have managed to cross several generations. They have found new audiences—and new adventures—through millions of books and magazines and "comic" strips, and through movies and radio and television (TV). Jack Armstrong, the Fat Man, and the "I Love a Mystery" crew have not been as lucky. Relegated essentially to United States network radio of the 1930s and 1940s (though Armstrong did headline a movie serial in 1949), those characters crossed the decades primarily in the nostalgic memories of their original listeners, and in the piles of sponsor-spawned promotional gadgets (badges, pins, toys, stickers, and more) that continue to be traded at flea markets and "collectibles" fairs throughout the country.[3]

Actually, though, the overall significance of such heroes both then and now should not be measured only by their ability to boost circulation figures or fill ticket counters single-handedly. The existence of many characters similar to those characters, and of many stories similar to their stories, are perhaps more important signs of collective social attention. Analysts of popular arts have long recognized that book, newspaper, comic book, record, movie, radio, and television materials often share patterns of characterization, setting, action, and values that transcend specific titles or series.[4] Take the Fat Man as an example. An obese detective also called Brad Runyon, he bore many of the personality characteristics of, and saw many of the same kinds of cases as, a choir of "hard boiled" private eyes who flourished in various mass media during the two decades before the Fat Man's appearance in 1947.[5]

Many volumes have been written to clarify the links binding various heroes and stories of "popular culture." Several fields—including the long-established disciplines of Sociology and Psychology, and the newer areas of Communication and American Studies—have converged upon these relatively recently respectable academic prey. Although it is rarely made explicit, the reference to "culture" in popular culture seems to resonate with Clyde Kluckhohn's definition: "A 'culture' refers to the distinctive way of life of a group of people, their designs for living."[6] And, indeed, a lesson one might safely draw from the fields' cumulative work is that the mass media of communication—television, radio, movies, records, newspapers, magazines, books, billboards—present worlds of people and their activities that are often so textured and patterned that they can very well be called cultures. Thinking back to favorite, or least favorite, books, TV dramas, or news programs reinforces this impression. The reader, viewer, or listener finds a world with richly portrayed lifestyles that may or may not resemble his or her own. At the extreme, the visitor may even plunge psychically into the mass media culture, if only for a while. A search for an analogy to this experience recalls a curious media-created attempt to portray its reverse: In Max Fleischer's "Out of the Inkwell" films from the 1920s, an animated Koko the Clown regularly materialized out of his cartoonist's inkwell or pen point and cavorted with the live setting around the drawing board. Probably the clown's wildest entrance took place in "Koko Gets Egg-cited," in which Koko took pen in hand to "draw"—and then interact with—the entire live-action background, including Fleischer, as if it were a cartoon.[7]

Koko the Clown never tried to analyze the "effect" the live-action environment had on his existence. By contrast, human beings have for centuries been debating, exploring, and worrying about the impact mass media content—both news and non-news materials—have on people (usually others) and on society. Particularly since the advent of the systematic investigatory tools of social research in the nineteenth and twentieth centuries, and since the parallel proliferation of media (records, movies, radio) that did not require literacy, the effects of mass media images have drawn steady attention from university professors, pressure group leaders, and government officials. Their concerns and findings have moved to the central legislative stage every so often as a result of periodic public paroxysms by media-conscious groups or lawmakers, usually about the effects of violence, sex, or stereotyped portrayals in the most pervasive medium of the day.

The energy with which researchers have been investigating the consequences, and the nature, of mass media materials has only recently begun to be matched by attempts to analyze the way those materials got there in the first place. It is not as if important basic questions have been lacking. What influences guide the creation and development of mass media material? Can patterns regarding those influences be observed across several mass media in a society? How does interaction among the many organizations in a mass media industry (such as the TV industry or movie industry) affect the selection, timing, and release of messages directed at the public? To what extent are conflicts, constraints, and opportunities within the organizations that produce the material relevant to understanding the spectrum of choice in the marketplace of ideas? These and other queries invite careful thought, discussion, and systematic research.

This book picks up their invitation. Its purpose is to set forth a systematic framework for understanding the production of mass media culture. And its aim is to do that by using a fruitful perspective that has not been applied to the subject before: the "resource dependence" approach.

A DEFINITION OF MASS COMMUNICATION

An appropriate place to start is with a definition of mass communication that will be useful in setting guideposts and directions. That means homing in on the organizational nature of mass communication. It can be argued that its organizational nature is mass communication's most distinctive feature. It is the organizational context of message creation that distinguishes mass communication from the individual speaker's presentation of a talk to a crowd and from exhibition of individually conceived, produced, and circulated books or video presentations. Historians generally agree that a revolution in the distribution of knowledge through writing took place in Western society when the machine and the organization became central elements in the marketplace of ideas.[8] By the nineteenth century, newspaper, book, magazine, and sheet music publishing firms had become the primary societal mediators between individual literary creators (call them reporters, writers, or "artists") and the public, by virtue of the firms' role of selecting and editing material, reproducing it quickly on expensive equipment, and arranging for its distribution. As a consequence, the writer had the potential of influencing more people than he or she could possibly reach by distributing the work through nonorganizational channels (standing with handmade copies on a street corner, for example). But for this privilege the artist had to devolve many important decisions—including the decision to display his or her talents—upon members of a publishing firm whose priorities might be quite different from his or her own.

From this standpoint, mass communication can be defined as the industrialized ("mass") production, reproduction, and multiple distribution of messages through technological devices. The word "industralized" means that the process is carried out by a mass media complex or industry—that is, by a conglomeration of organizations that regularly interact in the process of producing and distributing messages. "Industrialized" also implies the use of technology for production and distribution. It is a use that provides the potential for reaching large, separated, diverse groups of people. Note, however, that this definition does not set forth any requirements about the number and nature of the people attending to the messages. Whether and how the production process is influenced by the size and characteristics of the audience should be a matter of discussion and empirical examination; "audience" is a complicated term, as we will see.

The definition does posit that mass communication involves the technological creation of multiple copies of messages and the technological distribution of those messages to a variety of locations. It therefore excludes touring entertainment groups such as rock bands and symphony orchestras. While they often require several consistently interacting organizations to help them produce and exhibit their music on the road, they do not technologically copy themselves for performance in various places. If they do—on film, tape, or record—that becomes mass communication.

It will be convenient, and appropriate, to talk about particular mass media industries throughout this book. An industry, to quote the *Random House Dictionary*, is "the aggregate of manufacturing or technically productive enterprises in a particular field, often named after its principal product." So, we have the newspaper industry, magazine industry, book industry, and billboard industry. Of course, these "products" are also media, in that they convey symbolic material. Problems arise in a few prominent cases where the industry is typically described in terms of a medium that may or may not carry a product specifically created for it (broadcast TV, radio, cable TV, home video), or in terms of a medium (film, records) that can also be a product carried on other media. Conventional usage, however, tends to have even these cases mean both product and medium. So, for example, "the film industry" is taken to denote the production and distribution of movies as well as their actual projection in theaters of one sort or another. And, "the broadcast television industry" denotes the production, selection, and broadcast of any material to television sets.

We will follow this convention here, if only because it allows us to describe and analyze these industries more clearly than would otherwise be the case. At the same time, the definitional problem should alert us to some mass media industries' increasing use of material created by other mass media industries. One consequence of this activity is that the lines of mass media industries are increasingly blurred as producers long involved in one industry convey their material to other symbol producing and distributing domains. Such cross-fertilization, a result of two or more mass media interacting, is an important phenomenon that has received little attention. We will return to it later in the chapter.

The focus of this book is on the organizations of a mass media industry that directly control the production of material, and on their ability to present their material to ultimate consumers, the public. These production organizations are aided, constrained, or guided by other organizations that have the ability to affect the efficiency, even viability, of the material's creation and release to the public. In other words, entities in a production organization's environment have the ability to provide or withhold *resources* that can account for the success or failure of the mass media production organization's activity. Phrasing the situation in this way forces an awareness of the issue of *power*, both commercial and political, in mass communication.

RESOURCES AND POWER IN MASS COMMUNICATION

It was the Scottish patriot Andrew Fletcher who made the well-known statement, "Give me the making of the songs of a nation, and I care not

who makes its laws."[9] American song writer Irving Berlin, speaking with
more entrepreneurial and fewer governmental intentions, issued a somewhat similar note through the vocal chords of Al Jolson:

> What care I who makes the laws of a nation?
>
> . . .
>
> What care I, who cares
> For the world's affairs?
> As long as I can sing its popular songs?[10]

The two quotes point to the two pegs, politics and commerce, around
which the struggle over influence in mass communication revolves. Holding the pegs firmly in place is the generally accepted idea that widely
distributed messages have the potential to motivate large populations
politically and commercially. "Politically" implies a wide range of activities, from shaping social thought, to preserving the dominant social
hierarchy and values, to getting out the vote. "Commercially" also holds
broad meaning, not the least important of which is getting people to want
to pay for receiving certain mass media materials—books, magazines,
records, and the like. Of course, the success of a production organization
in selling its wares often prompts suppliers of materials that help create
those wares to fight with the producer, or with other suppliers, for a larger
part of the revenues. Thus the commercial struggle over influence in mass
communication takes on a secondary character in addition to the primary
battle between producers over markets.

The popular notions of mass media's political and commercial potential are not new ones. They hark to the dawn of widely reproduced and
distributed messages, and even before that. Andrew Fletcher spoke his
politically tuned words in the eighteenth century, the same period that saw
a commercial-minded Samuel Johnson proclaim in an early magazine
that "advertisements are now so numerous that it is therefore become
necessary to gain attention by magnificence of promises. . . .[11] It was also a
time when the novel, then a truly novel form, was generally held in low
esteem by European and American elites. Novels were regarded as
escapist at best, sensationalist at worst, and, overall, full of lies and
emotionalism.[12] The preferred type of prose writing was "history," the
true evidence of God's work on earth. Children and the poorest classes,
especially, were thought vulnerable to corruption by fictional versions of
life. But while the nature of message was a high concern, it was clearly not
the only one. Ben Bagdikian notes that an English writer in 1763 criticized
the religious schools that taught reading on the grounds that working class
students would afterward refuse "the drudgeries for which they were
born."[13] As Bagdikian points out, intellectuals such as James Mill and
Adam Smith argued that the mercantilists of their era should support

public education, but the business community ignored them. However, by the mid-nineteenth century the new industrialists were so alarmed by growing urban riots that they reversed their position and supported general education and literacy as vehicles for guiding the working classes to "govern and repress their passions."[14]

One does not have to search very hard for contemporary evidence of political or economic concerns about, and struggles over, various kinds of mass media material. The pages of mass media industry trade newspapers are continually filled with stories on the subject. Some of the reports bubble from there into the more general public media. Noisy political issues, particularly, grab the limelight—for example, the Moral Majority's attack on the alleged immorality of the American commercial television networks; Action for Children's Television's desire to eliminate commercials from children's TV; and attempts by various city governments to shut down pornographic movie theaters. Once in a while, too, primary and secondary commercial struggles intrude into the agendas of television news programs and weekly news magazines. Recall RCA's attempts to introduce its videodisc player and records into the United States market on a large scale; the strike against television and movie production companies by actors' unions hoping to get their members a larger portion of revenues from product sales to the videotape, videodisc, and cable industries; and RCA's auction of transponders on one of its entertainment-oriented satellites to the highest bidder. Obviously, even the many trade papers cannot cover all the goings on. The most important—"behind closed door"—negotiations, quarrels, and decisions rarely get reported anywhere publicly.

Organizations, Resources, and Power

These considerations lead to a key point that has been building for the past few pages. The point is that the struggle over the production of mass media material is essentially a struggle by organizations over a broad range of society's resources.

At heart, the proposition is not a new one. It is certainly reflected in examinations of the production of news that have flowered in Britain during the past decade and a half. British scholars, influenced strongly by neo-Marxist reflections on power, ideology, and society, have emphasized the production of mass media material in their research on mass communication.[15] Doing that has led them to deal in a richly textured manner with the way the distribution of two crucial social resources—property and wealth—shapes the production of culture. As Graham Murdock notes, these writers see "the structure of capital [in society] as determining production in a variety of ways and a variety of levels."[16]

Much of the British concern with the idea of resources is, however, implicit rather than explicit. When the notion is mentioned, it tends to pop up casually as a taken-for-granted aspect of a larger point. So, for example, Murdock and Peter Golding use the term "resources" fleetingly when discussing "market pressures and cultural domination." Their point is that media enterprises that are most likely to challenge the prevailing distribution of wealth and power will be "unable to command the resources needed for effective communication to a broad audience."[17] Similarly, to form a related argument, James Curran, Michael Gurevitch, and Janet Woollacott stated that "media organizations exist in a symbiotic relationship with their environment, drawing on it not only for their economic sustenance, but also for 'raw materials' of which their content is made."[18] But the idea of resources quickly falls by the wayside in their discussion, too.

By contrast, I argue that an explicit exposition of the relationship between organizations, resources, and power should be the starting point toward a many-leveled understanding of the production of mass media materials. A framework for doing that can be fashioned by merging two prominent perspectives from seemingly different fields—the "resource dependence" approach of industrial sociologist Howard Aldrich and the "power role" scheme of communication researcher George Gerbner.

Developing the framework so that it is clear and usable means coming to terms with the meaning of several key words that we often taken for granted—for example, organizations, resources, and power. One important goal of this chapter, then, is to lay out the meaning of relevant terms systematically, supported by a variety of examples from different media. That will yield a group of shared assumptions and perceptions with which to move through the rest of the book.

We start with Howard Aldrich's definition of organizations: *Organizations are goal directed, boundary maintaining activity systems.*[19] The key word pairs here are *goal directed, boundary maintaining,* and *activity systems.* By "goal directed," Aldrich means that organizations are purposive systems. To an observer, members of organizations behave *as if* the organizations have goals. "This is not the same as asserting that organizations *do* have goals, but only that much of the activity we observe appears directed toward some common purpose," as opposed to being purely friendly interaction.[20] "Boundary maintaining" implies that some persons are admitted to participate in the organization, whereas others are excluded. Modern organizations typically define members contractually; "maintaining the distinction between members and nonmembers involves establishing an authority, either exercised collectively or delegated to a specific role, empowered to admit some and exclude others."[21] Participants in organizations engage in "activity systems," that is, in interdependent behaviors (*roles*) revolving around the particular technologies the organizations possess for accomplishing work.

Aldrich's definition of an organization highlights its essential social nature; as he says, organizations are "products of, and constraints upon," social relations.[22] Interdependent activities describe and constrain a participant's role. The division of labor between activities leads to role differentiation and specialization of function. In large firms, each activity may constitute a different role, filled by a different person. In smaller organizations, role differentiation—people fulfilling different roles in the organization—may simply involve a difference between a leader or manager and other members.

The definition also points to the importance of an organization's *environment* to keeping the organization going. The environment comprises every person not admitted to participation in the organization (i.e., everyone outside its boundaries) and everything not already a part of, or a product of, the activity systems of organization personnel. Clearly, it is the environment toward which the organization directs the productions of its activities. At the same time, it is the environment that provides people for recruitment into the organization; supplies used in the performance of organizational activities; required information, permission, and services to help gain the acceptability, or permissibility, of its activities in that environment; and money to pay for it all.

People, supplies, permission, information, services, money. Very broadly defined, they represent the material and symbolic *resources* that must continually infuse an organization if it is to survive. Our characterization fits Yuchtman and Seashore's definition of organizational resources: "generalized means, or facilities, that are potentially controllable by social organizations and that are potentially usable—however indirectly—in relationships between the organization and its environment."[23] As this definition implies, organizations are continually in competition with other organizations for resources—be they money, people, supplies, permission, or information. Resources are not randomly distributed throughout the environment. Rather, they are concentrated in various areas of the environment and are often under the control of other organizations. Awareness that the consequences of this situation are quite broad is what Howard Aldrich calls the "resource dependence perspective":

> The resource dependence perspective...goes beyond the idea of simple exchange in arguing that one consequence of competition and sharing of scarce resources is the development of dependencies of some organizations on others. This proposition is the basis for Yuchtman and Seashore's definition of organizational effectiveness: the ability of an organization to exploit its environment in obtaining resources, while at the same time maintaining an autonomous bargaining position. The implicit assumption made regarding managerial and administrative behavior is that major goals of organizational leaders are avoiding dependence on others and making others dependent on

one's own organization. The general picture is one of decision-makers attempting to manage their environments as well as their organizations.[24]

Here, then, we arrive at the concept of *power* in interorganizational relations, since, as Richard Emerson notes, an organization's power resides in another organization's dependence.[25] Aldrich notes that from the resource dependence perspective on interorganizational relations "power is equivalent to the possession of resources." He adds that "influence [perhaps a better word is leverage] is the use of resources in attempts to gain compliance of others."[26]

The point applies clearly to mass communication. A mass media production firm cannot possibly generate internally all the resources it requires to ensure the viability of its creative and administrative activities. For example, money must be found; talent has to be hired; machines, videotape, film, paper, or other exhaustible materials have to be bought; the distribution or exhibition services of other organizations often have to be contracted; the favorable services of law firms and regulations of government agencies have to be ensured; the *in*activity of some pressure groups might have to be ascertained or negotiated; and information about the availability of appropriate talent, the activities of competitors, and the potential for the public's interest in planned or finished products has to be presented and evaluated. In other words, the production firm has to rely on entities in its environment for resources, and those entities might demand substantial recompense for their help. This will be especially true if other organizations are trying to compete for the same resources, or even if they are simply trying to block the producer from obtaining resources. That firm must consequently be able to cope with such demands by exchanging its own resources or dealing with its needs in other ways. This, then, is the interorganizational struggle that guides the production of mass media material.

A FRAMEWORK FOR ANALYSIS

A way to analyze this multipartner struggle is suggested by George Gerbner. Implicitly agreeing with the resource dependence perspective, Gerbner starts with the idea that the study of mass media industries shoud focus on the way that "the systematic exercise of power" within the industry guides and perpetuates the production of material and its release to the public.[27] He locates that exercise of power in the resource-controlling roles that certain organizations hold vis à vis other organizations. He adds that "a scheme designed to analyze this process needs to identify power roles of organizations or groups, suggest some sources of their powers, and specify those functions that affect what the media communicate. Power and its applications become relevant to this scheme as they affect what is being communicated to mass publics."[28]

Gerbner's power role scheme is presented with substantial modification in Table 1, but his basic approach remains. Note that each power role an organization might take on is characterized by a label for the role, the typical activities that describe it, and its leverage in the industry (that is, the way the organization can use resources to gain compliance from other organizations). Note also that these power roles are analytically distinct; it is possible for organizations to hold more than one power role. Another important aspect of this scheme is that it is essentially producer oriented. Roles 2–13 represent activities that allow an organization taking on a "producer" role to create and organize mass media material viably. It is true that organizations acting as distributors, exhibitors, patrons, unions, and the rest have relationships with, and thus provide resources to, organizations that have no impact on mass media producers. They all pay bills to the electric company, for example. Here, however, we are interested only in interdependent activities that affect the amount or nature of mass media material released to the public.

It warrants notice, by the way, that there are two power roles in Table 1—the creator and the public roles—that in their very concepts cannot be filled by any organizations. As the descriptions on the chart indicate, creators and publics are by definition unorganized. Creators are people who make individual decisions about lending their talents to production firms. Publics do not even join organizations. They are the consumers who, individually or (at most) in scattered small groups, make decisions whether to buy a book, whether to subscribe to a magazine, whether to watch a particular TV program. Clearly, such decisions have important implications for a producer's viability (and ability to employ creators). Directly or indirectly, publics provide a crucial resource—money. Still, it is worth stressing that when individuals go beyond making these kinds of yes/no consumer decisions or registering individual complaints and, instead, begin to band together systematically to affect production, distribution, or exhibition choices, they are not acting as "publics" any more according to this scheme. They are, rather, acting as organizations holding the "public advocacy" power role. Similarly, creators who band together take on the "union" power role.

As the foregoing comments imply, Table 1's power role scheme presents a view of mass media industries as *dynamic systems* in which a variety of forces taking one or more roles interact continually to accumulate and exert various kinds and degrees of influence. The following discussion will focus on specific influences that organizations in various roles have upon producers of mass media content, and on specific influences producers can have upon *them*. To keep the scope somewhat manageable, we will draw examples from mass media industries in the United States alone. The aim is not to present exhaustive descriptions of activities and leverages associated with these roles. In fact, several

Table 1 The Power Roles of a Mass Media Industry

	Power Role	Typical Activities	Leverage
1.	Producer	Create, organize, and reproduce material for release to the public via mass media. Set and supervise content and selection guidelines.	Control people and ideas that might get exposure to the public via mass media.
2.	Authority	Provide governmental (or governmentally sanctioned) regulation and arbitration among other power roles.	Political and military power.
3.	Investor	Contribute money in anticipation of production and purchase of material by patrons. Set general conditions for the supply of capital and operating funds.	Control over monetary resources.
4.	Patron	Make ongoing organizational purchases in support of specific products. Contribute to producers' most direct cash flow in exchange for mass media material created.	Control over monetary resources.
5.	Auxiliary	Provide material supplies and ancillary services to producers.	Control access to supplies.
6.	Creator	Provide producer with talent to conceive and arrange (but not necessarily reproduce) mass media material.	An individual creator's decision to join a production organization.
7.	Union	Regulate the provision of personnel to producers. Set work standards; provide worker protection.	Solidarity and threats of work stoppage.

8.	Distributor	Select and coordinate dispersal of material through channels to the point of exhibition.	Control over channels by which material can reach exhibition.
9.	Exhibitor	Offer material for public viewing or purchase.	Control over outlets through which the public chooses materials.
10.	Linking Pin	Move completed mass media material or people representing that material from production firms in one industry to production firms in another industry.	Control over access to new markets, new possibilities.
11.	Facilitator	Help production firms initiate, carry out, or evaluate mass media material.	Control over intermediary services.
12.	Public advocacy	Demand favorable attention, portrayal, policy support.	Pressure through boycott, appeal to authorities.
13.	Public	Purchase and/or attend to distributed messages in an unorganized fashion.	An individual decision to choose or not choose particular content. An individual decision to complain through legal or other channels.

NOTE: All but the *creator* and *public* power roles are typically carried out by organizations. See text for further details.

especially powerful roles will be introduced rather briefly, since later chapters will treat them at length. Roles that take up less attention later in the book, or roles that must be described in some detail now in order to develop key points later, will receive somewhat disproportionate attention in this chapter. The tack, then, is to set up avenues for further analysis and generalization.

The Producer Role

The producer is the focal power role in this interorganizational scheme. Production organizations in a mass media industry compete with one another for resources in the environment that must sustain them and help them grow. The fierceness of that commercial and political competition depends on two major considerations. At base, it depends on the extent to which the two producers have similar goals and activities. The more alike the two firms are in what they make and how they make it, the more fierce their competition is likely to be. The reason is that the producers would be competing for very similar, and by nature scarce, environmental resources. Given similar goals and activities, the fierceness of competition will additionally depend to a high degree on the nature of the environment that they share. The more difficult (or "expensive") it is to garner resources needed to support production, the greater the likely competition.

Take two publishing firms. Executives of both decide to produce an expensive title—a large "coffee table" book on candle making. Moreover, the executives of both firms decide that the best way to market the title is through book stores. Here are grounds for competition. Grounds for even fiercer competition might be imagined. Suppose, for example, that to make a good profit the firms must convince the top five national book outlets to carry their products, and suppose that each chain will carry only one such candle making title. In other words, a key resource—exhibition service—would be highly concentrated. Or, suppose that the number of people interested in buying expensive books on candle making in book stores is smaller than the number of books the two publishers must sell to make a profit; that is, that the environmental capacity is lean from the standpoint of another key resource—the public's money. Both these situations would increase competition between the two publishing firms.

Competition would be reduced if the companies did not have similar goals and activities (i.e., chose different kinds of books to sell). Similarly, competition would lessen if the environment's distribution resources were less concentrated and if a larger public willing to buy the book could be found. One way this might happen would be if one of the publishers decided to use book club rather than book store channels to reach potential customers. The book club strategy would allow the firm to use different outlets from its competition and, as a consequence, would provide a group of potential customers who might be quite different from book store browsers.

Let us assume that both publishers decide to produce only coffee table hobby books on candle making, car repairing, and flower arranging. One publisher aims at the book store market while the other aims at the book club arena. Under such circumstances, some organizational sociologists would say that each publisher had found its own rather specialized niche in the book industry.[29] The concept of a niche refers to a distinct combination of resources sufficient to support organizations with specific goals, boundaries, and activities. Generally, when one production firm perceives a niche, attempts to exploit it, and thrives, other firms enter to compete in the niche, to the point where no additional organizations find entrance profitable. One example might be the development of periodicals for upscale, "liberated" women in the 1970s. A market that offered *Ms.* early in the decade included by the late seventies, *Ms., McCall's, Working Woman, New Woman, Self, Working Woman,* and *Vital.*[30]

Howard Aldrich contends that identifying such niches in an industrial environment might be possible before the niches are actually exploited. He suggests that identification might be carried out deductively by considering six dimensions that characterize the presence and distribution of resources in a particular organization's environment. These dimensions are: environmental capacity (the level, rich-lean, of resources available); concentration-dispersion (the extent to which resources are controlled by a large or small number of organizations and individuals); homogeneity-heterogeneity (the extent to which resources are available from a large or small variety of organizations and groups); domain consensus-dissensus (the degree to which an organization's claim to particular resources is recognized or disputed by organizations, especially governmental, that have a right to supply permission to use the resources); stability-instability (the degree of predictability that certain resources will remain in the environment); and environmental turbulence (the extent to which it is possible to make predictions about, or understand, changes in resource availabilities in the environment).[31]

These dimensions along with the general idea of niche can be useful for considering the range of new products in a mass media industry that have the potential of succeeding, as well as for estimating an "equilibrium" level of expected competition in the production of certain kinds of material within a mass media industry. In addition, the notions suggest an approach to the competition of production firms across *different* mass media industries. Such competition involves organizations that require some of the same resources to survive despite their essentially different output. The more similar the niches that the organizations choose the exploit, the greater the interindustry competition. Often, such head-on clashing over niches occurs when a new medium enters the society. So, for example, television's entrance on the United States scene in the late 1940s brought about strong interindustry competition with radio as television broadcasters tried to woo the advertisers, artists, and viewers who had been lending support to radio. Television's emergence as the nation's most pervasive mass medium ultimately forced the radio industry to shift its focus to artists, advertisers, time periods, and publics that were different enough from those TV used to allow it to endure and prosper.[32] Certain magazines, however, also found themselves in competition with television and did not choose niches different enough to exploit successfully. *Look, Life,* and *The Saturday Evening Post*, general interest periodicals with publics as diverse as television's and advertisers with the same goals as television's, faded away as the TV industry juggernaut overran the fields those magazines had cultivated since the turn of the century.[33]

Despite the foregoing discussion, the situation is much more complex than the notion of niche and Aldrich's related dimensions imply. One important reason is that resources are sometimes not relevant to a mass media industry until a production firm risks using them. In other words, a niche might not exist until it is beginning to be exploited. Thus, for example, it was not at all clear that vinyl discs were relevant resources in the home video industry until technology firms began to develop marketable videodisc players. Another, related reason is that material or symbolic resources can actually be *created* at a particular point in time, a possibility that allows either for expansion of an existing niche (something that might not have been foreseen) or the creation of a new one. Take as an example the popularization of woman's liberation as a movement and a perspective in the early 1970s. Executives in magazine publishing firms perceived that with this development a new "public" resource became available to them—upscale working women with certain life styles who were attractive to magazine advertisers and who might subscribe to magazines that discussed their emerging interests and problems. As a consequence, the several magazines mentioned earlier came into being.[34]

Perhaps a more serious complication with the notion of niche is that it is not clear where one niche ends and another begins. The problem might be illustrated by extending the women's magazine example. When persuading advertisers to buy ads in their periodicals, most new "working women" magazines position themselves as different from others of their general kind. For example, *Savvy* calls itself "the magazine for executive women;" *Self* proudly avers that it speaks to "a new generation of American women;" and *Vital*, subtitled "The Magazine of Healthful Living," claims to reach a "higher targeted market of 19- to 44-year-old wives, mothers, and career women."[35] Do these magazines really share the same niche? If not, do they overlap niches? Does *Savvy* more likely share a niche with *Business Week, The Wall Street Journal*, and *The New York Times Magazine* rather than with *Self* and *Vital*? Clearly, the answers will depend on how narrowly or broadly one is willing to define a niche.

But niche is still a useful notion because it leads us to systematically consider the way in which an organization's environment influences its ability to produce and release certain kinds of material in certain ways. Not only does thinking about niches raise the issue of competition between organizations in producer roles, it also directs our attention to organizations and groups that hold other power roles by virtue of their ability to supply resources to, and withhold resources from, the producers.

The Authority Role

One of those power roles is that of "authority," an activity that involves legitimizing and regulating the other roles within a mass media industry. Simply put, authorities are governments. The most important resource they provide is permission—permission to publish, permission to broadcast, permission to film and record. Authorities can provide other resources as well—information that production firms might find impossible or too expensive to bring together by themselves, services that might help mass media industries, tax benefits that might improve cash flows of production firms, and even training programs to supply personnel, or laws to encourage the cheaper availability of personnel. Of course, authorities can also withhold permission, favorable tax arrangements, information, and other encouraging laws from production firms. Such broad abilities, plus the possible political and military leverage to enforce decisions, make organizations taking on the authority role important for mass media production organizations to have on their side.

"Authority" is an extremely general reference to a wide range of organizations with a wide range of specific duties and leverages. A variety of governmental arms—courts, legislative bodies, executive agencies, police—might be involved in setting policies or regulations, interpreting them, adjudicating them, or enforcing them. In the United States, moreover, various levels of government—federal, state, county, city— might have different, even intersecting, jurisdictions over different mass media industries or sectors of mass media industries. Thus, for example, licenses to broadcast commercial television signals in all communities across the nation are issued and regulated at the federal level, by the Federal Communications Commission (FCC). By contrast, franchises for cable systems are granted at the state and/or local (city-county) level, with the provision that those authorities adhere to minimum FCC guidelines. Similarity, expectations about the kind of material that can or should be carried on a local television station are broadly characterized by FCC documents; local complaints about programming are evaluated on a case by case basis. On the other hand, expectations about the kind of material that can or should be carried on a channel originating from a cable system are generally a nonfederal affair, though federal laws might prevent state or local authorities from proscribing certain programming.

Authorities may be said to regulate mass media industries on three levels: (1) structural, (2) technical, and (3) content. The *structural* level involves rulings that dictate actual organizational processes and relationships in a mass media industry. One example is the Federal Radio Act of 1927. In it, Congress recognized, essentially legitimized, the emerging configuration of the commercial broadcast industry and created a commission to oversee it.[36] An example narrower in scope was the 1945 decision by the United States Supreme Court striking down an Associated Press bylaw that permitted the wire service to grant exclusive service to a particular newspaper for a particular area.[37]

At the *technical* level, rulings relate to standards of a mechanical, electronic, or otherwise scientific nature that organizations in a mass media industry must uphold. A relevant case is the decision by Congress in the early 1960s to require that all television set manufacturers involved in interstate commerce equip the sets with receivers capable of receiving both UHF (Ultra High Frequency—channels 14–83) and the more popular VHF (Very High Frequency—channels 2–13).[38] More generally, postal edicts relating to weight, size, and construction represent technical regulations that affect the operations of book, newspaper, and magazine publishers, as well as mail order advertisers.[39]

The third level of regulation, the *content* level, involves specific messages and message policies. The Federal Communication Act's requirement that broadcast licensees program "in the public interest, convenience, and necessity," the Act's "equal time" provision for political messages, and the Commission's own "Fairness Doctrine" on noncommercial broadcast speech are but three examples of message policy regulations in radio and television.[40] Relevant to all mass media are content rulings concerning free speech and its limitations, on subjects such as libel, copyright, obscenity, pornography, and deceptive advertising.[41]

Clearly, content-level regulations have direct implications for the kinds of materials mass media organizations produce. Structural and technical regulations can, however, also hold consequences for content. For example, the determination by Congress in 1919 that United States broadcasting should be a commercial enterprise rather than the government monopoly desired by the Navy ignited a long and intricate chain of events that led to the radio and television networks, to the advertiser-supported system, and to the demographics-based orientation toward programming that still guided broadcast programming in the early 1980s.

Similarly, relatively lower postal rates for books, magazines, and newspapers compared to other commercial matter have historically helped foster the growth of those media. For example, postal laws have traditionally held that magazines sent to paying subscribers ("paid circulation magazines") may pay lower rates than magazines circulated free to a designated group of people ("controlled circulation magazines"). That is one reason many magazines prefer paid to controlled circulation. At the same time, magazine publishers wishing to be eligible for the lower ("second class") rate must make sure that the shape and orientation of their products conform to the technical standards the post office uses to define a paid circulation magazine:

1. It must be regularly issued at stated intervals, as frequently as four times a year. It must bear a date of issue and be numbered consecutively.
2. It must be formed of printed paper sheets, without board, cloth, leather, or other substantial bindings. Moreover, it may not be produced by the stencil, mimeograph, or hectograph process or in imitation of typewriting.
3. It must be originated and published for public dissemination, or devoted to literature, the sciences, arts, or some special industry. Too, it must have a legitimate list of subscribers. Also, it should not be designed primarily for advertising purposes, or for free circulation, or for circulation at nominal rates.[42]

These technical standards embody a perspective about magazines and magazine content that not only reflects what exists but also provides boundary rules for the entry of new periodicals.

Structural, technical, and content regulations that authorities in stable societies enforce regarding a mass media industry are generally the result of past struggles by various groups to achieve conditions favorable to them. Two broad factors operate in the United States to ensure that the most important of those regulations, those that affect the fundamental operating principles and relationships of the industry, are not likely to change dramatically. One factor is the self-perpetuating power of the groups that benefit most from the regulations. Those groups are likely to channel some of the profits they derive as a result of those regulations into making sure that they retain their powerful positions; the activity is often called "lobbying" or "public relations." The second factor is the logic of American jurisprudence, which places high value on precedents established by English common law, the United States Constitution, and previous decisions. Expressing this approach is the oft-heard legal phrase *stare decises et non quieta movere* (to stand by past decisions and not disturb things at rest). Its idea is that a judge should resolve current problems in the same manner, or along similar lines, as similar problems were resolved in the past. This factor, like the first, injects conservatism and predictability into the behavior of authorities.[43]

Such regulatory inertia means that authorities typically set conditions for the operation of mass media industries that producers learn to predict, accept, and integrate into the fabric of their operations. Doing so means the authorities are not major problems in day to day profit and loss decisions. Of course, challenges to this regulatory inertia will occur, and in such situations regulated firms will need to defend their traditional claims on resources. One example is the defense by the television networks against insistance of various public advocacy groups that the FCC force the networks to program certain kinds and amounts of material for children.[44] An unsuccessful case is the attempt by the motion picture studios of the 1940s to halt a Justice Department move to end the long-term ownership by those studios of film exhibition chains.[45] A struggle where battles were won but the war was lost involved the attempt by radio and television broadcasters in the 1960s and 1970s to stop Congress and the FCC from encouraging the cable television industry. The broadcasters' concern was that authorities not allow expansion of that emerging industry into territories that would threaten broadcasters' revenues.[46] Here was an interindustry struggle, caused by the perception that regulations favorable to one industry might be unfavorable to another.

The protective measures of production firms are usually carried out by personnel who specialize in dealing with authorities. Their argumentation with the regulators might stretch over a period of several months, or even years. In the meantime, people involved in the actual creation of mass media material by and large continue along traditional paths, though sometimes a few authority-pleasing modifications are engineered by the firms' most important policy makers. These defensive approaches provide maximum opportunity for the challenged production firms to redirect rulemaking to their favor without substantially affecting the ongoing creation of content. Failing this, the approaches provide the time the firms' policymakers need to plot long-term changes and integrate them into organizational activities with as few disruptions as possible.

The Investor and Patron Roles

The ability of mass media production firms to integrate authorities' expectations into the very fabric of decision making about content is a stable element in their production concerns. Less predictable, and there-fore more crucial, subjects in daily production decisions are the expecta-tions and activities of organizations that hold investor and patron power roles. The leverage investors and patrons hold is quite straightforward: They control the money producers need to make material for release to the public.

Investment organizations include banks, stock brokerage firms, insur-ance companies, government and private foundations, and investment syndicates. Generally, they provide money only when the expectation is that the production firm's overall activities will yield an attractive return (monetary or otherwise) on their initial outlays. Thus their power to veto or approve of a production company's long-range plans is enormous. Most specifically, producers know that to get solid investor support they must prove they can find patrons for their material that are acceptable to the investors on a long-term basis.

Patrons are organizations that provide money in support of particular products before the producer releases them for public consumption. Although the word patron sometimes refers to members of the public who pay to see a movie or read a magazine, I am using the word as it has been used in the production of culture. Historically, patrons were individuals or groups (like the Medici) who provided support for the creation of works *before* they were released to any audience at large. In the case of mass communication, individual members of the public do not typically have that power; giant organizations do. To use the word patron to refer to individuals, then, gives a wrong impression of the public's influence. In fact, that the patrons of mass communication are organizations rather than individuals indicates just how different this process is from the production of culture in earlier centuries.

By far the dominant patron group in American mass media is the advertising industry. So, for example, in many sectors of the magazine, newspaper, and broadcast television industries banks and stockholders invest in particular production firms on the conviction that enough advertisers will pay to be identified with the mass media material to make the investment profitable. Note, however, that in industries where advertisers do not hold significant sway, other organizations may take on the patron role. The "trade" sector of book publishing is a case in point. Investors provide capital to publishers with the expectation that a profitable number of stores will purchase the books and place them on sale to the public. For these publishers, these exhibition outlets are also the patrons.

In essence, then, patrons are the customers of producers. Dominant media patrons decide by their purchases whether particular mass media materials will be released to the public. It follows that the patrons' importance relates to their being most directly responsible for the production organizations' solvency. This pivotal position holds profound implications for both the process and the product of mass media producers. Chapter Two will examine those implications in detail.

The Auxiliary, Creator, and Union Roles

At this point, attention shifts from power roles that regulate or sponsor mass media production to roles that contribute to a production firm's technical ability to do its job—auxiliaries, creators, and unions. As in earlier sections, our interest is in the way these relationships may affect the amount and nature of mass media material released to the public.

And, in fact, there is much to consider about the ability of auxiliaries, creators, and unions to influence mass media content. Clearly, mass media material could not be created if auxiliaries did not provide producers with material supplies. Take, for example, the many supplies required to put together a movie. Of course, plumbing, air conditioning, telephones, and office equipment are needed to run the facilities from which the movie is coordinated. Typical preproduction as well as in-production demands include camera, sound, lighting, setting, wardrobe, makeup, hairdressing, and transportation equipment. Other production operations require equipment for editing, sound effects, and dubbing. Moreover, if the film is shot on location, many ancillary services will be needed. (Ancillary services are services that support, but do not contribute directly to, actual production procedures.) Transportation must be provided for cast and crew; hotel and meal accommodations must be established; preparations must be made to use the location setting; and facilities for screening daily "rushes" by the producer and director might have to be set up. Even if the entire movie is made in a studio, though, ancillary services as diverse as security, accounting, maintenance, and film developing will be required.

The ability of a production organization to afford auxiliaries' resources typically determines whether it will get them; that, in turn, might determine whether mass media material on the drawing board will actually be produced, or whether it will be produced in the manner originally conceived. Not too long ago, for example, sharply rising costs of silver boosted costs auxiliaries charged for photographic film, and that forced cancellation of some tightly budgeted movie projects. Of course, the chance also exists that auxiliaries will develop new supplies or services that will revolutionize the way mass media material is produced.[47]

A contemporary example can be found in the newspaper and magazine industries. There the relatively recent introduction of computer-based technology has helped create significant changes in the content produced.[48] The ability of auxiliaries such as IBM, Merganthaler, Compugraphic, and Atex to wed the data gathering, storing, retrieving, and printing capabilities of computers to newspaper and magazine situations has brought people in periodical production firms to act differently toward their products.[49] At one level, access to a computer has encouraged what some call "precision journalism." The *New York Times*, for example, has used its computer to analyze murder cases in New York, and the *Philadelphia Inquirer* computer-analyzed its city's criminal justice system.[50] At another level, a computer-run production system has encouraged editors to experiment with changes in the graphic design of periodicals much more than before. The reason is that the computer facilities allow them to translate new ideas into print without going through previously required time-consuming and potentially confusing intermediary steps involving composition and printing press workers.[51]

A computer-run production system has also allowed editors and writers in large firms to work closer to printing and distribution deadlines than ever before. Take the case of *US News and World Report*. Before the introduction of computer production into the weekly magazine's operation, the editorial deadline (the "closing") began at noon on Thursday and ended at 9:00 P.M. that day. Printing took place over the weekend. When the new equipment came in the mid-1970s, final page composition and printing took much less time. As a consequence, editors and writers did not need to *begin* closing until late Friday. This gain of more than a day, quite substantial for a weekly news magazine, allowed editors much greater leeway to update changing circumstances and integrate "late breaking" stories into the body of the periodical.[52]

The key impetus most newspapers and magazines have had for encouraging and adopting this kind of equipment was its ability to lower labor costs substantially. Of course, there still remain areas of content selection and creation where the substitution of machines for people is prohibitively expensive if it is not outright impossible. At the very least, people must participate in coming up with the ideas and supervising the machines. Among those people are individuals who hold the "creator" power role. They are involved in conceiving and initially arranging the material that is produced. Examples are magazine writers, TV actors, newspaper reporters, set designers, television producers, movie directors, movie stuntmen, newspaper photographers, book editors, and record producers.

Some mass media creators become recognized much more than others for their individual achievements. As a consequence, they take on power that makes them independent forces within their industries in the creation of mass media material. Actors such as Paul Newman, movie producers such as Woody Allen, movie directors such as Steven Spielberg, broadcast journalists such as Bill Moyers, writers like Norman Mailer, and cinematographers such as Gordon Willis have "clout" to personally initiate, shape, and finalize mass media works, clout that often exceeds the leverage carried by entire organizations that interact with production firms. That is the reason for including the "creator" power role in this essentially interorganizational scheme.

It is important to stress that the kind of leverage mentioned in the previous paragraph is held by a very small percentage of personnel in any mass media industry.[53] Most creators are buffeted by the constraints and opportunities they find within the production organizations that hire them on temporary or long-term bases. Indeed, the relative lack of leverage most creators find in their jobs has led them, along with other personnel, to form unions or guilds in attempts to wield collective power with respect to production firms.[54]

Thus we find that the ability of mass media production organizations to make use of an auxiliary's resources will sometimes depend upon terms that organizations holding "union" roles negotiate with the producers about the use of those resources. This pont has been most dramatically demonstrated in the newspaper industry, where craft union anger over producers' intention to replace linotype machine operators with computer-run machines has led to bitter disputes. In a flurry of incidents during the late 1960s and the 1970s, the International Typographical Union and the National Newspaper Guild attempted to use the leverage of solidarity they had with union workers both inside and outside the composition and printing rooms to set standards for retaining printers and regulating the arrival of new technologies. These arguments over the proper introduction of automation generally led to viable compromises. In a minority of cases, however, the disagreements led to bitter strikes that, for a combination of reasons, resulted in the suspension or merger of newspapers, particularly in large metropolitan areas. By the late 1970s, it was becoming clear that the traditional newspaper craft unions were being forced to give way to automation. Some writers even suggested that the best hope for them to survive and serve their members effectively in the current technological revolution was for them to merge.[55]

Most union demands revolve around defining and ensuring satisfactory wages for their members under nonexploitative working conditions. One way to do this is to limit the number of workers qualified to carry out needed production tasks and, by making these resources scarce, drive up their minimum price. A way to do that is to develop industry standards for creative or technical quality that a very small percentage of the potential worker population can meet. Sometimes, union admission requirements and apprenticeship tracks protect these standards and regulate worker entry. In turn, the "professional" look and content of the finished product reflect these standards.

The ability of unions to fix specific minimum wages and other terms for their members varies within and across mass media industries. In book publishing, for example, the Authors' League has created a "model contract" for royalty terms and other aspects of writer-publisher agreements. However, the contract has no binding value, and many publishers successfully negotiate terms less generous to authors.[56] By contrast, the Writers' Guild, which operates in the movie and television industries, has successfully established minimum rates producers must pay for a "treatment" (a brief description of a proposed screenplay), for an actual screenplay, and for revisions. In addition, the Guild has helped create rules about the on-screen credit that writers will be given and about the kinds of rights over an original screenplay that a writer may retain when a producer buys his or her material for a movie.[57] At the same time, the Writers' Guild has tried and failed to get production firms to agree that the writer of a movie screenplay retains creative control over that screenplay even after he (or she) delivers it to the production firm. Production firm executives have insisted that the writer is simply an employee, not an executive. They have maintained the right to alter a screenplay any way they wish once they have paid for it.[58]

In the nature of things, compromises must be made. A union's bargaining position toward a compromise is only as strong as the collective importance, and cohesion, of its members as production resources. Many of the resolutions ultimately influence the kind of content that is created. The most drastic consequence of negotiations or work stoppages over minimum wages might be producers' decisions not to produce certain kinds of material at all because of high costs. The producers might, however, respond to the higher costs in one or more of the following other ways: They might scale down the material to versions more in line with current costs. They might keep the material unchanged but raise its price to the public to meet extra costs. They might keep the material unchanged but raise the price of advertising inserts to help defray expenses. Or, they might keep the material unchanged but create it in ways that reduce reliance on the unions.

One way to get around the union involves turning to auxiliaries for substitutible automated resources. Another way is to create the material in places where union regulations are absent or not as stringent. Both these strategies might have substantial consequences for the content produced. We have already seen that the use of new technologies can themselves lead to important changes in mass media material. Choosing a production location because of a favorable union environment also may affect what the public sees, hears, or reads.

Just such a circumstance obtained in television from the late 1950s through the 1970s. During that period, TV production shifted dramatically from New York to Los Angeles, and the location of stories and outdoor scenes shifted as well. An important part of the reason lay in the union situation in the two cities. During that time, producers generally considered the major New York union, the International Alliance of Theatrical Stage Employees (IATSE), to be more troublesome and a lot more expensive than its counterparts on the west coast. That, plus a parallel decline in available studio facilities, encouraged producers to forsake the "Big Apple", birthplace of TV production, for Hollywood. In the early 1980s, however, as part of a bid by the mayor's office to attract motion picture and television work to the city, the management of the IATSE became much more flexible in approaching TV production. Moreover, a second union became prominent, and competition between the two created an even more flexible attitude toward production. An umbrella organization, the Conference of Motion Picture and Television Unions, was formed to provide a forum for production executives and members from both unions to discuss problems of mutual concern. These activities, along with an increase in studio space, helped establish near parity in production costs between New York and Los Angeles. By extension, the activities helped to increase the number of series, specials, and movies with a New York City backdrop.[59]

The Distributor and Exhibitor Roles

Along with concern by producers of mass media material about the costs and implications of auxiliary and union resources must come an awareness of the critical importance of distribution and exhibition. For if garnering the specific resources to create a product is a necessary early step toward influence and profit, placing that product in front of the people who will potentially choose it is the equally necessary later step. Consequently, to remain viable, production firms in every industry must exert control in one way or another over decision making relating to the distributor and exhibitor power roles. Here we are concerned with the way such controls, combined with leverage in the other direction by distributors and exhibitors, can influence the amount and kind of mass media material producers make.

The subject, put concisely, is spectrum of choice. For executives in a production firm the question is this: How can we ensure that the spectrum of materials which the public gets to choose from in our industry will include our company's products? One logical answer is for them to oversee an entire chain of activities leading to the marketplace, from production to distribution to exhibition. This kind of "vertical integration" is, of course, common practice in many industries, symbol-producing or not. A logical next step is to maximize the chance that the public will choose the company's product by inhibiting competition at the production, distribution, or exhibition levels.

In the United States, the clearest attempts to obtain monopolistic or oligopolistic control over the chain of mass media production, distribution, and exhibition activities took place in the late nineteenth and early twentieth centuries. Reverberations of those activities still influence the industries today. One tactic companies used in their attempts to achieve market control was simply to buy up the available mass media material in a particular field. Another related to government-issued patent rights. That idea was to win, purchase, or pool patent rights over a particular medium so that any firms wanting to exploit the medium would have to pay license fees to the patent holder. Thomas Edison used the latter tactic with the phonograph.[60] His firm carried it to more sophisticated heights with the movie camera and projector to form the Motion Picture Patent Company in collaboration with a number of other early movie powers.[61] In a similar vein, the United States Navy and American Telephone and Telegraph coordinated the pooling of patent rights in the wireless area to form the Radio Corporation of America as a production-to-exhibition monopoly granting licenses.[62] While that tactic was useful with new media, the other strategy attracted interest in publishing, where the basic technology (fundamentally Gutenberg's) could not be patented. Two examples stand out. In the late 1880s, the American Book Company bought the plates and stock of twenty-one publishers to become the largest publisher in the United States. Around the same time, the United States Book Company did the same in the textbook field.[63]

None of these operations lasted much more than a decade in their original manifestations. Vigorous courtoom disputations in the record industry and government trust-busting in the movie and radio industries made it clear that patent rights would not provide the airtight producer-to-public control the firms originally thought they had. Nor did control over plates and backlists in book publishing amount to total control. Changing public tastes and competition from new books of other publishers ended the dominance of the two book companies rather quickly.

Over the next several decades, another tactic aimed at total control took hold in the movie industry. A small number of production companies (Paramount, Warner, Twentieth Century Fox, RKO, and MGM) managed to reduce their risks greatly by owning (or being owned by) both the dominant distribution firms and the major theaters in which movies were exhibited throughout the country. By the 1950s, however, the United States government, claiming antitrust concerns, had forced those film industry "majors" to divest themselves from their exhibition interests.[64] In the movie industry, as in others, it seemed that somewhat different strategies would have to be developed to make the route from production to exhibition as certain as possible.

The strategies that have evolved have varied by industry and by firm size. By and large, the tendency of dominant production firms has been to hold on to a substantial, sometimes oligopolistic, share of distribution channels. This has been true, for example, in the movie and television industries, where specific decrees continue to prevent the buying up of exhibition arenas (theaters and local broadcast outlets) by major producers and distributors. The movie industry is the most extreme case. In 1978, the Washington Task Force on the Motion Picture Industry argued that "the major producer/distributors are effectively limiting competition by maintaining tight control over the distribution of films, both by their failure to produce more films and by their failure to distribute more films produced by others."[65] Thomas Guback added the next year that the domination of distribution by the majors has brought about "a pattern of circularity that has become a closed ring in the film industry."[66] Guback estimated it cost each of the majors about $20 million a year to maintain a distribution operation and sales force worldwide. The monetary requirements to sustain such operations, the difficulty newer companies would find competing at that level of operations, and the leverage the majors have on exhibitors because of the majors' abilities to mobilize huge film production resources all converge to dictate the movies prominent theatrical exhibitors carry:

> Major distributors know they can get the bulk of their films booked—and booked widely—because there are exhibitors who need them, and large national and regional circuits with centralized decision-making are the guaranteed customers with thousands of important screens. The rules of the system dictate that an exhibitor try to book the most commercial film, and this means that pictures with little perceived commercial value stand in line far behind blockbusters. The majors are often the ones with well-performing commercial films, but they are well-performing sometimes because they are booked widely.[67]

Producers who cannot convince one of the fewer than ten majors to pick up their films (and they cannot if they have no previous record of commercial success) might be able to find smaller, independent distributors to disseminate their material. Or, the producers can try to distribute material themselves. Typically, this approach has meant finding a niche in the marketplace that the major producer/distributor firms have not elected to fill. "In practice, this yields G-rated films for the children's market, exploitation and sexploitation films for drive-ins, X-rated films for adult theaters, or motorcycle/trucking films and the like for some regional audiences."[68]

A similar lock on the dominant distribution channels—with analogous influences on producers not tied to them—has obtained for years in the broadcast television industry. Three commercial and one public television network have sat astride the channels linking the great majority of television exhibition outlets in the United States with the programs produced; of 988 television stations broadcasting in 1979, only about 100 were independent of the networks.[69] The commercial webs, older and more powerful than the public broadcasting service, function not only as distributors but as producers as well for much (though by Justice Department edict not all) of their programming. Although some research shows that it is "rather easy" for television producers to enter the network's chosen production circle,[70] it is also true that such entry is contingent upon suggesting program ideas that fit network-approved formats, time requirements, and strategic needs at a particular point in time.[71]

As a rule, producers choosing to sell new programs "off network" have to go the syndication route if they want their ideas to reach most Americans' homes. That is, they have to distribute their programs to individual stations or to station groups market by market with the hope of obtaining enough reach and advertiser support to make the project viable. There is a problem, however: If an ambitious prime time syndication project costs about the same as a network prime time project (as it likely would in competing nationwide with network prime time fare), more than the present number of independent stations have to carry it for it to succeed monetarily. That means some network affiliates would have to preempt network programs. Affiliates do have an incentive to do this once in a while (particularly with network shows that are not doing well in the ratings) because with syndicated pickups the station will not have to share advertising time and revenues with the network. For the same reason, however, the networks try to discourage syndication. Their generally powerful leverage lies in an ability not to renew the station's biennial affiliation contract. That would stop the station's continuous supply of expensively mounted programs that reach large audiences and attact local and national advertisers. During the late 1970s each network provided sixty-five percent of its affiliates' daily programming. Since affiliates in the very largest markets are owned by the networks themselves, and since all affiliates generally "clear" every prime time program the networks offer, syndicating a prime time show successfully is very difficult.[72]

When prime time syndication has been carried out it has been done by a coalition of powerful station groups and a major Hollywood production studio. Even in these circumstances, though, the material has consisted of short-flight series or single program specials, undoubtedly so that affiliates will not incur too much network wrath. Actually, it turns out that affiliates (and independents) have only limited incentive to carry newly made syndicated material even when they are not carrying network fare. More profitable is their airing of inexpensive old movies made by the Hollywood majors, and reruns of programs the networks used to show. On stations and time slots where production firms can sell syndicated fare, the desire by stations for low cost investment with high immediate returns forces the producers, like their movie counterparts, into niches that reward relatively inexpensive formats and ideas—talk/variety shows ("Merv Griffin"), game shows ("Family Feud"), nature programs ("Wild Kingdom"), and magazinelike information and interview shows ("PM Magazine").[73]

Of course, one could argue that production firms that cannot work with the broadcast networks can turn to one of a growing number of cable-related distribution channels that are reaching into an increasing number of United States homes via local cable outlets. Some have, although the largest satellite-to-cable channels of the early 1980s (e.g., Home Box Office, Showtime, Cable News Network, and Nickelodeon) were generally getting original programming from the same production firms that were selling to the major broadcast networks and theatrical distributors. Even more often, though, the channels were either producing programs themselves, purchasing second-run rights to American theatrical movies, or finding use for European (or South American) television reruns.

Still, many observers predicted that by 1990, many production firms that do not own distribution channels will have attempted to release scores of program services to a wide variety of narrowly defined publics. Yet, in 1981, media analyst John Reidy of the Drexel, Burnham brokerage firm augured that "the fragmented audiences won't support all this programming" and that "more money will be lost on programming for cable TV in the next five years than will be made in the next ten."[74] And, in fact, with "programming" coming to mean filling an entire channel daily, the largest program developers in the cable industry were already realizing that the true chance for success lay in controlling distribution and/or exhibition as well as the creation of programming. In that way they could ensure that the programs they originated could at least have the potential of being delivered to an economically viable number (or type) of people.

Take Westinghouse as an example. In 1981, the firm ensured its ability to deliver its programming to a large national audience by acquiring Teleprompter, the second largest multiple system operation (MSO) in the industry. That was the biggest merger of two communication companies in United States history, and it gave the TV programmers of Group W—backed by the enormous financial and technical resources of parent Westinghouse Electric—ready access to 1.5 million homes. At the same time, the firm bought ten transponders on the new Westar satellites. These valuable keys to distribution clout allowed Westinghouse programmers to link up with Teleprompter systems around the country.[75]

Such ability to move programming from creation through to distribution and exhibition under one corporate umbrella—an ability also enjoyed by other communication giants such as Time, Inc., Times-Mirror, and Warner Amex—not only enhances a single company's position but makes it harder for other less endowed producers or distributors to compete. Seasoned observers noted that it also is beginning to result in less competition in cable programming. In 1981, writer Martin Koughan quoted Sam Simon of the National Citizen's Committee for Broadcasting as contending that "the vertical integration of cable system owners controlling program suppliers has the effect of freezing others out of the marketplace."[76] Ted Turner, independent owner of the Atlanta "superstation" and the Cable News Network, concurred: "Right now there are almost no independent satellite networks not owned by the big MSOs. And the MSOs will not carry competing services."[77] In fact, the competition over production, distribution, and ultimate exhibition was such that important producers were freezing each other out. Here is an example Harold Horn of the Cable Television Information Center gave during Congressional testimony in 1981:

> When Times-Mirror began its new movie service, Spotlight, it was acting as a publisher. However, when it removed [Time, Inc.'s] HBO from most of its systems and substituted Spotlight in its place, I don't believe it was acting as a publisher, but rather as a vertically integrated monopoly.[78]

In the *print* publishing areas, and in other mass media industries, the importance of distribution for maintaining a producer's access to exhibition outlets is not as dramatically evident as in the cable television, theatrical movie, and broadcast television industries. This does not mean that control over the distribution process by a producer is not important, but it does mean that many more producers have an opportunity and ability to exert control. The reasons seem to be several, and intertwined: (1) The relatively low cost of production and promotion that is possible; (2) the relatively greater number of units of material that outlets will accept; (3) the relatively large number of outlets that exist to exhibit the material; and (4) the relatively large variety of outlets that exist to exhibit the material.

Comparing the theatrical movie industry with book publishing will illustrate these points. Books are a lot less expensive to create than movies; book stores, libraries, and schools will carry more new titles a year than will movie exhibitors; there are more outlets for new books in the United States than there are theatrical movie outlets; and the variety of book outlets (book stores, libraries, schools, a wide spectrum of commercial locations, book clubs, and direct-to-home sales) is much greater than the variety of first-run theatrical film outlets (essentially "hard top" movie houses and drive-ins).

In magazine publishing, the ability to distribute material to consumers directly through the mail, as well as through racks in stores, also makes it more difficult for a small number of companies to own all distribution routes. Similarly, the situation in radio, though once comparable to the contemporary TV and movie industries, is closer today to book publishing in its range of outlet diversity and production costs. The change came about as a result of two parallel developments that began in the mid-1950s. One was the new advertising role for radio that emerged during the rise of television—reaching narrower publics than TV for short periods of time. The other was the increased government allocation of AM and (particularly) FM licenses. By 1981, over 8,000 radio stations existed in the United States. While the traditional radio networks (Mutual, CBS, ABC, and NBC) certainly exhibited a strong presence (particularly in news and sports), a plethora of other production and distribution services with a wide variety of short and long programming forms were entering the marketplace to compete for licensees' interests.[79]

Note, however, that a general atmosphere of easy entry for producers at both the distribution and exhibition levels of a mass media industry does not mean that all segments of the industry are so competitive. To the contrary, it is quite likely that even in these industries distribution channels to certain types of outlets are controlled by a small number of production firms. Mass market paperback publishing—a sector of book publishing in which a variety of retail stores are the major outlets—serves as a good example. In 1977, North American sales of mass market paperbacks amounted to an estimated $477 million, about fifteen percent of the approximately three billion dollar North American book industry. Within the mass market area, Bantam Books, a producer and distributor, accounted for eighteen percent of the sales.[80] Moreover, eight publisher/distributors—Bantam, Dell, CBS, New American Library, Ballantine, Pocket Books, Avon, and Warner—together accounted for eighty-four per cent of the sales. Parallel examples could be brought from the general book store ("trade") outlet sector of book publishing and the record store area of the record industry.

A variety of distribution channels not locked up by a small number of firms can serve to encourage wide diversity of materials within the industry. The reason is that it allows a greater number and variety of producers to try to reach the public. So, for example, a small firm wanting to market a magazine about toys might be able to convince magazine distributors in different cities to carry the magazine; some distributors might carry it, and some might not. Failing that, the firm might be able to succeed by advertising and selling the magazine through the mail. Or, perhaps the firm will decide that the best distribution approach will be in toy stores, where another kind of distributor will carry the material. One actual magazine distributed through nontraditional retail outlets in 1981 was It's Me!, a bimonthly aimed at large women. While it was being marketed on a test basis through magazine stands in Chicago, It's Me! was released in Los Angeles, New York, and Chicago through stores of its charter advertiser, the Lane Bryant clothing chain for larger women.[81]

The implication of several of the foregoing remarks is that in industries where a few production firms do not dominate distribution, the leverage of the exhibitor in deciding what to accept and what not to accept is greater than in industries with producer-distributor oligopolies. This does not mean that the major movie companies or the three commercial networks do not pay any attention to the outlets that carry their programming. They do, and sometimes the exhibitor/distributor relationship can strongly influence the material released to the public. For example, in 1981 objections by NBC affiliates derailed that networ's plans for an hour-long weekday evening newscast. Still, exhibitors have more direct control over the spectrum of outlet choice (and, thus, more leverage) in industries where control over production and distribution is more contested and more fluid. What that means is that there, especially, producers must develop ways to reduce the uncertainty over whether outlets will carry their products. Paul Hirsch has noted three "coping strategies" that production firms employ to deal with this kind of uncertainty: deploying "contact" personnel to organizational boundaries; overproducing and differentially promoting new items; and coopting mass media gatekeepers.[82] To them might be added a fourth strategy—by-passing outlets altogether through direct mail marketing.

The first strategy, deploying contact personnel to organizational boundaries, involves sales representatives (the contact personnel) who curry favor with and carry information to buyers in the outlets organizations or influential distribution organizations. "Currying favor" might range from building friendships and trust with outlet personnel regarding sales suggestions to gaining influence over them through monetary or drug-related "payola." "Carrying information" might mean persuasion through material that supports high sales optimism for the product, through assurances about impressive advertising campaigns that will bring the public to the outlet in search of the product, or through special discounts that accrue to outlets or distributors carrying the product.

The second coping strategy, overproduction and differential promotion of new items, means producing and selectively promoting a large number of items in the hope that at least some will be accepted by distributors and outlets and, ultimately, by consumers. For example, R. Serge Denisoff pointed out in the mid-1970s that despite the control by five record conglomerates of over fifty percent of the business, those firms found it imperative to follow what Denisoff called "the buckshot theory of record releasing." As his explanation suggests, the approach had important consequences for new artists hoping to break through to success:

> CBS Records, with its plant and catalog, must produce an enormous amount of product to keep its various bureaus, agencies and departments busy. Of every 10 records released, only 2 or 3 will sell. Consequently, large companies must produce massive amounts of product to sustain their large corporate bodies. Huge investments are made and must be maintained. A concentration upon proven talent, coupled with the 7 to 3 ratio, motivates the larger companies to treat newcomers indiscriminately, at the same time competing with each other for surefire sellers.... Capitol [Records] operates on what [an executive] calls Formula 10, which is nearly identical to Columbia's 7 to 3 ratio. Capitol's advertising department head believes that in 10 releases at least one should be gold with several others bringing in a sizable return.[83]

The third strategy Hirsch mentions, coopting mass media gatekeepers, is likely to be used in conjunction with other strategies. Gatekeepers are people who make decisions about whether or not to select certain material for production. Thus, coopting mass media gatekeepers means convincing gatekeepers of particular media to promote mass media material that is available for sale elsewhere—in retail outlets or through mail. Examples are easily found: a record promoter who persuades a radio station's program director to play a particular record; a public relations agent who convinces a talk show coordinator to schedule the author of a new book on the show; and a movie studio publicist who convinces television network programmers to produce a special about how a new movie was made.

The Linking Pin and Facilitator Roles

The examples in the foregoing paragraph point to activities that are often underestimated, or even ignored, when sociologists speak of influences on mass media production. Borrowing a term from industrial sociology, we will call these activities *linking pin* activities. They involve the movement of completed material or people representing that material from production firms in one industry to production firms in another industry. They are key aspects of a mass media cross-fertilization process that serves to tie together publics that otherwise might have little in common. Consider how often you have seen certain people or subjects appear on television, in magazines, on book covers, and in the movies during a particular period. Not only does this phenomenon exist regarding "hard news" (the governmental, economic, and crime reports of the day), it holds true for "soft news" (tales of ordinary people and discussions of the arts) and fiction.[84] Brooke Shields might appear in a new movie, on a magazine cover, and on a TV talk show in the course of the same week. Similarly, Tom Wolfe might discuss his new book on TV's "Good Morning America," on Mutual radio's "Larry King Show," and with *Time* magazine on the same day.

As the several examples suggest, much linking pin activity is "promotional" from the standpoint of the organization that initiates the interindustry connection. Production firms that want to ensure that the largest possible number of people find out about their creations often turn to others mass media to spread the word. Often, they will devolve this linking pin power role upon public relations or advertising agencies specialized in this task. Other times the production organizations themselves act as linking pins; special units arrange to tout the firms' creations in other media. In the case of large media conglomerates, transactions might even take place among various arms of the company. An example is when *Time* magazine carries a piece about the programming of Home Box Office, a cable television subsidiary of Time, Incorporated.

But not all organizations promoting interindustry links are advertising or public relations agencies or divisions. Sometimes they may be production organizations pursuing the output of other media for their own uses. They might do so because they want assuredly popular material, or because they find that borrowing from other media is the easiest way to fill time or space in their own medium. Thus producers of TV's "Phil Donahue Show," who need to come up with controversial guests for five hour-long programs each week, might rely on a variety of magazines and books for suggestions. And a movie production firm might purchase the movie rights to a popular new novel in the hope that its popularity will carry over to a planned film. Certainly, firms that are the object of such linking pin pursuits usually do not discourage the situation. Richard Snyder, president of the Simon and Schuster book publishing company, recognized the importance of interindustry connections when he said, "In a certain sense, we are the software of the television and movie media."[85]

Probably the most important linking pin organizations in the world are the major international news wire services—the Associated Press, Reuters, United Press International, Agence France Presse, and TASS. These firms are producers in what might be called "the raw material news" industry. That industry generates thousands of nonfiction stories that are sold across mass media boundaries as building blocks for newspapers, radio and TV newscasts, magazines, even books. Examples of a few other linking pins in the raw material news industry are the investigative journalism collectives (the Community Information Project, the Center for Investigative Reporting, and the Better Government Association) which sell their reports to newspapers, magazines, and television networks;[86] the major international picture agencies (Sygma, Magnum, Gamma-Liaison, Sipa, Black Star, and Contact) which, for a fee, will help photographers sell their work to newspapers, magazines, and book publishers throughout the world;[87] and picture libraries, such as the Bettmann Archive, which rent historical pictures on a wide variety of subjects to production firms in various mass media industries.

The role of linking pin organizations is to move mass media material, or people representing that material, across, then through, other mass media industries. By contrast, organizations that take on *facilitator* roles work *within* mass media industries to help initiate, carry out, or evaluate mass material in the first place. The kinds of organizations and specific activities we are talking about run a wide gamut. They include representation agencies that suggest artists to production firms and negotiate their contracts; law firms that help production firms in dealing with investors, authorities, and distributors; consulting firms that help producers create certain mass media material; and market research firms that survey the environment for production firms, determine how previous material has fared, project how current material might do, and suggest why.

The consequences of these facilitation activities for mass media material can sometimes be profound, as forthcoming chapters will show. Consider, for a start, the position of a large talent agency (say, William Morris or International Creative Management) in the process. On a rudimentary level, a talent agency's purpose is to serve as a negotiating intermediary between a particular creator-client—for example, an actor, director, composer, or writer—and the production organization. The agency's mandate is to get the client work, and then the best deal possible from the firm that wants the client's services. Over the years, however, large talent agencies have parlayed their influential client lists into an ability not only to suggest and negotiate for individuals, but actually to come to a production firm with a package of talent.

A *package* is a coalition of two or more elements useful in creating a mass media product. Through its writer-clients, the talent agency knows what manuscripts are available, or potentially available. At the same time, through its producer, director, and actor clients it can keep close tabs on needs and desires in their creative bailiwicks. Putting together some of these elements might yield a plan for a movie or television series using the agency's clients that a production firm might find very attractive. The latter, for its part, might appreciate the agency's packaging activities, since it saves the firm a good deal of time, effort, and money trying to do the same thing.[88] In fact, talent firms often act as linking pins as well as facilitators, since they frequently parlay particular groups of talent into packages that cross media boundaries. Thomas Whiteside has described that activity well:

> A script is an "element," so is a writer, so are a book, a producer, an actor or a group of actors, a director. In contrast to simpler times, in which it was taken for granted that a published book originated with the author...[the package] does not have to take place in the mind of a writer; it can occur around a conference table in the office of a producer or an agent, who may then add to it "elements" including the writer, who is "acquired" sooner or later in the packaging process.[89]

Not all "packaging" deals are consummated, of course. Such negotiations are very delicate, since they involve placing value on every element in the package, as well as on the package as a whole. In addition, production firm executives might not want certain individuals in the package, preferring to substitute their own choices in those creative slots. Nevertheless, use of talent agencies to facilitate the production of material has become a pervasive fact of life in mass media industries.

The Public Advocacy and Public Power Roles

The last two power roles in Table 1—the public advocacy and public roles—have already been introduced earlier in this chapter. Little more will be said about them here. That is because the task of drawing out their actual implications for mass media material is so great that it demands a separate chapter (Chapter Three). At this point, we will stress only that publics come into existence when scattered groups or individuals share certain mass media material. By contrast, public advocacy organizations emerge when those individuals or groups systematically band together to demand that producer, distributor, or exhibitor organizations change certain procedures or policies regarding mass media content. While the public's leverage includes individual consumer purchasing decisions, viewing decisions, and complaints, public advocacy power might be expressed through boycotts of offending organizations (or their investors and patrons) and through political clout with authorities that regulate the offending entities. Note that the word "audience" has not been mentioned. Chapter Two will take up the meaning of "audience" and the surprising importance it has for illuminating mass media process.

SOME IMPLICATIONS OF THE FRAMEWORK

I hope that the usefulness of the power role framework for studying the interorganizational activities within and across mass media industries is now apparent. Certainly, using the scheme to draw further illustrations regarding the roles can be very instructional; it can also go on forever. At this point, it will be more helpful to step back and approach the framework as a whole after becoming familiar with its parts. The reason is that the power role framework and its underlying resource dependence perspective carry with them crucial implications for the production of mass media material in society that could very well be missed when carrying out specific role analyses.

One basic point to stress is that the roles represent interdependent *activities* of organizations and groups; they are not organizations or groups per se. A corollary of this point is that organizations may take on more than one role within a mass media industry. Earlier examples have already shown that producers are sometimes also distributors, exhibitors, and linking pins; that linking pins are sometimes also facilitators; that exhibitors are sometimes also patrons. The overlapping of other roles might be harder to imagine—for example, the convergence of producer, patron, and auxiliary roles. However, in today's world of many-tiered, vertically integrated conglomerates—and in countries outside the United States—such combinations are not at all out of the question. Only the public, public advocacy, and creator roles are, by the very nature of their definitions, not able to be carried out by organizations that also act as producers.

The accumulation of roles by an organization means an accumulation of the organization's ability to garner resources. That, in turn, means an accumulation of the organization's ability to exert leverage within (and possibly across) mass media industries. Organizations can also increase their influence by forming role coalitions with other organizations for short or long periods of time. Thus a union might increase its leverage with a producer by marshaling the support of another union, or of an auxiliary organization. The latter two might agree to help the union out of genuine concern for its cause, or out of an assurance that reciprocal help will come forth in the future. This view of mass communication as, at base, a dynamic interorganizational struggle over resources with sometimes shifting power centers and alliances should put to rest any notions that mass media material results from the straightforward process of "giving the public what it wants." Certainly, the public is a factor in an industry's scheme of things.

But it is only one factor. Other power roles may at times be more salient, and carry more leverage, than do scattered, individual consumers.

In every established mass media industry there is a pattern of roles that the organizations maintain with one another. That role pattern is what we mean when we refer to an industry's *structure*. The broadcast television industry's structure, for example, is found in the rather predictable relationships that networks, Hollywood production firms, communication law firms, market research firms, pressure groups, and other entities have with one another. As earlier sections of this chapter imply, an important step toward understanding the structure of an industry lies in understanding the historical events that have caused the various elements to coalesce in a certain way. Relationships not developed, leverage possibilities not pursued, resources not exploited—these and other omissions may have their roots in critical incidents, power struggles, and national philosophies that shaped the industry at its birth or at later critical junctures.

The structure of a mass media industry ultimately reflects the overall power relations of the society in which it emerges and develops. That is because the dominant interests that guide the economy are, by extension, the ones that set the basic terms on which resources become available to organizations wanting to produce and disseminate messages publicly on a large scale.[90] Those vested interests will not allow the basic industrial relationships and perspectives that shape the shared messages of the society to deviate fundamentally from mainstream industrial relationships and perspectives. The tendency is clear in any system, whether it be capitalism, state socialism, or a mixed economy. Thus it is inconceivable that the contemporary United States would have its most pervasive media free of corporate, commercial involvement just as it is inconceivable that the contemporary U.S.S.R. would allow commercial interests independent of the government to control its television, radio, movie, newspaper, and magazine complexes.

These implications of the power role framework and resource dependence perspective will, together with specifics presented throughout this chapter, serve as both a first step and constant backdrop to the discussions that follow. The next two chapters will continue the present industrial bent, focusing in some depth on the influence of patrons, the public, and public advocacy groups on mass media material. The chapters following them will shift from the essentially interorganizational level of analysis to one that deals more specifically with the organizations and people that actually produce mass media material. Toward the book's end we will return to the industry-wide focus. Through it all, the resource dependence approach will remain a crucial aid in helping to find pattern amid complexity, and in helping to show that the creation of mass media culture cannot be truly understood without reference to the broad industrial and social environment in which the production of symbols takes place.

REFERENCES

1. Jim Harmon, *The Great Radio Heroes* (New York: Signet, 1967), p. 8.

2. Quoted in Melvin DeFleur and Everette Dennis, *Understanding Mass Communication* (Boston: Houghton Mifflin, 1981), p. 354.

3. See Russel Nye, *The Unembarrassed Muse* (New York: Dial Press, 1970); and Raymond Stedman, *The Serials* (Norman: University of Oklahoma, 1977).

4. See Nye, *The Unembarrassed Muse*, for example; also see John Cawelti, *The Six Gun Mystique* (Bowling Green: Bowling Green University Press, 1972).

5. John Dunning, *Tune in Yesterday* (Englewood Cliffs: Prentice Hall, 1976), p. 196.

6. Clyde Kluckhohn, "The Study of Culture," in D. Lerner and H. Lasswell (eds.), *The Policy Sciences* (Stanford, Calif.: Stanford University Press, 1951), p. 86.

7. Leonard Maltin, *Of Mice and Magic* (New York: New American Library, 1980).

8. See, for example, John Tebbel, *A History of Book Publishing in America*, vol. 1 (New York: Bowker, 1972); Richard Altick, *The English Common Reader* (Chicago: University of Chicago, 1957); Ronald Fullerton, "Creating a Mass Book Market in Germany: The Story of the 'Colporteur Novel' 1870–1890," *Journal of Social History* 10 (Spring 1976), pp. 265–283; Edwin Emery and Michael Emery, *The Press and America*, 4th ed. (Englewood Cliffs, New Jersey: Prentice Hall, 1978); Dan Schiller, *Objectivity and the News* (Philadelphia: University of Pennsylvania, 1981); and John Tebbel, *The Media in America* (New York: Crowell, 1974).

9. Andrew Fletcher, *Conversation concerning a Right Regulation of Government for the Common Good of Mankind* [1703] Quoted in John Bartlett, *Famous Quotations*, 15th ed. (New York: Little Brown, 1955), p. 290.

10. Irving Berlin, "Let Me Sing and I'm Happy."

11. Quoted in Edwin Emery, *The Press and America*, 3rd ed. (Englewood Cliffs, New Jersey: Prentice Hall, 1972), p. 55.

12. An interesting discussion of this issue is in Martin Battestin, ed., *Joseph Andrews*, by Henry Fielding (Boston: Houghton Mifflin Riverside Edition, 1961), pp. xix–xl.

13. Ben Bagdikian, *The Information Machines* (New York: Harper and Row, 1971), p. 7.

14. Bagdikian, p. 7.

15. For two important overviews of this research, see James Curran, Michael Gurevitch, and Janet Woollacott, eds., *Mass Communication and Society* (London: Edward Arnold, 1977); and Michael Gurevitch, Tony Bennett, James Curran, and Janet Woollacott, eds., *Culture, Society and the Media* (London: Methuen & Co., 1982).

16. Graham Murdock, "Large Corporations and the Control of Communication Industries," in Gurevitch, Bennett, Curran, and Woollacott, eds., p. 144.

17. Graham Murdock and Peter Golding, "Capitalism, Communication, and Class Relations," in Curran, Gurevitch, and Woollacott, eds., p. 37.

18. James Curran, Michael Gurevitch, and Janet Woollacott, "The Study of

Media: Theoretical Apporoaches," in Gurevitch, Bennett, Curran, and Woolla-cott, eds., p. 20.

19. Howard Aldrich, *Organizations and Environments* (Englewood Cliffs, New Jersey: 1979), p. 4.

20. Aldrich, p. 4.

21. Aldrich, p. 5.

22. Aldrich, p. 4.

23. Ephraim Yuchtman and Stanley Seashore, "A System Resource Approach to Organizational Effectiveness," *American Sociological Review*, vol. 32 (December 1967), p. 900.

24. Aldrich, p. 267.

25. Richard Emerson, "Power-Dependence Relations," *American Sociological Review*, vol. 27 (February 1962), p. 32.

26. Aldrich, p. 268.

27. George Gerbner, "Institutional Pressures upon Mass Communicators," *The Sociological Review, Monograph 13* (1969), p. 243.

28. Gerbner, "Institutional Pressures upon Mass Communicators," p. 243.

29. Michael Hannan and John Freeman, "The Population Ecology of Organizations," *American Journal of Sociology*, vol. 82 (March 1977), pp. 929–964; and Aldrich, *passim.*

30. See *Advertising Age*, April 20, 1981, p. 81: *Advertising Age*, October 19, 1981, p. S27; and Cecilia Lentini, "Balancing Act in Women's Magazines," *Advertising Age*, October 19, 1981, pp. S62–S64.

31. Aldrich, p. 63–70.

32. Erik Barnouw, *The Image Empire* (New York: Oxford University Press, 1970).

33. Otto Friedrich, *Decline and Fall* (New York: Harper and Row, 1970).

34. Lentini, p. 562.

35. See *Advertising Age*, December 14, 1981, p. 75 and *Advertising Age*, October 19, 1981, pp. S-5 and S-27.

36. Erik Barnouw, *A Tower in Babel* (New York: Oxford University Press, 1968).

37. Richard Allen Schwarzlose, *The American Wire Services* (New York: Arno Press, 1979), p. 239.

38. Kenneth Cox, "The Federal Communications Commission," *Boston College Industrial and Commercial Law Review*, vol. xi (May 1970), pp. 605–66.

39. J.W. Click and Russell N. Baird, *Magazine Editing and Production*, 2nd ed. (Dubuque, Iowa: William C. Brown, 1979), pp. 280–287; and Ernest C. Hynds, *American Newspapers in the 1980s* (New York: Hastings House, p. 157.

40. Erik Barnouw, *The Golden Web* (New York, Oxford University Press, 1968), pp. 311–347; and Kenneth Cox, p. 631.

41. See Don R. Pember, *Mass Media Law* (Dubuque, Iowa: William C. Brown, 1977).

42. Click and Baird, p. 281.

43. Pember, pp. 3–4.

44. See, for example, Barry Cole and Mal Oettinger, *Reluctant Regulators* (Reading, Massachusetts: Addison-Wesley, 1978), pp. 243–288; and Joseph

Turow, *Entertainment, Education, and the Hard Sell* (New York: Praeger Publishers, 1981).

45. Thomas Guback, "Theatrical Film," in Benjamin M. Compaine, ed., *Who Owns the Media* (White Plains, New York: Knowledge Industry Publications, 1979), pp. 179–250.

46. Christopher Sterling, "Cable and Pay Television," in Benjamin M. Compaine, ed., *Who Owns the Media* (White Plains, New York: Knowledge Industry Publications, 1979), pp. 293–318.

47. Lewis Jacobs, *The Rise of the American Film* (New York: Teacher's College Press edition, 1968), pp. 302–335 and 433–453; and Arthur Knight, *The Liveliest Art* (New York: Signet edition, 1957), pp. 142–187 and 274–312.

48. Click and Baird, pp. 204–220; and Hynds, pp. 261–282.

49. Hynds, p. 273.

50. Hynds, p. 279.

51. Click and Baird, pp. 214–220.

52. Click and Baird, p. 215.

53. Muriel Cantor makes this point specifically with regard to the broadcast television industry in Muriel Cantor, *Prime Time Television* (Beverly Hills, California: Sage Publications, 1980), pp. 85–91.

54. Charlton Heston, "Actors as Union Men," in A. William Bleum and Jason Squire, eds., *The Movie Business* (New York: Hastings House, 1972), pp. 136–139.

55. Hynds, p. 164.

56. John Dessauer, *Book Publishing* (New York: R. R. Bowker, 1974), p. 34.

57. M William Krasilovsky, "Motivation and Control in Creative Writing," in Bleum and Squire, eds., p. 33.

58. J. Kenneth Rotcap, "The Story Editor," in Bleum and Squire, eds., p. 22.

59. Amy Kaufman, "It's Easier Now Than It Used to Be," *Emmy Magazine*, vol. 3 (Fall 1981), pp. 38–41.

60. Ronald Gelatt, *The Fabulous Phonograph* (Philadelphia: Lippincott, 1955), pp. 40–45.

61. Jacobs, pp. 81–95.

62. Barnouw, *A Tower in Babel*, pp. 52–74.

63. J. Kendrick Noble, Jr., "Books," in Benjamin Compaine, ed., pp. 254–255.

64. Guback, p. 183.

65. Guback, p. 186.

66. Guback, p. 186.

67. Guback, p. 201.

68. Guback, p. 200. In the early 1980s, the majors, often in partnership with other media giants, began to exert strong distribution control over movie markets that were growing in importance—videocassette, cable, and videodisc. At the time, these markets were still considered ancillary or subsidiary. That is, the most promising product was material that had already done well in theatrical distribution. So theatrical distribution was still considered very important for a film's success. The majors, however, were acting to ensure that power over possible mainstream distribution channels of the future would not elude them.

69. *Broadcasting Yearbook, 1979*, pp. A-1 and D-49.

70. Christopher H. Sterling, "Television and Radio Broadcasting," in Compaine, ed., p. 201.

71. See, for example, Les Brown, *Television: The Business Behind the Box* (New York: Harcourt, Brace, 1972); Sally Bedell, *Up the Tube* (New York: Viking, 1981); and Joseph Turow, "Unconventional Programs on Commercial Network Television," in D. Charles Whitney and James Ettema, *Mass Communicators in Context* (Beverly Hills, California: Sage, 1982).

72. Sterling, "Television and Radio Broadcasting," in Compaine, p. 107–108.

73. Sterling, "Television and Radio Broadcasting," in Compaine, p. 105. In 1983, Metromedia, a powerful station group that potentially could reach about 24% of the population through six independent television outlets and one network affiliate, seemed convinced it had the clout to successfully syndicate prime time series. The company's effort centered on mixing old and new episodes of two series that had recently been canceled by the networks, "Fame" and "Two Close For Comfort." For details on this exception that proves the rule, see *Electronic Media*, August 4, 1983, p. 22.

74. Quoted in Martin Koughan, "The State of the Revolution, 1982," *Channels*, vol. 1 (December, 1981–January, 1982), p. 25.

75. Koughan, p. 25.

76. Koughan, p. 25.

77. Koughan, p. 25.

78. Quoted in Henry Geller, "Law Review: Putting the Lock on Cable," *Channels*, vol. 1 (December 1981–January 1982), p. 62.

79. *Variety*, January 12, 1983, p. 74. Several of the new radio networks ultimately failed.

80. Noble, "Books," in Compaine, p. 284.

81. "New Women's Magazine Aiming Big," *Advertising Age*, March 2, 1981, p. 40.

82. Paul Hirsch, "Processing Fads and Fashions," *American Journal of Sociology*, vol. 77 (January 1972), pp. 639–659.

83. R. Serge Denisoff, *Solid Gold: The Popular Record Industry* (New Brunswick, New Jersey: Transaction Books), pp. 97–98.

84. Joseph Turow, "Local TV: Producing Soft News," *Journal of Communication*, vol. 33 (Spring 1983), pp. 111–123.

85. Quoted in Thomas Whiteside, *The Blockbuster Complex* (Middletown, Connecticut: Wesleyan University Press, 1981), p. 70.

86. Ron Powers, "Behind Mike Wallace," *TV Guide*, December 19, 1981, pp. 5–10.

87. *Time*, December 28, 1981, pp. 28–29.

88. Lew Weitzman, "The Literary Agent: The Large Agency," in Bleum and Squire, pp. 20–21.

89. Whiteside, p. 70.

90. Aldrich, pp. 297–350; and Anthony Giddens, *The Class Structure of Advanced Societies* (London: Hutchinson, 1973).

Two

The Key Connection: The Producer-Patron Relationship

"Money talks." Maybe that well-worn phrase is the best short way to explain this chapter's title. The idea is that the relationship mass media production organizations have with patron organizations is typically the most important relationship they maintain with their environment. Of course, *all* the power roles discussed in Chapter One exert influence on the activities of producers. Authorities are unquestionably crucial, since they set the basic terms under which all mass media operate. The argument here, though, is that once the most basic of the authorities' conditions are set, the interactions between patrons and producers take over as the most pivotal interorganizational forces shaping day-to-day change and continuity in mass media material.

The reason for this contention lies in what patron organizations do. Recall that patrons make purchases in support of existing products before those products reach the public. For example, advertisers purchase space in newspapers and magazines in the hope that readers will buy their products, book stores purchase books from publishers with the aim of retailing them profitably, and record stores buy discs and tapes to sell profitably to the public as well.[1] In acting as patrons, these organizations provide production firms with the cash flow that is most directly responsible for their survival. In fact, dominant mass media patrons decide by their purchases whether particular mass materials will be released to the public. By extension, the patrons also help determine the kinds of materials producers will create in the first place.

The purpose of this chapter is to support these propositions, and to extend them. The examination of the producer-patron relationship will show that while the phrase "money talks" may be a rough indicator of patrons' importance for producers, a better way to phrase their relationship is that money starts an interorganizational conversation. Indeed, influence in the producer-patron relationship runs both ways—from producers to patrons as well as from patrons to producers. Too, the influence runs deep, even to the decision making structures of production organizations and to the images producer and patron executives hold of their audiences.

THE VARIETY OF PRODUCER-PATRON RELATIONSHIPS

The examples of patrons in the newspaper, magazine, book publishing, and record industries that we used at the start of this chapter can be recycled here to make another point: There is no uniformity to the kinds of organizations that take on the patron role. In fact, even within an industry one sector may have different kinds of patrons from another sector. Take the book industry as an example. While book stores as a broad class are important to the solvency of many publishers, there are also many publishers that rarely turn to book stores as key monetary supporters of their products' public release. Libraries are crucial to publishers of certain technical monographs, digests, encyclopedia, and other volumes; school boards and schools are crucial in the elementary and high school ("el-hi") market; and wholesale independent distributors are the chief purchasers and store rackers of books in the paperback mass market.

But the complexity does not stop here. Even within a sector of an industry different kinds of patrons may exist, and they may hold different levels of importance. Trade book publishers that have book stores as their major clients may also sell a fair amount to public libraries. Similarly, children's book publishers that aim mostly at the library market may, at times, find that stores are also profitable clients for some titles. It is useful, then, to speak of *primary* and *secondary* producer-patron relationships. Whether a type of patron is primary in a producer's scheme of things can be gauged using two criteria: (1) the contribution of that type of patron to the solvency of the production firm (or the division of the firm that is under study); and (2) the independence of that patron from other kinds of patrons when it purchases material from the firm. The more important the client is to the producer's solvency, the more likely that it is a primary patron to the producer. And, the more independent the client is, the more likely that it is a primary patron to the producer.

The second criterion can be illustrated by referring to the general trade and el-hi sectors of the book industry. In both arenas, jobbers, or wholesale distributors, act as efficient middlemen between the publishers and the outlets; schools and book stores often buy from them.[2] Consequently, one jobber may very well purchase more textbooks than might many schools, and it might purchase more trade books than might many book stores. Still, the jobber should not be considered the primary patron. That is because to a very large extent the jobber's purchasing decisions depend upon the menus of books the schools and stores wish to present to their publics. Usually, then, the schools and stores are the primary patrons. Of course, exceptions can be noted. One kind of exception occurs when a jobber takes on the responsibility of stocking trade book shelves of department stores or groups of book stores. In that situation, the jobber's role in the sector can be considered equivalent to that of book stores.

Typically, the most prominent sectors of American mass media are associated with one of three kinds of patrons—exhibitors, distributors, or advertisers. The general trade sector of book publishing is a case where organizations that hold the exhibitor power role often serve as primary patrons. A different situation obtains in the United States movie industry. There the major distributors, rather than the exhibitors (the theaters), take on the primary patron role. Seven powerful distribution firms—Columbia, Paramount, Twentieth Century Fox, MGM/United Artists, Universal, Warner Brothers, and Buena Vista (Disney)—direct about ninety per cent of Hollywood's product to the overwhelming number of American movie theaters and subsidiary outlets.[3] As noted in Chapter One, the theaters generally have little to say in this matter. Probably the most important commitment the majors feel to exhibitors is to supply an ample number of films to keep the screens reasonably busy and prevent independent distributors from intruding, particularly during peak (holiday) movie-going periods.

Drawing on money they made on previous films and on long-term bank finance arrangements, the major distributors provide cash for the making of films to their own production firms. They get the cash primarily from film distribution revenues and from revolving credit with banks. This form of in-house patronage in itself accounts for a substantial proportion of Hollywood product. However, because of the increasing costs of creating theatrical movies (a 1981 film averaged near ten million dollars), the majors have been interested in devolving some of the risk upon a small cadre of independent production firms (often called "minimajors") that use their distribution arms.

So, for example, in the late 1970s, Lorimar Productions inked a pact for fifteen films to be distributed by United Artists; Orion Pictures and the

Ladd Company signed agreements with Warner; Rastar had an agreement with Columbia, and Casablanca arranged a distribution deal with Universal. Such arrangements benefit both parties. The distributors get an increased diet of movies from reliable suppliers to circulate, and a cut of the box office gross that usually begins at thirty-five per cent. The minimajors forego that wopping royalty for the privilege of plugging into the most efficient and powerful method of distribution available. Very often, too, the distributor's cut is raised even higher, or other favorable arrangements are made, for guarantees of monetary support by the distributor. Such support often comes in the form of a loan. For example, in the 1970s Warner put considerable financing behind the newly formed Ladd Company for an exclusive right to distribute the firm's product. At other times the distributor helps by guaranteeing an independent producer's bank loans. A case in point is Warner's co-signing of the $100 million line of bank credit for Orion Pictures that helped the firm get off the ground. Frequently, the patronage comes indirectly as well. When a bank finds out that a major distributor has agreed to carry several films by an independent producer, the firm's success becomes more plausible, and the bank is more willing to extend credit for the making of those films.[4]

The third form of media patronage—advertising—is without question the most pervasive form in the United States. Advertising involves payment for calling attention to a product, service, or need. Whether the subject is Coca Cola, a cleaning store, or the United Way, the goal of advertising is straightforward—to persuade people to purchase or otherwise support the product, service, or need. Advertising is sometimes carried out by itself, separately from other kinds of mass media material. Mass-produced billboards, handbills, catalogs, audiocassettes, records, even videodiscs, and part of a blizzard of media that carry only advertising messages.[5] At the same time, advertisers find it useful to place their announcements alongside material that does not carry overtly persuasive intent—material such as newspaper and magazine articles, radio programs, and television shows. Their hope is that the people using those media will also attend to the commercial messages and act favorably in response to them.

Clearly, then, advertisers' patronage of mass media is a direct outgrowth of their desire to reach people who might respond favorable to their messages. The monetary outlay for this rather simple desire is stratospheric. In 1980, the 100 companies that led in United States advertising spent an estimated $13 billion on that activity. Most of that money was used to purchase time or space among attractive nonadvertising material on television, radio, in magazines, or in newspapers. For example, the 25 top newspaper advertisers spent $616 million; the 25 top magazine advertisers spent $887 million; the 25 top local radio advertisers spent $281 million; the 25 top network TV advertisers spent a bit over $2 billion.[6]

Note that these numbers do not reflect the media patronage of thousands of companies that spent much smaller amounts on advertising. Still, it is worth paying particular attention to the largest mass media customers, since their largesse might be of particular significance to the solvency of production firms within a mass media industry, or even of the industry as a whole. It is hard for television executives to ignore Procter and Gamble, for example, which spent about $650 million on advertising in 1980, sixty-six per cent of it going to network TV and twenty-two per cent going to local stations. Similarly, newspaper executives might find it difficult not to consider the Loew's Theater Corporation, which placed about forty-one per cent of its $113 million ad budget into that medium. Even more difficult to ignore are classes of advertisers—food firms, airlines, automobile manufacturers, tobacco companies, and the like—that pack a lot of financial clout in certain mass media industries. For example, only five airlines (TWA, United, American, Eastern, and Delta) together contributed about $92 million to newspaper coffers in 1980. And only four food companies (General Foods, Dart/Kraft, Norton Simon, and Campbell Soup) provided about $85 million of support to magazines in the form of advertising space purchases.[7]

Less obvious, but even more concentrated in their ability to direct the flow of cash to mass media, are the leading advertising agencies that service the national advertisers. These organizations clarify, crystallize, even create, the advertising plans of their clients. They produce advertising material based on those plans, purchase media space or time for the material, and evaluate the success of the efforts with the aid of market research firms (which they sometimes own). In the process they direct hundreds of millions of dollars toward various mass media industries. They also spend tens of millions more to produce mass media material that vies for public attention alongside material by the production firms they patronize. In 1980, twenty-six advertising agencies each paid over $200 million to various United States mass media for carrying their commercial announcements. The range of manufacturers whose cash the agencies controlled was quite broad. For example, J. Walter Thompson, second largest United States agency with just over two billion dollars in ad placement billings, operated in support of firms as diverse as H & R Block Income Tax, Kellogg, California Milk Producers Advisory Board, and Ford Motor Company. The agency allocated forty-five per cent of its billings to network television, twenty-three per cent to local ("spot") television, eighteen per cent to magazines, six per cent to newspapers, one per cent to outdoor (billboard) advertising, and two per cent to other media (presumably including cable and new media technologies). Other agency leaders doled out money in rather similar proportions.[8]

The interconnection of advertisers, advertising agencies, and market research firms in supporting the production of newspapers, magazines, television programs, and other mass media material indicates that when it comes to advertising, the "patron" is an industry itself, rather than a single type of organization. While advertisers put up the money to proclaim their products, services, or needs, advertising agencies often set the agenda for that money's use, frequently with the aid of market research firms. Small wonder, then, that many production firm executives see the major advertising agencies as the key forces within the United States media's major support system. Undoubtedly this idea was on the mind of Don Lachowski, a vice-president of sales at Turner Broadcasting System, which is heavily committed to ad-supported cable. Speaking to a group of advertising industry executives in 1980, Lachowski complained that some major ad agencies have been so reluctant to take risks that they have deliberately played down the probable impact of the new forms of video technology on conventional TV in the decade to come. He contended that advertiser initiative, rather than agency initiative, has provided the greatest thrust toward sponsor revenues for both Turner networks—the Cable News Network and the satellite—transmitted "superstation," WTBS, Atlanta. The frequent agency attitude, he said, has been that "if we ignore it [the new technologies] and pretend it doesn't exist, maybe it will go away."[9]

THE RELATIONSHIP AND MASS MEDIA MATERIAL

Lachowski's concern about the flow of advertising dollars into his sector of the cable industry points to the clearest influence of the producer-patron relationship on mass media content. Simply, if there is no money to create the material, it will not be created. It warrants mention that Lachowski's comments came at a point in the cable industry's history when the advertising industry was still unclear as to how broad and deep a commitment it was willing to make. Still, the general problem is not unusual. Every year, book publishers, magazine publishers, record producers, and newspapers publishers go out of business because patrons will not support them. Once in a while, entire niches within mass media industries also see their patron resources dry up. Overall, though, many mass media producers do thrive. It is to the influence of the producer-patron relationship on their output that we now turn.

The Relationship as a Communication System

Before investigating specific influences in some detail, it will be useful to explore the very idea of such an interorganizational connection. What does it really mean to talk about a relationship between production and patron firms within a mass media industry? At times in this book we have described dealings of one organization with another organization as just that—the exchanges between faceless entities. Of course, we have always assumed—and often noted—that people make up these organizations and carry out their tasks. Here, however, it pays to be more systematic and careful about this point, since it bears strongly on an understanding of the producer-patron relationship.

To start, we should return to the definition of organizations that we adopted from Howard Aldrich in Chapter One: Organizations are goal directed, boundary maintaining activity systems. Recall that activity systems are interdependent behaviors—roles—carried out during the process of accomplishing work. This feature of organizations highlights their essentially social nature. People hired to work in an organization learn the basic activities that are expected of them. They learn from descriptions of their jobs and through dealings with people already established in the organization. And, in the process of learning, the newcomers take part in creating their roles. That is because the way they go about their activities helps shape the way other organizational members act toward them. And, since roles are not static descriptions but, rather, mutually dependent behaviors, it can be said that roles are continually acted out and reinforced through this kind of communication.

The two-way, reciprocal process that is involved in defining roles within an organization can also be found in dealings of organizations with one another. Indeed, the key to understanding the influence of the producer-patron relationship lies in conceiving it as a communication system involving members of the patron and production organizations of mass media industry. The function of such a communication system for each organization in the relationship can be further specified by recalling Aldrich's proposition that "major goals of organizational leaders are avoiding dependence on other [organizations] and making others dependent on one's own organization." It is also helpful to consider a prominent body of material on the sociology of work that stresses the importance of developing role-related routines.[10] Routines allow people to work much more efficiently than if they had to consider every task, every problem, anew. Of course, in order to develop routines organizational members try to ensure that their activities carry with them at least a minimal level of predictability. The reason is basic. If you cannot predict what will happen, you cannot develop routines for managing it.

One class of concerns that all organizational leaders try to manage relates to the various entities that control resources in their organizations' environments. Mass media production firm executives worry particularly about their firms' primary patrons because they affect the solvency of the firm quite directly. These patrons become what William Evan has called "normative reference organizations."[11] That is, they become entities that production executives see as generating requirements that they must incorporate in their work or change if they are to succeed. Production executives usually aim to do some of both. To achieve this, they assign special "boundary" employees (salespeople, public relations personnel, technical personnel) the specific task of representing the organizations successfully to patron firms. The production firm leaders and their agents recognize that executives in patron organizations need to derive benefits from their support of producers. Exactly what the clients need depends on the kind of patron organizations involved. Sometimes (as when book or record stores are patrons) the overall goal is the profitable retailing of patronized products. Other times (as when advertisers are the clients) the goal is to reach people who will respond favorably to certain messages.

We have in this interpersonal tango the kind of mutual dependence that we would expect to lead to the development of roles in a sustained relationship. In view of the executives' general desire for independence and predictability regarding their environment, we would expect that boundary personnel and high level executives of production firms would try to cultivate role definitions with boundary personnel and executives in patron organizations that would be both manageably predictable and profitable for the production firms. Too, we would expect that patron executives and their boundary personnel would try cultivate role definitions with boundary personnel and executives in production firms that would be manageably predictable and profitable for the patron organizations. The influence of the producer-patron relationship, then, would flow from the continual interactions of the parties that make up the relationship. Those interactions would comprise a communication system through which the requirements and opportunities posed by each party regarding the other would be perceived, negotiated, assimilated, and acted upon.

A couple of corollaries to this perspective on the producer-patron relationship should be introduced here. One stems from the idea that the relationship is continually in the process of reenactment. A proposition to draw from this idea is that knowing how a producer-patron relationship got to a particular point has relevance for explaining its present situation. A second corollary is that every relationship involving one production and patron organization must necessarily be different from relationships involving any other producer-patron pair. That is because the perceptions a given organization's executives hold regarding the environment will inevitably be at least somewhat different from those in other organizations. The differences emerge simply by virtue of the different people involved, their history together, the tradition of their organization, and the history of their organization's interactions with other organizations.

At the same time, it would be incorrect to make too much of the differences between relationships that involve the same type of established producers and the same kinds of established patrons in a particular niche. Doing so would be like seeing trees but not the forest. Certainly, there are differences in the relationships, but there are also important similarities.

The similarities stem from needs by the same kinds of organizations to compete for the same resources and, in the process, engage in parallel, optimally competitive activities. Moreover, emphasizing similarities will lead us to suggest generalizations about the influence of the producer-patron relationship on the creation of mass media content.

Setting General Boundary Conditions for Producer Activity

One generalization that can be suggested with certainty is this: The continual interactions of producers and primary patrons play a dominant part in setting the general boundary conditions for day-to-day production activity. That is, the interactions are important in determining the range of approaches production firm executives might take toward their creations and still maintain the survival of their operation.

It would be wrong to ignore the position of authorities in this aspect of things. By developing regulations and enforcing them, authorities play a profound role in guiding the behavior of mass media industries generally and mass media producers specifically. As noted in Chapter One, the structural, technical, and content regulations that governments promulgate fundamentally shape the manner in which organizations taking on other power roles within a mass media industry may interact. Still, as also noted in Chapter One, the most important actions of authorities in stable societies are generally marked by a conservatism, by a regulatory inertia that encourages the long-term perpetuation of basic government perspectives and edicts. This means that producers can integrate the relevant conditions authorities set into their operations so that those conditions are predictable, not major problems in day-to-day profit and loss decisions. By contrast, the daily expectations and activities of patrons are inherently less predictable since in patronizing particular producers, patrons do not emphasize principles of continuity over change. Rather, they tend to base their media purchasing decisions on shorter-term profit and loss considerations, market strategies, and/or political expediencies. The upshot is that patrons typically provide production people more to weigh and deliberate daily regarding general boundary conditions than do authorities.

The producer-patron relationship helps set general boundary conditions in three areas: (1) the kinds of people that are the targets of the mass media material; (2) the frequency at which the material is released to those people; and (3) the amount it costs to produce and release the material. These boundary conditions are set whether or not members of the production organizations fully realize it. The reason has to do with competition between producers. The number of patrons and the amount of resources they use to support mass media are, of course, limited. Patrons present their resources to producers in exchange for resources the producers provide. Usually, the producers provide the patrons with the ability to reach publics from whom they can derive certain benefits. For example, the benefits might be in the form of profits earned through distributing or retailing the mass media material to publics, or they might be in the form of profits earned by persuading publics to buy certain products through ads. Whatever the way, the kinds of people a production firm presents to clients, the frequency at which it presents those people, and the cost it charges for reaching them (based on the cost of the material) can directly affect the client's ability to make a profit. So, of course, producers presenting patrons with the greatest opportunities to make a profit through their publics will receive support while those that cannot compete on this score will not survive.

This "survival of the fittest" scenario does not mean that a handful of mass media production firms releasing a narrow variety of material will necessarily result. When a large number or variety of patrons interested in a broad range of publics exists, executives in production firms will find it a lot easier to gather support for their ventures than if this heterogeneity were absent. Even in relatively rich resource situations, however, production firm executives will still have to present patrons with products that will bring the kinds of benefits the patrons are seeking at a price they are willing to spend. If the public that a firm's products reaches is of no interest to patrons, the producer will have to fold its operation. Similarly, if the cost of reaching the public is too high for interested patrons to accept, the producers will not be able to continue that approach. And, if some patrons are interested, but not enough of them to sustain the very frequent production of material for that public, the producer will have to release its material less frequently.

These points can be illustrated by looking briefly at the "consumer magazine" area of the United States magazine industry. Consumer magazines represent the segment of the magazine industry that is aimed at the general reading public. "They are called consumer magazines because their readers buy and consume products and services that are sold at retail and may be advertised in those magazines."[12] Advertising represents a crucial vehicle of support in the great majority of these magazines, although an increasing amount of money is earned through reader subscriptions and, sometimes, newsstand sales. Generally, consumer magazines derive about sixty per cent of their revenues from advertising, forty per cent from readers.[13] Judging by the number of consumer magazines that exist in the United States, the environment for supporting this activity is rich indeed. According to *Folio*, the trade magazine for magazine publishers, there were 1,659 magazines distributed in the United States in 1979.[14] The fields of interests were broad—from "girlie" magazines to periodicals about boxing, wrestling, and karate, to those dealing with sewing and crafts, to news magazines and business magazines. Still, the environment for support by advertisers and readers is not unlimited. *Folio* reports that only ten per cent of the approximately 300 magazines started each year in the late 1970s survived a year.[15]

If one trend could be said to encompass the consumer periodical area in the early 1980s, it would be the increased movement to specialization in subject matter and readership. The trend is clearly associated with shifts in advertiser interests away from large general interest magazines during the mid-1960s through the 1970s.[16] Until then, and since the turn of the 1900s, consumer magazines with huge, heterogeneous readerships (e.g., *Life, Look, Coronet, The Saturday Evening Post*) had been very attractive to national advertisers. Magazine publishing firms had tried to build huge circulations by offering readers very low subscription rates. Advertising rates were set to cover the costs of the magazines and profits, provided enough advertising was sold. Advertisers were satisfied with this situation, since it allowed them to use just a number of magazines to reach the kinds of widespread audiences that only network radio could duplicate; and radio could not carry pictures. To satisfy producers and patrons, magazine circulation figures were systematically audited by an independent agency, the Audit Bureau of Circulation (ABC). In addition, to facilitate cost comparison of two periodicals, both parties used an "efficiency" measure, "cost per thousand" (CPM). CPM was (and is) simply the price an advertiser paid to reach a thousand people through a full page, black and white ad.

With the advent of television, however, the situation changed. By the late 1950s, eighty-six per cent of all United States homes had at least one TV set; the number jumped to ninety-three per cent in 1965.[17] Advertisers, attracted to the audiovisual capabilities of TV, realized that the new medium reached basically the same heterogeneous audience as the general consumer magazines at about the same cost. That was the beginning of the end of those periodicals, despite their large readerships. For example, in 1963 *Coronet* ceased publication while carrying a circulation of 3.1 million.[18] *Life, Look, The Saturday Evening Post*, and others of that ilk also died a bit before or during that decade.

Magazine publishing surged back beginning the late 1960s, but it was in a new relationship with advertisers. Many advertisers saw that television filled their needs for reaching giant, diverse segments of the population quickly. Magazine executives, recognizing that the head-on battle with TV was lost, tried to persuade advertisers that certain kinds of periodicals were still worth their advertising dollars: the ones that helped them reach narrower social segments (often the wealthy segments) with specially tailored messages. The magazine executives noted that quality-looking magazines could be produced much less expensively than could prime time television programs. CPMs could therefore be reasonable even if subscribers numbered only in the tens of thousands. That was particularly true if the magazine passed more of its costs along to readers in subscription fees.

Clearly, that procedure lowered page costs and thereby made the magazine more attractive to sponsors. In addition, magazine executives contended that passing more costs on to readers indicated that subscribers would read the magazine (and its ads) more seriously, since they had paid significant sums to receive it. J. W. Click and Russell Baird reflected the advertiser's point of view on this trend: "The efficiency of carrying advertising within a specialized area to persons obviously interested in that activity appeals to advertisers catering to such an area and makes these magazines ideal media for their ads at lower overall cost and with minimal waste circulation."[19]

As a result of this perspective, the advertising industry supported special interest consumer magazines that could prove the worth of their readership, and that area burgeoned. From *Psychology Today* to *Essence* to *National Lampoon* to *Smithsonian* to *Money* and *Omni*, the 1970s saw magazines with circulations in the hundreds of thousands or less (instead of the several millions) become strong objects of Madison Avenue support. As the key to this producer-patron relationship became efficient specialization, leading magazine publishing firms, advertising agencies, and the Magazine Publishers Association began to devise more studies and measures that reflected the value of a magazine to a sponsor. Magazine executives wanted to present their periodicals to advertising agency people as better buys than other periodicals or other media (especially television). Agency executives, for their part, wanted to be able to justify their media buying decisions in quantitative, "scientific" terms that would be difficult for their bosses to question. Consequently, over the past few decades both parties joined forces to develop various numerical measures that go beyond the still important circulation and CPM to chart various characteristics of the readership, including self-rated personality attributes. The process led to still more specialized magazines, and thus still more research. As William Dunn, publisher of *U.S. News and World Report*, noted, "because there are so many magazines, advertisers have demanded more demographic and readership information. In turn, that has helped sharpen and focus the editorial product of many magazines." George Green, president of *The New Yorker*, added: "Magazines today are often designed around the advertising, particularly with specialized magazines. [Research] studies are getting so specific that you can design magazines around readers so you can have more clearly defined target audiences for the advertisers."[20]

Magazine research has regularly come under attack within the industry and outside it for methodological and statistical sloppiness.[21] Actually, though, for our purpose of understanding the two-way influence of the producer-patron relationship, it matters little whether the information reflects the outside world or not. Dissociated from their methods and presented neatly in graphs, bar charts, and tables, the measures have an aura of certainty about them. More important, they create a consensus about reality with respect to certain readership categories that magazine and advertising executives agree are important. Here, for example, is the way *Soap Opera Digest* touts its fine points to advertisers:

> ...Every two weeks, about 700,000 women...buy a copy of SOAP OPERA DIGEST at their checkouts or newsstands. With a Simmons pass along rate of 4.48. Most of them are married with children, and all of them are spenders. Name the product, and our readers buy it, everything from make-up and cigarettes to toys and toiletries. Though their median age is 30, our readers span the critical 18–49 age group. Critical because this segment is expending fast—right along with our circulation base. From a monthly only three years ago to a tri-weekly, now as a biweekly—with two increases in cover price—and the sales success continues. But you probably want to know about our first milestone: today SOAP OPERA DIGEST delivers more women in the 18–49 category at a lower CPM than any other women's magazine....[22]

Articles in the trade press, regular discussions with agency people, and other intelligence sources indicate to magazine publishers and editors the categories, and the ratings on the categories, that are desirable to advertisers. Changes in these evaluations might occur. For example, advertisers may show preferences for different readership groups as population shifts bring about changes in income and consumption. Keeping up on such things, magazine executives can use their research data to tout their periodicals to advertisers. Or they might rely on the research to adjust their periodicals and readerships to make them more attractive to advertisers. Or they might do both.

What they do and how they do it depends to a large extent on the magazine executives involved, on their organization's tradition, and on their magazine's history. The producer-patron relationship sets the parameters for survival, not necessarily the motives for creating certain products. And, in the magazine business, the range of motives and interests can be wide, since the number of advertisers that are interested in reaching specialized publics efficiently is large. So, for example, George Green can eschew readership research for his venerable *New Yorker*, arguing that "our readers are looking in on what our editors feel is important," and still attract much Madison Avenue money because of a general feeling that "*New Yorker* readers must be upper class."[23] Similarly, Hamilton Fish, publisher of *Nation*, can reach 52,000 people with the perspective that "we say what we feel should be said and if someone doesn't like it, they cancel," and still attract advertisers because "we have a specialized audience we have been able to identify...people who generally read highbrow publications."[24]

By contrast, executives in less politically or culturally committed organizations often rely heavily on market research to make sure they have carved a viable readership from the marketplace and can prove it to advertisers. Thus, before deciding to put out a test issue of a potential new (and ill-fated) magazine called *Families* in 1980, the Reader's Digest Association (RDA) polled potential advertisers. According to writer Joseph Winski, the RDA went ahead with the test after advertisers agreed that the magazine would make a good advertising vehicle and sixty of them agreed to purchase ads in the trial issue. Along the same lines, a Meredith Corporation executive contended that her firm did not encourage the renewal of subscriptions by certain kinds of readers for Meredith's *Metropolitan Home* magazine. That, according to editor Dorothy Kalins, reflected the publishing firm's "decision to forgo its nonmaterialistic audience in favor of its more established affluent readers—those who have money to spend on magazines and advertised home products."[5]

It is important to note that the development of specialization as the key to advertiser interest in consumer magazines durng the 1960s and 1970s was a two-way street. Magazine firms did not simply respond to Madison Avenue's dictates. They actually joined with the advertising industry to devise studies, measures, and visions of reality that would justify the existence of their medium in the television age. Once the basic pattern of operation began to be set, the producers had even more to lose from advertisers' abandoning it than did the advertisers, since the producers' solvencies were based on it.

From this perspective, the various advertisements by magazines that tout their audiences, the various seminars and conferences that the Magazine Publishers Association holds for advertisers, and the various discussions in the trade press by magazine executives about the future of their medium are individual and collective attempts by the producers to celebrate and reinforce the basis of their relationship with their patrons. The more powerful production firms—Time Inc., Conde Nast, and *Reader's Digest*—have the clout to stand apart sometimes from the overall pack of producers. By themselves they can guide other magazine publishers and the ad industry to accept certain approaches to readership, space charges, or other aspects of the relationship. Sometimes, their desire to hold on to their dominant positions brings them to champion certain perspectives and special relationships with patrons that prevent competitors from achieving greater ad revenues and inhibit new firms from entering the field. For example, in the early 1970s the larger periodicals were roundly accused of influencing certain kinds of readership research so that it often showed their periodicals to best advantage and downplayed the worth of magazines with smaller circulations.[26] The situation can be generalized: Having organized the basic approaches to their material, activities, and power bases around the current rules of the producer-patron relationship, producers large and small try to maintain their power by maintaining those rules.

Although the particulars are different in other segments of the magazine industry and in other mass media industries, the general points that the last few pages illustrate hold for those areas as well. One could, for example, start with journalist Les Brown's reflection that "programs come into being to deliver...[an audience] to advertisers."[27] Then one could show how this fundamental patronage situation has over the years influenced the number and kinds of people that the three major commercial networks have targeted as their viewers; the frequency at which the networks (and producers) create and release new shows as well as the amount of television time the networks take up with their programming; and the cost of the programs the networks show at different times of the day. The analysis would have to take into account a two-step patronage flow that often occurs—from the advertisers to the networks, and from the networks to TV production firms. In the movie industry, similar careful analysis about the relationship between production companies, the major distributors, and the conglomerates that own the majors would elucidate Garth Jowett and James Linton's contention about the industry's approach to films in the 1970s. They argue persuasively that developments in the mainstream producer-patron relationship led producers to create "a smaller number of blockbusters (with higher production costs and larger audience requirements) rather than...a larger number of 'lesser' movies (with lower production costs and smaller audience requirements)."[28]

The popular record industry stands out as a fascinating exception to this producer-patron pattern. As noted earlier, the primary patrons are record stores. By all accounts, though, the radio stations are the forces in the popular record industry that exert the influence we have attributed to patrons, even though they are not patrons.[29] The reason is not difficult to perceive. Stores, while generally not providing the public with players to hear the new songs, nevertheless expect that people will be familiar with the popular records they carry when people decide what to buy. This imperative forces record producers to try to publicize their music so that stores will want to carry it. Purchasing advertising time on television and radio to play all new songs would be prohibitively expensive for any production firm. However, the presence of popular music formats on radio allows the firm's boundary personnel to do the next best thing. They try to convince radio station programmers to play their music for free, as part of their formats. The stores and producers have evolved a general understanding that records played often and widely have a better chance of being carried in the stores than records played not so often and not so widely. In a large sense, then, stores have devolved much of the record patronage influence upon the radio stations. No wonder, then, that these facilitators have the clout generally reserved for patrons.

Setting Content Criteria

In many cases, setting the kind of general boundaries for the production of mass media material that we noted in the magazine, TV, and movie industries may be only the beginning of the producer-patron relationship's influence. For in many media organizations, the ramifications of "the key connection" extend beyond setting broad boundaries to setting quite specific criteria about actual content. How specific such guidelines are in certain organizations, or even in certain industry sectors, is hard to determine. In general, tracking the breadth and depth of the producer-patron's influence is very difficult. One reason undoubtedly relates to the sometimes quite subtle nature of these influences, a subtlety that writings on production processes in mass media industries rarely tap. Another is the seeming reluctance of executives in producer and patron organizations to talk in public about their cooperation in creating content. Rare are stories in the popular press that even broach the subject of advertiser influence on production. Discussions of the less obvious forms of media patronage are nearly unknown in the popular press. Generally, only industry trade papers or memoirs of disgruntled employees let loose brief mentions of the subject. By contrast, a wide spectrum of channels trumpet Nielson ratings, movie revenues, record sales, and book sales. It is as if executives want people to ignore producers' transactions with other organizations and, instead, believe that the artists who create mass media material respond solely, or at least overwhelmingly, in terms of what they think the public wants.

Drawing on our earlier discussions of organizations, we can suggest the following proposition: The extent to which a particular mass media production firm molds its material to needs of its primary patrons depends to an important extent on three factors—the production firm's tradition, its executives' interests, and, not least, its executives' perceptions of the requirements of the producer-patron relationship. Things can get even more complex, though. Recall that production firms are involved in shaping the typical demands and opportunities of a producer-patron relationship within their sector of an industry. Consequently, in some situations a powerful production firm or group of production firms might have participated in originally setting guidelines that present-day executives see as required and immutable. The executives may be afraid to challenge certain notions about patron expectations that they have inherited. As Karl Weick points out, it takes considerable courage to overstep perceived boundaries in a relationship to see what will happen.[30] Sometimes, if the transgressor is lucky, he or she will be surprised that the repercussions are not nearly as great as was anticipated. An example can be taken from the recollections of John H. Johnson, the pioneering black publisher who launched *Ebony* magazine in 1945.[31] Noting *Ebony's* reliance on advertising for its survival, Johnson recalled that in the 1950s he hesitated to carry an article titled "Was Abraham Lincoln a Segregationist?" and, later, to devote an entire issue to the "white problem" in America. His fear was that advertising executives (most of whom are white) would take offense and withdraw their support. Johnson let both pieces run, however, claiming that his anguished decision finally turned on a feeling of moral responsibility ("I've got to go forward with this"). At this writing, *Ebony* is still thriving.

Stories such as this one are the kinds of nuggets that one can find scattered through textbooks on the history and practice of various media. Presumably the hope is that students will find the tales inspiring and emulate the unorthodox trailblazers, in the process bringing new distinction to their professions. It may be cruel to throw cold water over a neophyte warm with enthusiasm, but a wide body of literature on the production of mass media material indicates that such maverick questionings of fundamental relationships are rarely tolerated within and across mass media organizations. More realistic is the following generalization advanced by J. W. Click and Russell Baird in their text *Magazine Editing and Production*: "Editorial integrity is much easier to maintain if the [magazine] is in solid financial condition and does not need to desperately woo advertisers."[32]

When speaking of a breach of "editorial integrity," Click and Baird mean a publisher's direct offering of editorial support for a product, service, or idea in exchange for an advertiser's commercial support. They bring an example from the declining days of *The Saturday Evening Post*. In order to secure $400,000 worth of Ford automotive advertising for the periodical's October 5, 1968 issue, *Post* executive Martin Ackerman promised the client's admen that Henry Ford's picture would grace the cover of the issue.[33] Click and Baird assert that such goings on are uncommon among large, prestigious magazines, for quite pragmatic reasons. "When one advertiser is obviously favored, others will justifiably be irate. And there can even be a backlash or boomerang effect against the favored advertiser, because a competitor might get a better deal next time."[34]

Click and Baird fail to consider that a publishing firm might routinely peddle editorial-advertising deals so that all sponsors would feel they are getting an even break. Overall, though, the authors' discussion of advertising influences on magazines seems to agree with the following proposition that derives from the resource dependence perspective: *Production people tend to tailor their material to patrons more when they perceive a narrow variety of patrons as crucial to their survival than when they perceive a wide variety of patrons as interested in supporting the venture.* A narrow variety of patrons means clients that are perceived by production executives to hold similar guidelines regarding the kinds of mass media material that are most conducive to the sales of their products. The guidelines might be quite specific (and encompass few patrons) like printing articles on certain subjects, or they might be very broad (and encompass many patrons), like not introducing violence into the material. Similarly, "tailor their material" can hold an array of meanings, depending on the particular industry, industrial sector, and even the particular producer-patron relationship.

When speaking about media that are supported predominantly by advertising, "to tailor" means, in its broadest sense, to create an environment that will enhance the effectiveness of the advertising. In women's magazines, this might mean making sure that recipes exist to stand beside all-important ads from food companies; in daily newspapers, it might mean creating a special business section to attract both an important upscale business readership and the advertising that will be lured to it; and in industry trade magazines, it might mean generating special inserts devoted to various industry sectors with the aim of attracting the advertising money of companies in those sectors. Behind such tailoring lies the strategy of using editorial matter to attract the kind of readers who are likely to buy from certain kinds of advertisers.

Of course, one can argue that this kind of activity benefits readers as well as advertisers and producers. The purpose here is not to dispute that conclusion. Rather, the purpose is to point out that such material is often created in response to sponsors, not necessarily or even primarily in response to readers. Inserts and sections that would not tie in with advertisers' needs, or would have negative things to say about potential advertisers, would be rather unlikely to appear. It is difficult to imagine, for example, that a series of articles about deceptive labeling by major food brands would show up in a homemaker-oriented women's magazine that relies on food sponsorship for support. Similarly, in view of the crucial importance of supermarket ads to daily newspapers, it would be very surprising if a newspaper routinely initiated stories exposing abuses in price and quality in area food stores. Moreover, production firm executives understand that their advertising counterparts sometimes show reluctance to sponsor material that, while having no relationship to their products, carries political and moral viewpoints that might reflect badly on them. Speaking about *Penthouse* in a 1981 issue of *Advertising Age*, an unnamed advertising official noted frankly: "Many agencies and corporations consider it an endorsement of an editorial product if you avertise in a magazine." He added that many of the companies find *Penthouse*'s photography too sexually explicit for their tastes.[35]

We should stress that we are not talking here about censorship. Censorship is the active attempt by an organization or group to suppress material that a producer has already created or wants to create. Censorship often represents a stormy episode in the relationship between the two parties. It often results in a new understanding by production executives of the environmental demands on them, and of the limits of their powers. On the other hand, tailoring material to create an attractive surrounding for ads represents the accepted fulfillment of the demands and opportunities of the producer-patron relationship as perceived by production firm leaders. The extent to which, and the way in which, that kind of tailoring weaves through aspects of the product will vary with the firm, with its need for certain advertisers, and with its perception of demands from those advertisers. So, for example, adherence to certain tenets of journalistic professionalism might lead executives of a news organization to print balanced stories about supermarkets or other issues sensitive to them if they were initiated by reputable third parties intent on exposing public problems.[36] And, of course, sometimes a production firm's executives will choose to alienate certain advertisers in order to maintain their organ's point of view and readership. Clearly, *Penthouse* survived 1981 despite the absence of some national advertising support; its advertisements to the advertising trade proclaimed that it is "provocative and proud of it."[37] Much less reputable "girlie" and "true confession" magazines have managed to get along without General Motors, General Foods, and General Electric for decades.[38] Still, *Penthouse*'s associate editor did say toward the end of 1981 that in order to win over more sponsors the staff had instituted "subtle evolutionary editorial changes" along with surveys to prove reader loyalty toward products advertised in *Penthouse*.[39]

A feel for the overarching influence of the producer-advertiser relationship on the creation of mass media material can perhaps be conveyed through a brief sketch of that relationship's implications for prime time commercial television in the early 1980s. As noted earlier, we have here a "two-step" patronage process. Advertisers purchase time during shows on the three major networks, ABC, CBS, and NBC. They create the program schedule and, in turn, support production firms that create programs that are the building blocks of that schedule. Sponsorship considerations pervade both levels. One need only begin with that basic TV viewership gauge, the Nielsen ratings. Broadcasters and advertisers have encouraged the development of Nielsen measurement categories (notably the number of households viewing as well as the sex and age of individual viewers) that directly reflect the specific marketing concerns of sponsors.[40] The number of households the networks reach with their shows are very important to sponsors. Both groups have tended to make capturing extended blocks of households' viewing times, rather than winning a half hour slot here and there, an important criterion for success. Winning the year in a time block (whether it be morning, afternoon, evening, or latenight) means being able to charge substantially more for commercials in that block at the start of the next year. For many national advertisers, however, the age and sex of viewers during those time blocks are also very important. The most attractive target for the past decade or so has been 18- to 49-year-olds, since they hold more discretionary spending money than do younger or older people. Prime time—the 8:00 PM to 11:00 PM block that is generally the most popular viewing period— presents the networks with the best opportunity to reach 18- to 49-year-olds, since most of them are home from work during those hours. Consequently, each network's executives try to create a prime time schedule that will attract the largest possible number of households for the entire prime time period while they simultaneously try to grab the highest percentage of 18- to 49-year-olds of the three networks.[41]

Explaining how networks executives try to do that explains to a considerable extent the shape and content of the prime time schedule. For example, with the aim of "winning the night," ABC, CBS, and NBC programmers set up their schedules to maximize "audience flow" from one show to the next. At 8:00 PM, the start of prime time, they choose programs designed to lure both children and their parents, since children are thought to control the set at that point in the evening. After 9:00 PM, they schedule shows that are more "adult" in theme (since by that time many children have abdicated set control to parents), but which still fit into an overall tone or approach to the evening's schedule, to maintain that flow. Because of advertiser interest in 18- to 49-year-olds, the executives choose programs that they believe, or determine by research, will particularly attract that group along with others. "Counterprogramming" may occur if a competitor seems stubbornly successful at holding on to one segment of the desired audience. So, for example, when one network's football game on Monday night attracts a large percentage of 18- to 49-year-old-males, another network may build its night around "women's" movies and series to lure 18- to 49-year-old females, and advertisers interested in them.

One more example of the producer-patron relationship's influence on prime time's shape and content might be of interest: All three networks developed one minute "newsbreak" spots, which they insert before the top of each hour. They did that to take advantage of an industry rule of the time that allowed broadcasters to exceed the six-minute limit on commercials in an hour if they were airing "news and public affairs" programs.

Just as important as the material ABC, CBS, and NBC schedule during prime time is the material the networks have learned not to schedule in that period as a response to the producer-patron relationship. Programs aimed exclusively at youngsters are unacceptable, as are programs for people over fifty. The reason is that the networks can attract much more advertising money at that time of day trying to lure 18- to 49-year-olds. Similarly, programs that are not upbeat in at least some basic way, or are too provocative or controversial, are frowned upon by network executives. The reason is that most advertisers feel that such programs do not provide the best environment for their commercials.[42] Program production executives have picked up this criterion, as they have the general advertiser-oriented network perspective. Consequently, over the years, they have negotiated specific production rules and general guidelines with the networks that make their ideas for shows much more likely to be accepted for the schedule. The guidelines extend to the very structure of the programs. So, for example, the plot must be created with natural breaks about every ten minutes so that commercials can be inserted. Too, the regular characters of a series should reflect (or attract) viewers whom the networks are hoping to draw for advertisers. An 8:00 PM "family" adventure show must therefore have a child for the youngsters in the house to like, a good-looking male lead for women to ogle, and at least one pretty woman in tight (though not terribly revealing) clothes for male encouragement. A lot of action (cars bumping, people yelling, though in the very early 1980s not much actual "violence") is desirable if the show is not a situation comedy. The reason is that many important advertising agency decision makers believe their research shows that action added to programs increases viewers' recall of commercials.[43]

This thumbnail sketch can convey only some flavor of the way the producer-patron relationship permeates the actual creation of material. But it is important to point out that such influence is not confined to media where advertisers are the patrons. Take elementary and high school textbook publishing as an example. There the primary clients are various state and local school systems around the United States. Often, a central administration will periodically create a list of the only books that educators throughout the area can choose. Teachers will then choose from that list. As might be expected, textbook publishers are eager to get their textbooks on the "approved" lists in as many places as possible. As a result of the need to get school board approval of texts, and in view of the several fiery public controversies that have swirled about the moral values that certain texts convey, publishing firm representatives and editors pay extremely close attention to the educational and moral guidelines school board members articulate. They pay attention, too, to the way text advisory panelists inspect the books. A popular inspection technique, for example, is the "flip test," whereby an evaluator flips the pages of a text to note the kinds of activities that are illustrated, as well as the number of whites, blacks, Hispanic Americans, Native Americans, and Asian Americans who are named or drawn. The editors pass along their conclusions about school system desires to authors of the texts in the form of written and verbal guidelines.

The strictures that get passed on will tend to represent a homogenized compilation of boundary personnel perceptions regarding several states.[44] Because publishing firm executives want to keep in the running in as many places as possible, they try to tailor a least common denominator of text and pictures that will be acceptable everywhere. The list of "dos and don'ts" for authors thus becomes long, broad, and specific. Here are just a few policies from a confidential guidesheet that a major textbook publishing firm expected all its authors to follow in 1981:

Brand names, commercial identification—Do not use or show.

Death—Do not include except in anthologies and only there if well balanced by other materials.

Divorce—Do not include.

Evolution—Avoid, except in science texts where it is a necessary part of the curriculum. Make sure all reference is to theory, not fact. Include statement required by Texas in front matter.

Mixed marriages, religious or racial—Do not show.

Religion—Do not show symbols of. Avoid all references to unless it is the theme of a story of exposition. If it is central to the piece, consider leaving the piece out. Avoid topics considered by some to be antireligious, e.g., evolution, witchcraft, secular humanism.

For materials in preparation this year, represent minorities in the following minimum percentages—whites, 68%, blacks, 15%, Hispanic Americans, 10%, Asian Americans, 1%*, Native Americans 1%.*

* In each case, the percent may have to be higher to be visible in a flip test.

THE RELATIONSHIP AND ORGANIZATIONAL STRUCTURE

A wealth of additional examples could illustrate the influence of the producer-patron relationship on content criteria. At this point, though, the discussion should move forward with a new proposition. The proposition is that the interactions of a production firm and its class of primary patrons are crucial not only in setting both boundary conditions and specific criteria for the creation of material. More than that, the interactions play an important role in shaping the way people who select and compose the material for the production firm (the "creators") are actually organized to do their work. Recall that the roles that these creators take on while doing work comprise part of the *structure* of their organization. What the proposition argues, then, is that the part of an organization's structure that relates to the creation of mass media materials is influenced strongly by the producer-patron relationship.

The idea flows directly from this chapter's earlier discussion of the relationship. Drawing on writings by Howard Aldrich, Karl Weick, and others, we noted that the interactions of producer and patron organizations are comprised of interactions by both executives and specialized boundary personnel who carry out roles that guide them toward managing profitability and predictability for their organizations. These interdependent behaviors across organizations affect the criteria that production and patron members both use in deciding about content. In production firms, carrying out the perceived criteria of the relationship can mean the difference between a step toward success and a step toward failure. Therefore, we might expect production leaders to try to ensure that the activities they want artists to carry out will maximize the chances for fulfilling the demands and opportunities of their major producer-patron relationship. William Evan seems to expect that, too. Evan writes about the "set" of organizations that make up a "focal" organization's environment, He suggests that an important class of "normative reference organizations," which is what a group of primary patrons is, might very well help explain the "internal structure of the focal organization."[45]

Supporting this idea requires close examination of the ongoing relationship of a particular mass media production organization and its primary patrons. Unfortunately, such examinations are extremely rare. In fact, when I conducted a comparative case study of children's book publishers and outlets in 1976 to explore the ramifications of the producer-patron relationship, I could find no similar investigation of any mass media industry. Here it might be useful to review some of my findings, not only to illustrate the influence of the producer-patron relationship on organizational structure, but also to show how that influence is connected to other repercussions of the key connection.

First, a bit of background: In the mid-1970s, general children's (nontext) book publishing contained two separate sectors with distinct, usually nonoverlapping, production and exhibition organizations. The *library* market consisted mostly of nonprofit institutions whose selectors purchased books from library-oriented publishing firms. The commercially oriented *mass* market for children's book was dominated by department, chain, and book stores, which purchased the overwhelming majority of their titles from a different group of publishing firms. In both producer-patron relationships, the patron organizations (libraries or stores) were the most important exhibitors of publishers' books to the children and/or their parents.

To explore the influence of the producer-patron relationship within these two publishing industry sectors, I conducted a comparative case study.[46] I examined one important publishing organization in each market, one patron organization from the library market, and two patron organizations from the mass market. The goal was to trace the factors guiding selectors of content within each publishing and each outlet organization and, in the process, gauge the influence of producer-patron relationships on the decisions of editors and buyers for stores and libraries. At the production end, the firms studied were large publishing houses whose children's book divisions have strong sales records and good reputations. At the distribution level, the nationally prominent juvenile division of a metropolitan public library system was examined, as were two mass market distribution outlets—a book store chain and a department store chain in the same city. I conducted interviews with sixty-two people connected to the five organizations; administered a questionnaire survey to fifty librarians; and categorized the new titles released by the two publishers and purchased by the outlet organizations during approximately the same time period. In addition, I interviewed about forty people in other areas of the children's publishing industry who, I felt, could contribute knowledge and viewpoints about the subject. Too, I examined historical records on the interactions of production firms and exhibition outlets in the children's book industry.

The investigation showed that the producer-patron relationship in each sector brought about systemwide consequences that guided very different book production and exhibition policies in each sector and that resulted in very different ranges of choice for children and their parents. This brief overview will concentrate on the relationship's influence on the publishing firms. By the mid-1970s, the division of the children's book industry into firms that produced books for retail sale and others that produced for libraries had been long-standing; it traced back to the development of those markets during the late nineteenth century. In the two companies that were studied, the producer-patron interactions had been shaped (and continued to be shaped) by three major considerations— the tradition of the publishing house and interests of its editors; the environment of selection in, and economic nature of, the marketplace; and the possibilities for feedback from the environment as well as for book promotion in the environment. Both the interviews and firsthand observation of activities in the two publishing houses suggested that workers' different conceptions of the producer-patron relationship had become major influences in bringing about and perpetuating differences between the firms in (1) the *overlapping roles* people designated to make creative decisions held; (2) *the process* those people carried out in selecting books to be published; (3) the *guidelines* they used in choosing content; and (4) *the types of titles* that their firms actually published.

The Library Market Case

Illustrating these points can begin with the library market publishing firm. The people interviewed in that firm clearly understood the "bottom line" economic significance of libraries and librarians for their work. The children's division's publisher, for example, noted that "librarians are very important to us because they are the ones who bring books to children." Interviewees also were quick to suggest that to simply imitate past successes is a sure way to fail in this market, because librarians shun formulaic material, despite its original appeal. The general consensus was that librarians are professionals who have been trained to select what people in this industry sector characterized consistently as "good books." An editor and a promotion director agreed that even in times of budgetary crises with limited book buying funds, a librarian's first priority is "quality," not price.

These respondents' view of the library market's requirement that they publish "good books" was consonant with their own publishing interests and their division's award-winning tradition in the library market sector. Experience with the promotional and feedback environments in which they operated made them quite confident of their ability to publish successfully "innovative" children's literature falling in the "good books" category. The library market environment encompassed direct and indirect avenues of contact with the library world. Indirect avenues included visits by editors, the promotion director, and the seven-person promotion team with librarians and library school teachers (who influence the opinions of future librarians). That happened at libraries, at faculty offices, and at conferences.

The firm's marketing director and an editor both described their acquaintance with librarians as being most frequently used for promotion of books rather than for guidance prior to selection for publication. Stories told by several employees of the firm's success in promoting unusual or avant garde books highlighted their belief that the publishing community can initiate new trends and, within limits, shape the views of the library community as to what is "good."

The conceptions members of the firm had developed about their relations with clients were also seen to affect the firm's structure of artistic decision making. For example, the children's division employed several "readers" to conduct a preliminary examination of every manuscript submitted and suggest to the editors whether any warranted more serious consideration. One of the aims of this review (the greatest portion of which covered unsolicited manuscripts from "unknowns") was promotional—to show librarians that the firm was indeed actively searching for the best in children's literature wherever it could be found. But one editor pointed to somewhat more concrete demands from the marketplace for going to great lengths to review all arrivals: The vogues of the library market were changing frequently because librarians were emphasizing new directions as well as simply replacing old books. Editors, therefore, had to discover new writers and illustrators as well as ensure that the division's backlist continued to feature books that would circulate well and retain a reputation for "quality."

Concerning the number of new books chosen each (fall and spring) publishing season, several editors mentioned that a triennial assessment of the market had produced a current guideline of approximately twenty-five to thirty new books per season. All interviewees stressed, however, that their year-round evaluation of manuscripts and the necessity of relying on authors to originate and deliver acceptable works made it impossible to dictate the exact size of the list. At the same time, it is important to note that this library-oriented children's division was less subject to marketing and sales department approval for the publication of new titles than any other division in the company. One reason for the independence was the absence of any substantial role for the firm's trade force in this division's activities, since librarians ordered directly from institutional wholesalers.

Book content guidelines, too, reflected the producer-patron relationship. Two words used by several editors to characterize the guidelines they use in selecting books were "variety" and "balance." A primary reason for the varied assortment of new books was a feeling that librarians might be loath to buy several books on the same topic or directed at the same category from a company's list. The editors added that since they know librarians classify children according to different interests, the division should try to balance these categories in the hope that librarians will need all the books on the list. An added impetus toward a "varied" list in terms of age (or grade) levels and subject matter lay in the different interests of the division's editors. Although every editor admitted to certain likes and dislikes in developing manuscripts, all stressed a preference for working on different kinds of books to vary routines and expand their creativity.

The editors maintained they select individual titles without any formal guidelines. This state of affairs would be consonant with their producer-patron relationship, since adhering to specific guidelines could be construed as taking a formulaic approach to what both librarians and these editors liked to portray as an artistic endeavor. However, the editors did state that plot, writing style, characterization, and illustrations (in picture books) are the most important characteristics. The nonformulaic, individual nature of each title was stressed. Broad leeway was allowed for plot (required to be successful "on its own terms"). A personal style was demanded of author and illustrator. And "depth" and "believability" were required in characterization. One editor noted a general dislike for portrayals where animals act human. All agreed that series books and easy readers produced from word lists were likely to be hopelessly formulaic. Cartoonish illustrations were similarly seen to be generally unacceptable.

Regarding a work's moral point of view, the editors decried titles that are obviously "dogmatic" or "moralistic." They did note, though, that a book that has no redeeming moral or social value will be rejected. Drugs, abortion, racial discrimination, homosexuality, and other controversial subjects had been treated in library market oriented children's books. The confidence of the editors in dealing with such sensitive areas could be traced to an aspect of the client relationship that was mentioned by several respondents. Librarians were giving publishers support by acting as buffers between them and complaining community groups.

The Mass Market Case

Answers to the same interview questions by editors for a book publisher oriented to retail sales reflected a very different conception of the producer-patron relationship and of a "children's book." This publishing division's orientation to the mass market was intimately connected to a trade book tradition for the entire company. The children's division was created with the intention of relying on the firm's already effective sales force to place juvenile titles in the same book, department, and chain store outlets that carry the company's popular adult books.

Editors for the mass market publisher described an environment quite different from that portrayed by the library market's staff in conceptualizing their producer-patron relationship. Both groups did note a dearth of advertising and promotion by both types of children's book publishers (which continued for reasons of cost and industry inertia). However, the library market people pointed out that, in place of direct promotion, they rely on librarians to introduce their books to children and parents. The mass market oriented interviewees, by contrast, stressed that clerks in most of their outlets—stores—have little knowledge or time to introduce particular titles to customers.

This situation in the mass market led to a demand from buyers (representing outlets or jobbers who buy books from publishers) that the juvenile works they purchase essentially "sell themselves." *Lines* (groups of titles in similar forms) and—more rarely—individual titles that had proven sales records were bought repeatedly by outlets. Exterior characteristics (format, cover attractiveness, general subject) took on primary importance. Buyers' criteria also included color and competitively low prices (about $4 lower than in the library market) as crucial factors for acceptance. The importance of a book's similarity to others with good mass market track records was underscored by respondents, for it was much easier to sell a new title to a store or jobber representative when the title was introduced as an addition to a popular line. And, as one mass market publishing executive noted, "if you get them in [stores, particularly enough stores to justify the necessarily low price], you can sell them."

The importance of salespeople for this publisher was another feature that distinguished it from the library oriented firm. Here, the sales force was crucial for getting books into the stores and to the jobbers. The salespeople who serviced major accounts did not even usually talk to buyers in terms of lines. Rather, they dealt in "programs"—packages of books that had been tailored to the individual "turnover" and profit requirements of each outlet. The strong influence of the sales department placed the editors for the mass market in the position of having to convince their sales force to recommend their new titles wholeheartedly to buyers as books that sell themselves. In view of this aspect of the firm's producer-patron relationship, it should not be surprising that these editors, in contrast to the library market's, believed their division to the *more* dependent on the opinions of the marketing and sales force than any other in the company.

In this particular firm, the marketing orientation was further strengthened by the dual assignment of the company's marketing vice president to the position of juvenile division publisher. While he suggested that this combination of roles was an historical accident, the sales manager and others mentioned the importance of the publisher's marketing expertise in helping the division respond quickly and properly to the mass market environment. This contrasted with the library market (where the publisher was an editor) and pointed up the different primary requirements of the two producer-patron relationships. Other structural contrasts also reflected differences in the relationships. For example, recall that the library oriented firm's editors and readers were allowed to work on different types of books with the aim of fostering creativity. By contrast, editors for the mass market oriented publisher were assigned to one of four separate sections which, for reasons of efficiency and predictability, produced particular lines targeted for particular age levels. In two of these sections, the editorial supervisors also perceived their role as that of marketing expert.

These appropriately different organizational responses to very different producer-patron relationships fostered divergent approaches to the selection and production of juvenile books. The library oriented firm's procedure was a strict selection process in which special readers and editors chose manuscripts by authors who frequently publish through the firm, by other known talent, or even by "over the transom" discoveries. The division's publisher here mainly confirmed (making sure that a manuscript was an economically feasible "good book") and oversaw (making sure the list was "balanced"). In the mass market case, though, most of the titles were originated by the editors and section heads themselves, at the specific request of the division's publisher (who tied the particular number of books needed to reports on what buyers were willing to lay out). Reliable talent was then recruited to complete the job; sometimes, the editors themselves wrote picture book copy. Such a procedure allowed for a high degree of control over the final product. Just as important, it helped reduce costs, since the writers or illustrators could be paid lump sums or very small royalties for following directions or well-plotted formulas. In those cases where the books did not originate with the firm's editors, they were usually developed by several "name" author-illustrators who were under long-term contract and whose names bespoke "track record" to salespeople and buyers alike.

The guidelines all creators of mass market books were expected to follow were well understood by all members of the firm. Besides having the already noted requirements regarding price and color illustrations, the mass market personnel preferred easily recognizable and admittedly formulaic stories and characters; favored cartoony drawings and anthropo-morphic characterizations; and championed the series book format. These and other guidelines (quite at odds with those favored in the library market) served to cultivate the "instant appeal" (and, hence, self-salabi-lity) of lines. Writing style and character depth, both considered extremely important in the library market, were not deemed important by the mass market oriented editors. They seemed to feel that since these content characteristics were not evident to the stores' agents (who, unlike librarian reviewers, did not read the books) nor probably to the adult or child customers (who were "sold" immediately on the subject and other visible "track record" elements), they could be sacrificed in favor of reduced costs (through the hiring of inexpensive writers).

On the Use of Case Studies

This rather long-winded "brief overview" of the children's book study underscores the wide-ranging ramifications of the producer-patron rela-tionship for the creation of mass media material in all its phases. A comparative case study is the best way to chase these kinds of revelations. What the researcher loses in across-the-board generalizability of specific findings, he or she gains in an ability to see particular organizational processes in action and to trace interorganizational behaviors to their functions for individual organizations. Note, though, that comparative case studies should not be catchall fishing expeditions. Rather they should be guided by specific lines of inquiry that spring from previous bodies of knowledge or investigations of the area. New findings then confront old findings and force the investigator to come to terms with differences and similarities at an acceptable level of generality. The process has been called *retroduction*.[47] Formally put, retroduction is the activity of deductively applying ideas from certain bodies of knowledge and emerging frameworks to case studies and then inducing from findings of the case studies the extent to which (and the manner in which) the bodies of knowledge and emerging frameworks should be altered. Carrying out this activity in the children's book industry led to still another trail of insight on the producer-patron relationship, this one involving the audience. Coming to terms with the notion of audience in two publishing sectors that create very different kinds of books for children sparked an awareness that put previous sociological writings on the audience in a new perspective. Along the way, it established a crucial interorganizational basis for the whole idea of a mass medium's audience.

THE RELATIONSHIP AND THE AUDIENCE

The role of "the audience" in the production and distribution of mass media material has been one of the least understood aspects of the process. Despite the cliché that "people get what they want," very little research has been conducted about the part the audience plays in decisions to produce, select, and distribute messages through books, newspapers, magazines, records, television programs and theatrical films. Moreover, the literature that does exist points to contradictory conclusions. One group of writers contends that the significance and nature of mass communication are determined in large part by notions that the creators (often called "communicators") have of their audience. For example, John and Matilda Riley note that "writers, broadcasters, and political speakers all select what they are going to say in terms of their beliefs about the audience."[48] Ithiel De Sola Pool and Irwin Shulman conclude from a study of "newsmen's fantasies" that "the messages sent [by a communicator] are in part determined by expectations of audience reactions. The audience, or at least those audiences about whom the communicator thinks ... play more than a passive role in communication."[49] And Raymond Bauer, perhaps the most vocal champion of the view that the audience strongly influences the communicator, calls in a 1964 review on the subject for a view of mass communication as a transactional process in which both audience and communicator take important initiatives.[50]

Another group of researchers, growing larger in recent years, has tended to minimize the importance of the audience to producers of mass media content. In a pioneering study of "social control in the newsroom," Breed notes that "a newsman's source of rewards is located not among the readers who are manifestly his clients, but among his colleagues and superiors."[51] Walter Gieber, in a somewhat later study of the selection of wire service news by "telegraph editors" at sixteen Wisconsin dailies, concludes that the editors were not guided by considerations of the audience but by "the number of news items available, their size, and the pressures of time and mechanical production."[52] Subsequent studies of newspaper reporters, television news selectors, and television entertainment program producers expand the conclusions of Breed and Gieber and broaden their generalizability. Even when researchers from this group note that producers do consider audience images along with other factors when making decisions, the researchers are careful to stress that such images are based on little actual information. Dennis McQuail makes this point about British Broadcasting Company television producers.[53] And, Muriel Cantor observes that while the Hollywood television producers she interviewed had images of their programs' viewers, these images were often limited to stereotypes of broad social characteristics and did not even match the findings of "audience research."[54]

Findings about "the audience" from the children's book study point a way toward incorporating and transcending the seemingly contradictory perspectives that have just been presented. Actually, the children's book industry is an appropriate area to explore the influence of the audience upon producers of mass media content because people in the two sectors, the library market and mass market, purported to aim at the same audience, children. Consequently, two questions in every interview dealt specifically with this issue—"What image do you have of the people who read your books?" and "How do you arrive at that image?" The answers, and other facets of the study, revealed that children did form a group that was important to editors, publishers, and other content selectors when they chose material for books. At the same time, it became quite clear that the images of children that publishing personnel used when making decisions were shaped by the organizational environment in which they worked; specifically, by considerations of the producer-patron relationships.

A concise discussion of these findings must suffice here.[55] Right off, it should be said that all the editors and marketers in both firms discussed guidelines and operated as if they had clear impressions of their ultimate audience. In the library market firm, for example, one broad notion about the selection of book ideas and manuscripts was that the nature, extent, and complexity of a work should vary with the expected age of the reader, according to general conceptions of childhood and childhood interests. In the mass market firm, the editors' discussions of making sure a book has "instant appeal" to children and parents, and the concentration on exterior characteristics of the books, on cartoony drawings, on anthropomorphic characterization, and not on writing style might also imply that the personnel have concrete images of their ultimate readers.

Wrong. When editors and marketers in both firms were asked about their images of the people who read their books, all uniformly denied any direct knowledge of them. A library market editor, for example, said "I have no image. They're the great invisible face out there." One mass market editor observed, and people in the library market also noted, that no market research is carried out and "we're really flying by the seat of our pants." Another mass market editor characterized as "parlor wisdom" his colleagues' assumption that parents usually choose books for younger children (with or without children present) and that adolescents buy books on their own.

Upon reflection, it becomes clear that the implicit images of children that the library market and mass market publishing people were carrying were largely reflections of the requirements and opportunities that those people perceived in their firms' interactions with patrons. For example, when asked where they got their "general conceptions of childhood interests," many of the library market people mentioned their dealings with librarians. Along similar lines, when three of the library market editors did try to characterize their audience, they simply projected an image of readers who would logically correspond to their firm's book list (e.g., "multifaceted," "probably pretty good readers," and "not necessarily the average child"). Mass market publishing personnel did the same thing. For example, the requirement of store agents for low price and high turnover was interpreted by the company's marketers and editors as a mandate to reach the widest possible audience. Too, the cartoons, anthropomorphism, and other content elements they use to reach the audience are usually chosen from the range of previously successful materials—materials the store agents perceive as being self-salable and forming a "track record."

Interesting to note, representatives of each sector, relying on their producer-patron relationship, claimed that the books that *they* publish are generally what children want. One of the library oriented editors insisted that children who visit the library get more "of what they really want" than in a department store, since librarians choose books that they know from experience children will like. However, the mass market company's trade publicity director contended that because parents know their children better than librarians do, mass market books are likely to give children what they really want.

Perhaps the images of children that the publishing personnel inferred from the requirements and opportunities of the producer-patron relationship accurately reflected the differences in children who attended the mass market or library market outlets. Actually, it was by no means clear that those publishers' outlets served customers (children or parents) who were so different that the outlets had to establish different book selection criteria. Rather, detailed interviews with personnel in a large public library, a large department store chain, and a large book store chain revealed that organizational requirements help shape their perspectives of children, too. Purchasing agents from the stores freely admitted that they have little contact with the people who choose to buy juvenile books in their outlets. From their remarks it was clear that their desire for titles to sell quickly despite clerks' ignorance about children's books cause them to demand books that "sell themselves." Because such material, comprising the primary range of choices in the stores, does sell well, the agents insisted that their audience is interested in unsophisticated and formularized material.

The librarians interacted a lot more with children. However, they too approached their audience and book selection duties with a generalized conception of children that was shaped by the environment in which they trained and in which they worked. Previous library school training and pressures by heads of their libraries (who are continually influenced by editors from library market publishing firms) lead them to adopt a view of children as having aesthetic and social needs. Librarians emphasized the "need" of children for emotional and aesthetic enrichment through "quality" (i.e., mostly library market) literature, as well as the need to consider the sex, reading ability, racial and ethnic backgrounds of their branch patrons. The head of the children's library decried the notion of buying only titles that have track records; she said the track record simply indicates "what seems to be what children want by what they say they want to take out" in view of the choices they have at the time. She insisted that every day brings proof that high quality titles can be successfully introduced to children if a good librarian is doing the introducing.

The Constructed Audience

These findings point to another important generalizable idea—the notion that an "audience" is necessarily a concept, an abstraction. In theory, there is an infinite number of ways to look at children; there is an infinite number of ways to look at *any* people who come into contact with mass media content. Rather than seeing the audience as an external group that exerts influence upon them, the producers of content perceive their audience as a grouping of particular categories (sex, education, interests, etc.) which they hope (or know) are being reached by messages. The audiences that are "constructed" (that is, the categories of potential consumers that are focused upon) by key production decision makers are ultimately the result of the ongoing relationship between those decision makers and counterparts in the organizations that affect them most directly, the patron organizations. Both sides expect that the mass media material will attract individuals with specific characteristics, or people who can be made *aware* they have those characteristics. Some of the artists (writers, reporters, directors) may very well hold personal audience "fantasies"—idiosyncratic conceptions of certain people or things—when they do their work. Ultimately, though, the product they come up with has to attract the constructed audience that production personnel who select content for release (they may be editors, marketing directors, programming vice-presidents) hold in response to organizational demands. Those selectors try to make adjustments in the material they release to provide the most popular options within the initially established range of content choice. Audience research, when conducted, does not provide a more accurate image of the true audience. Rather, audience research elaborates upon and makes explicit the categories of the target population that are of greatest interest to members of the producer-patron relationship.

Clearly, the point also applies to industries where organizations other than outlets are the patrons. Executives at advertiser-supported media, for example, construct their audiences based on demographic and other data that they feel their sponsors will need in order to justify buying space or time. A medium's *pervasiveness* and *concentration* would seem to determine how detailed the picture of that audience must be. For example, broadcast television is very pervasive (it reaches ninety-eight per cent of American homes)[56] and very concentrated (over eighty per cent of the population still watches the three networks during prime time).[57] Because they can easily reach huge numbers of people efficiently, TV oriented advertisers and their agencies are willing to accept as basic rating data raw audience size estimates, together with a number of breakdowns regarding age and sex, in various viewing times. Magazines, radio programming, and newspapers, on the other hand, are quite a bit less pervasive and concentrated than TV. To be advantageous to advertisers, they must show their patrons that they can target for them specific groups that other media (especially television) cannot reach as efficiently. They do that by commissioning audience research that taps the kinds of categories their potential advertisers might desire—information about buying habits, more detailed demographic and attitudinal profiles, analyses of their specific purchasing habits and even of their particular media use. Actually, during the past few years, advertisers facing rising TV commercial prices have begun to demand that executives in even that medium construct more detailed audiences than they traditionally have constructed. Some local station groups and advertising agencies have hired market research firms—Quantiplex, Petry, Strategy Research, and Yankelovich, Skelly, and White are examples—to generate pictures of viewer buying habits, watching habits, and program loyalties that go beyond the basic rating information. As one station manager explained, "In the game of numbers, we need anything we can get that will help make profitable decisions for our clients."[58]

This view of the production organization's audience as a construct based on the requirements and opportunities of the organization's producer-patron relationship has many implications for research on mass media industries. It suggests that research emphasis be placed on the way different people within mass media industries construct their audiences, on why they construct them the way they do, and on how such constructions may be altered to better serve public and/or professional goals. The perspective also underscores the notion that "an audience" for a mass medium is not the same as "the public" for that medium. "Audience response" is the activity of people in terms of the categories and concerns that producers and patrons designate as important. "Public response," on the other hand, is the activity of people in terms of categories and concerns that they themselves define and that may or may not feed the producer-patron relationship. It is to the influence of this public response, organized and disorganized, that we now turn.

REFERENCES

1. Generally, book stores and record stores do have a "returns" provision on some of the merchandise they buy. That is, they may return a percentage of the goods they do not sell and receive credit on their accounts. This does not mean, however, that the stores can be casual about the goods they purchase. They only have a certain amount of floor space, and the books and records must move off the racks in a reasonable time if they are to make a profit.

2. John Dessauer, *Book Publishing* (New York: Bowker, 1974).

3. *Variety*, December 30, 1981, p. 1; *The New York Times*, January 20, 1982, p. 29; and Garth Jowett and James Linton, *Movies as Mass Communication* (Beverly Hills, California: Sage, 1980), pp. 25–64. See also Janet Wasko, *Movies and Money* (Norwood, New Jersey: Ablex, 1982). Wasko traces the importance that banks (investors) and major distributors (primary patrons) hold for production firms. She quotes a Bank of America executive as stating in 1974 that "the majors have become the [key] bankers for the industry" (p. 160).

4. David Less and Stan Berkowitz, *The Movie Business*, (New York: Vintage, 1981), p. 81. In the early 1980s, Home Box Office, Time, Inc.'s powerful cable service, began to help fund theatrical films in much the same way the majors were doing. They did it in exchange for the right to show the film exclusively on their channels after it had made its first theatrical run. The movie majors, seeing this patronage as a way that HBO could get around paying the theatrical distributors (i.e., the majors) for cable rights to the films, were balking at distributing such HBO-financed films. It was all part of a battle over the expanding cable programming and distribution turf.

5. *Advertising Age*, December 24, 1980, p. 68.

6. *Advertising Age*, September 10, 1981, p. 36, 40, 50, 58, and 64.

7. *Advertising Age*, September 10, 1981, p. 12.

8. *Advertising Age*, March 18, 1981, p. 32.

9. *Advertising Age*, November 24, 1980, p. 68.

10. See, for example, Gaye Tuchman, "Making News by Doing Work: Routinizing the Unexpected," *American Journal of Sociology*, vol. 79 (July 1971), pp. 119–131; and John March and Herbert Simon, *Organizations*, (New York: John Wiley, 1958).

11. William Evan, *Organization Theory*, (New York: John Wiley, 1976), p. 123.

12. J. W. Click and Russell N. Baird, *Magazine Editing and Production*, 2d ed. (Dubuque, Iowa: William C. Brown, 1979), p. 4.

13. *Advertising Age*, October 19, 1981, p. S-18.

14. Cited in Leonard Mogel, *The Magazine* (New York: Spectrum, 1981) p. 2.

15. Mogel, p. 3.

16. Click and Baird, pp. 25–30.

17. Christopher Sterling and Timothy Haight, *The Mass Media: Aspen Guide to Communication Industry Trends* (New York: Praeger, 1978), p. 372.

18. Click and Baird, p. 2.

19. Click and Baird, p. 24.

20. Both quotes found in *Advertising Age*, October 19, 1981, p. S-6.

21. Chris Welles, "The Numbers Magazines Live By," Barry Orton, William

Vesterman, eds., *American Mass Media* (New York: Random House, 1978), pp. 218–225.

22. *Advertising Age*, July 13, 1981, P. 12.

23. *Advertising Age*, October 19, 1981, p. S-6.

24. *Advertising Age*, October 19, 1981, p. S-4.

25. *Advertising Age*, October 19, 1981, p. S-32.

26. Welles, p. 220.

27. Les Brown, *Television: The Business Behind the Box* (New York: Harcourt Brace Jovanovich, 1972), pp. 49–50.

28. Jowett and Linton, p. 39.

29. See, for example, Clive Davis with James Willworth, *Clive: Inside the Record Business* (New York: Ballantine, 1976); Charlie Gillett, *Making Tracks: Atlantic Records and the Growth of a Multi-Billion Dollar Industry* New York: Vintage, 1976); and Michael Gross, "The Hits Just Keep Coming," in Robert Atwan, Barry Orton, and William Vesterman, eds., *American Mass Media* (New York: Random House, 1978), pp. 316–321.

30. Karl Weick, *The Social Psychology of Organizing* (Reading, Pennsylvania: Addison-Wesley, 1979).

31. Click and Baird, p. 263.

32. Click and Baird, p. 263.

33. Click and Baird, p. 262.

34. Click and Baird, p. 263.

35. *Advertising Age*, October 19, 1981, p. 28.

36. Harvey Molotch and Marilyn Lester, "Accidents, Scandals, and Routines: Resources for Insurgent Methodology," *The Insurgent Sociologist*, vol. 3, (1973), pp. 1–11.

37. See George Gerbner, "The Social Role of the Confession Magazine," *Social Problems*, vol. 6 (Summer 1958), pp. 29–40.

38. *Advertising Age*, October 19, 1981, p. 60.

39. *Advertising Age*, October 19, 1981, p. S-28.

40. For an explanation of Nielsen ratings and programming strategies, see Charles Clift, III and Archie Greer, eds., *Broadcast Programming: The Current Perspective* (Washington, D.C.: University Press of America, 1979), pp. 1–114; and Susan Tyler Eastman, Sydney Head, and Lewis Klein, *Broadcast Programming: Strategies for Winning Television and Radio Audiences* (Belmont, California: Wadsworth, 1981), pp. 163–207.

41. Joseph Turow, *Entertainment, Education, and the Hard Sell: Three Decades of Network Children's Television* (New York: Praeger, 1981), pp. 50–55.

42. Erik Barnouw, *The Sponsor: Notes on a Modern Potentate* (New York: Oxford University Press, 1978), pp. 106–107.

43. Interview with Seymour Banks, Vice-president of Leo Burnett Advertising, Chicago, 1978.

44. Paul Goldstein makes this point about el-hi textbooks in Paul Goldstein, *Changing the American Schoolbook* (Lexington, Mass.: DC Heath, 1978).

45. Evan, pp. 122–123.

46. Parts of this section are drawn from Joseph Turow, "Client Relationship and Children's Book Publishing" in P. Hirsch, P. Miller, and F. G. Kline, eds., *Strategies for Communication Research* (Beverly Hills, Calif.: Sage Publications,

1978), pp. 79-92. For a full length review see, Joseph Turow, *Getting Books to Children* (Chicago: American Library Association, 1979).

47. L. Spencer and A. Dale, "Integration and Regulation in Organizations: A Contextual Approach," *The Sociological Review*, vol. 27 (Winter 1980), pp. 679–702.

48. John Riley and Matilda Riley, "Mass Communication and the Social System," in Robert Merton, Leonard Broom, and L. S. Contrell, Jr., eds., *Sociology Today* (New York: Basic Books, 1959), p. 566.

49. Ithiel De Sola Pool and Irwin Shulman, "Newsmen's Fantasies, Audiences, and Newswriting," in Lewis Dexter and David M. White, eds., *People, Society, and Mass Communications* (New York: The Free Press, 1964), p. 143.

50. Raymond Bauer, "The Obstinate Audience: The Influence Process from the Point of View of Social Communication," in Wilbur Schramm and Donald Roberts, eds., *The Process and Effects of Mass Communication* (Urbana, Illinois: University of Illinois Press, 1971), pp. 326–388.

51. Warren Breed, "Social Control in the Newsroom," *Social Forces*, vol. 33 (1955), pp. 326–335.

52. Walter Gieber, "News is What Newspapermen Make It," Dexter and White, p. 176.

53. Dennis McQuail, "Uncertainty about the Audience and the Organization of Mass Communication," *The Sociological Review Monograph*, vol. 13 (1968), pp. 75–84.

54. Muriel Cantor, *The Hollywood Producer* (New York: Basic Books, 1971), p. 166.

55. For a longer exposition, see Joseph Turow, "The Role of 'The Audience' in Publishing Children's Books," *Journal of Popular Culture*, vol. 16 (Fall 1982), p. 90–100.

56. Sterling and Haight, p. 372.

57. ABC Annual Report, 1981, p.33; and Ronald Kaatz, *CABLE: An Advertiser's Guide to the New Electronic Media* (Chicago: Crain Books, 1982), p. 41.

58. *Advertising Age*, February 1, 1982, p. S-12.

Three

Producers and the Public

In Chapter Two, we developed the idea that a mass media production firm's audience is a construct based on requirements and opportunities that the firm's executives perceive in their dealings with primary patron organizations. We noted that when production executives think of their audience, they are thinking of people in terms of categories and concerns that those executives and their counterparts in patron firms consider important. And, we distinguished audience response—the activity of people in terms of producer-designated categories and concerns—from public response, the activity of people in terms of categories and concerns that they themselves define. In this chapter, we take these notions a step further and try to understand their consequences for the creation of mass media material. What is the influence of individual consumers, and organized groups of consumers, on that material? Under what circumstances are they likely to have clout? The answers lie in the resources consumers carry along with their demands in a mass media industry.

To follow through on this idea, it is helpful to extend some ideas on organizations that were introduced in Chapters One and Two. One theme that has been woven through the pages of this book is the dependence of a mass media production firm on its environment for the resources it needs to create and release mass media material to the public. It has also been clear that these resources are not randomly distributed and that entities in the production firm's environment often claim the ability to provide or withhold resources that can account for the success or failure of the firm's activity. We have noted that major goals of production firm leaders are consequently likely to be (1) avoiding dependence on environmental entities and, instead (2) making environmental entities dependent on the production organization. In order to respond to and manage the environment profitably and efficiently, production executives develop routines for themselves and for specialized boundary personnel. They recognize that in order to take resources from entities in the environment, they have to give resources in return. What they give and how much will depend upon their evaluation of the importance of the resources, the availability of the resources, the power of the entities to control them, the competition among production firms (and other firms) for them, and alternative ways of getting the same resources or substitutible ones.

In general, the discussion in previous chapters has centered around the response of production firms to formally established organizations in their environments. That is because these entities predominate in mass media industries. However, the principles noted above are as readily applicable to individuals who confront production firms and to loose coalitions of individuals as they are to long-standing "public advocacy" organizations or coalitions of organizations. Of course, the results of their interactions with production firms might very well be different, as the following discussion will show.

PRODUCERS AND INDIVIDUAL CONSUMERS

It might be logical to start at the most basic level—the response production firms have to direct comments or suggestions about mass media material by individual members of the public. Such offerings are certainly not rare. Several studies of mass media production firms have noted the substantial number of reader, viewer, or listener phone calls, postcards, and letters that stream through the organizations continually. For the most prominent media, that stream can be very large indeed. For example, Kalman Siegel noted in the early 1970s that letters to *The New York Times* editor averaged 40,000 or more a year. Of course, the fact that some of those letters would be printed on the editorial page might have been a strong incentive for some readers to write.[1] Still, the count appears to be high even when people do not see their names in print or on a screen. Herbert Gans counted 351 letters to NBC television news anchor John Chancellor in one month.[2]

During the past several decades quite a bit of research has been devoted to investigating the kinds of people who contact mass media organizations and to noting what they say.[3] Here we are concerned not so much with the characteristics of individuals who contact production organizations about mass media content but with the influence they have on the creation and release of materials they are calling or writing about. Remarkably, very little research has been carried out on this subject. One way to come up with generalizations that predict a mass media production firm's response to individual consumers is to look toward the resource dependence perspective. The basic question to ask is this: What can an individual consumer offer the production firm that the firm cannot get elsewhere without giving up as much independence of action to that consumer?

The answer will, of course, vary depending on the particular situation. All other things being equal, people in a production firm will likely feel that an unknown letter writer or call implicitly can offer (or take away) very little compared to an important political office holder. And, *ceteris paribus*, people in a production firm will likely feel that acting positively on consumer ideas that flow with organizational plans and policies involves giving up less independence of action than does acting positively on consumer ideas that force changes in those plans and policies. The last point is important to underscore. Production personnel are much more eager to get requests and comments that allow them to treat contacters as "audience members"—people who use terms and categories that the producer finds useful—than to get requests and comments that prod them to challenge or derail current approaches. Ideas that production personnel perceive as constructive, easily usable, and fitting their organizational imperatives may be welcomed and adopted in one way or another. On the other hand, ideas that require organizational personnel to depart from basic accepted approaches or to admit *their* lack of creativity will likely be rejected as irrelevancies, nuisances, or threats.

Earlier, we noted that in order to respond to and manage the environment profitably and efficiently, production firm executives develop routines for themselves and specialized boundary personnel. This idea can be applied to an understanding of the way production organizations respond to contacts from members of the public. We would expect any producer regularly receiving comments from consumers to develop an organized set of responses that will be used when such comments appear. James March and Herbert Simon have called this kind of routinized response pattern a "performance program."[4] The performance program a media organization develops for public contacts may be simple, involving a couple of steps and people, or it may be elaborate. The *New York Times*, which receives thousands of "letters to the editor" a month, has a special department consisting of a number of people who sift through that mail, select some for publication, and respond to them all. According to Kalman

Siegel, the head of that department in the early 1970s, a routine for dealing with such contacts is well established there:

> All letters are read, screened and recorded as to issue and position. Anonymous letters are ignored. So are obscenities and obvious cranks.... Letters signed with pseudonymns are considered, but rarely used.... Open letters, letters addressed to public officials and those elsewhere simultaneously or generally circulated are not considered for publication at *The Times*.... Letters that are not used—and this accounts for some 93 out of every 100 letters received—are acknowledged with a series of forms.[5]

A couple of related points about this procedure warrant notice. First is the idea that a regularly appearing letters area is a traditional part of a paper, combining marketing, journalistic, and public relations functions. Kalman points out that "every responsible newspaper" has a letters section, that such a section is usually among the most widely read parts of the paper, and that *Times* editors have long believed that the letters section "is one of the paper's great responsibilities in helping to form public opinion."[6] A second point to make is that the *Times* letters department keeps total control over the use and disposition of the material it receives. The goal is to "reflect a balance on most issues," but only with letters that fit the criteria regarding anonymity, obscenity, exclusivity—and more: "Good letters are generally brief, clearly written, pegged to the news, free of vituperative attack, issue-oriented, and offer constructive informative comment or criticism."[7] Too, because "professional letter writers tend to hog short letters space," they are "discouraged by imposition of a limit, generally two a year for a single writer."[8] Letters from people who seem to be part of an organized letter writing campaign ("they generally come from the same place and [contain] similarity of phrasing") also tend to be excluded. Kalman does not say it, but his preface and the letters he chooses for the anthology called *Talking Back to the New York Times* give the distinct impression that famous people and people in power will have easier access to the letters section than will members of the public without such influence. Clearly, prestigious letter writers reflect prestige on the paper.

Actually, *Talking Back to the New York Times* is only a partially correct title for the book. While many of the letters it contains argue with *Times* editorials and columnists, a good many more simply comment on events that the newspaper had been reporting. None explores in any depth possible reasons for *Times* coverage of certain issues in certain ways. None critically analyzes the power the paper as an organization and a product has in United States society. It is impossible to know from the anthology whether the *Times* ever received any such letters, Still, their absence reinforces and extends a generalization we can derive from our previous discussion of the desire by a firm's executives to maintain their firm's autonomy: Production firms that use citizen feedback in their material tend to (1) limit the feedback that can appear by circumscribing it into certain prearranged spaces or (in broadcasting) time slots, and to (2) limit possible threats such feedback might pose to the organization by circumscribing the debate it reflects to issues that will not critically examine the existence and process of the production firm itself.

In testing this generalization, consider the editorial replies that are broadcast over local television and radio stations; the vox populi spots that some TV stations occasionally air in place of ads; the letters that "Sixty Minutes" and "Meet the Press" hosts read every week; and programs such as "Letters to CBS" that appear every once in a while. Magazine letters to the editor seem overwhelmingly to fit the generalization, as do periodicals' "op-ed" and open contributor pages, such as "My Turn" in *Newsweek*. One important difference between print and broadcast media in the United States is important to note here. Print has traditionally been free of prepublication regulation through safeguards dating to the earliest days of the Republic. The broadcast industry has not been so lucky. There, regulation mandates an individual's right to usurp air time under certain narrow circumstances. The Equal Time provision of the 1934 Federal Communications Act requires broadcasters to allow announced candidates who are qualified for public office "equal opportunities" to state their views, at the station's cheapest rates. The Fairness Doctrine of the Federal Communications Commission, which was inserted into the Federal Communications Act in 1959, requires broadcasters to "afford reasonable opportunity for the discussion of conflicting views on issues of public importance."[9]

Broadcasters are generally allowed to decide the way they will present such views, and the frequency, duration, and place on the schedule the views will appear. Still, as one might expect, broadcast executives have balked at both the Equal Time and Fairness obligations. The requirements, they have openly contended, have led stations and networks to inject *less* controversy into their medium than would otherwise be the case. The argument is that executives have avoided controversy as much as possible so as not to be forced to give up valuable commercial time—and decision making independence—to contentious individuals. Consequently, the Washington broadcast lobby worked hard to eliminate the regulations when responding to a rewrite of the Communications Act that was proposed in the late 1970s. As of the early 1980s, however, they had not succeeded at convincing Congress to get rid of the rules without asking radio and TV station owners to surrender economic and competitive advantages in return.[10]

Production executives in record, movie, billboard, book, and catalog companies are free of requirements to present individual public viewpoints. Moreover, unlike magazine and newspaper counterparts, they do not even feel compelled in most cases to carry citizen feedback (like letters) in their material.

But what of consumers' suggestions to media executives that are meant not to be shared publicly but, rather, to be acted on by members of the company in a private and positive manner? Here, too the approach described earlier is likely to hold: Creative suggestions that production personnel perceive as constructive, easily usable, and fitting their organizational imperatives may be welcomed and adopted in one way or another. Suggestions that require organizational personnel to depart from basic accepted approaches or to admit *their* lack of creativity will likely be rejected as irrelevancies, nuisances, or threats. Suggestions that production personnel accept are not much of a problem, except perhaps to company lawyers who might have to figure out how to adopt (or adapt) the idea with least payment to its originator. Suggestions that production personnel reject may or may not cause them problems, depending on the nature and tone of the suggestions.

The nature of the organization might be relevant as well. For example, it seems clear that executives at a radio or television station would likely view a complaint or strong demand for program control much more seriously than would executives in a newspaper or magazine firm. The reason is that broadcasters, unlike print firms, operate as public trustees of the airwaves and must renew their licences every few years. Connected to this point is the requirement by the Federal Communications Commission that obliges broadcasters to establish a public file of all complaint letters to the management, and to solicit letters for the file. Radio and TV executives therefore have a strong incentive to limit the number of citizen complaints they receive and to defuse threats. Production executives in other mass media industries might also try to mollify an individual contacter's anger, if only to retain a consumer's good will and to forestall the possibility that disgruntled individuals might eventually come together in organized protest.

A study I conducted in the mid-1970s provides an example of the performance program a broadcast firm might use to respond to critical citizen feedback directed at its management.[11] The organization I observed is a network-affiliated radio station in a major American city. News and public affairs are broadcast regularly, and at the time on-air audience participation was encouraged through talk show programs. The purpose of the investigation was to concentrate on the radio station's response to complaints and demands for change (rather than to fan mail or personal remarks directed at an individual). So, the letters to the station or the station manager—and the way the station handled them—became the focus of the investigation.

The criteria for success that the principals of the radio station used with regard to feedback letters could be inferred from remarks by the station manager about the importance of letter writers to his organization. He noted an FCC requirement to respond to every complaint and underscored his desire not to alienate any member of the audience. At the same time, he said that his feeling, and the feeling of executives within the parent firm, is that sentiments of letter writers are not at all representative of the audience as a whole. Audience ratings, he emphasized, are the only form of listener feedback that influences station policy and operations. In fact, when asked specifically about the dismissal of a radio personality who had been inciting angry mail, the station manager (and, later, the program director) denied that the letters had any effect on the individual's forced departure. The executive added that if ratings of that person's program had been climbing over the past several years instead of remaining low with an undesirable (i.e. old) audience, he would still be on the air.

As implied by this example, the necessity of responding to every letter without alienating the correspondent sometimes confronted the equally crucial goal of not allowing angry or demanding feedback letters to alter or disrupt station activities. That such a confrontation was the rule rather than the exception can be inferred from Table 2, which presents a breakdown of the topics found in 100 letters received by the station during a two-month period. The range of topics that was represented in the sample of letters (all but six of which were devoted to only one subject) also represents a wide variety in the degree to which the correspondence threatened the station's autonomy. The guideline for comparing topics in terms of threats to organizational autonomy is whether one subject, if pursued through the formal regulatory and legal channels, could, more likely than another subject, cause the station to relinquish some or all of its programming decisions to the plaintiff. The categories in Table 2 are arranged with this guideline in mind, in an order ranging from "no threat" (Topic I) to "substantial threat" (Topic VII). Both the station manager (who assumes final responsibility for the replies) and the editorial director (who writes them) agreed that the ranking presented in Table 2 is the correct order of

Table 2   Breakdown of Feedback Letter Topics

		Number	Percent
I.	Favorable remark about the Station's on-air personality	22	21
II.	Nonstation related request	10	9
III.	Opinions and proposals relating to current events	17	16
IV.	General complaint about a personality's actions	24	23
V.	Specific complaint about a personality's actions	17	16
VI.	Complaint about station policy	7	7
VII.	Complaint about a specific station action	9	8
		106	100

"the types of letters we'd rather receive," from "most rather" to "least rather." The editorial director also stated that the sample of letters examined for this study is fairly typical of most months. Such predictability regarding feedback, the fact that a majority of the letters are at least somewhat threatening, and the organizational requirement to respond to all letter writers without alienating any of them point to a performance program that divorces the letters from the mainstream of station operations while using rhetorical skill to disguise this fact.

These expectations proved to be well founded. An established routine for handling feedback letters and replying to them could be observed, a routine that severely limited their circulation within the station. Only two nonsecretarial members of the firm—the station manager and editorial director—participated in the performance program. The station manager contended that he read every letter that was addressed to him. However, he was not as informed as the editorial director with regard to the frequency with which letters on different topics are received. He admitted he delegated almost all the responsibility for dealing with the letters to the editorial director, though he added that he consulted with her on responses to some particularly thorny complaints.

In the overwhelming number of cases, the editorial director composed and typed her own reply to every letter in the station manager's name, and he simply signed them. The editorial director also typically answered letters referring to many aspects of the organization without consulting the people involved. Not even the program director was informed about the letters or their responses even though he would, by virtue of his close involvement with daily station fare, be an important individual to weigh complaints and suggestions if consideration as to their implementation were desirable. No tallies were kept on the amount of mail on various topics.

In discussing how she composed responses to feedback letters, the editorial director (who had been working at the station for a year at the time of the study) stated that the reply process could devour all her time if she had to write a newly conceived message to every correspondent. She also stressed her mail-answering function as secondary in importance to her task of writing daily editorials to be read over the air by the station manager. Consequently, she said, a systematic reply procedure grew out of a necessity to answer the letters efficiently; at the time it had been used for several years. While every letter received a personal reply (in that the salutation was directed to the letter writer and the topic of initial correspondence was mentioned in the body of the reply), a model for the reply was taken from a loose-leaf notebook of past responses to similar letters.

An analysis of the letters that were sent by the radio station to eighty-three of its correspondents revealed this patterned approach. Sandwiched between a fixed introductory thanks for the writer's comments and a fixed final hope that the writer would continue listening to the station were remarks that attempted to deal with the particulars of the complaint, demand, praise, or question. These remarks were usually brief: of the 83 letters, 73 (88%) comprised 7 or fewer sentences (including the fixed introduction and conclusion). Even the longest letter was only 11 sentences in length. Because of the brevity of the replies and propositional nature of many of the statements (which were often lifted verbatim from notebook samples), it as possible to categorize the answers in terms of single statements. An analysis of the coincidence of the topics in the initial feedback letters with those reply statements revealed an exact association, as Table 3 shows. The table also shows that the ordering of topics in terms of their increasing threat to the radio station's autonomy was accompanied by a parallel movement of the replies from what might be called as "accommodation" stance (characterized by openness and encouragement towards action or continued letter writing) to a "rule invocation" stance (characterized by rigidity and the blocking of action).

As can be seen in Table 3, "rule invocation" was an attempt to defuse potential or actual threats through the direct or indirect association of station programming and policy with fundamental tenets against which the plaintiff would not be likely to argue. For example, the tenet of cultural democracy was invoked when, in reply to a negative opinion of a station personality (Topic IV), the "station manager" said that "thousands of

Table 3   Association of Feedback Topics with Station Replies

Topic	Reply
I.	"Always happy to hear from a satisfied listener."
II.	"Here is some information that may help you . . ."
	"Write to this government agency to get information."
III.	"Why don't you call our talk shows and present your ideas on radio."
	"Since we feel that your idea is most interesting, why not present it as a rebuttal to our editorial? Contact our editorial director . . ."*
IV.	"Our moderator is among the best-informed in the country."
	"Thousands of listeners feel different from you."
V.	"Our moderators often take positions they don't really believe for the sake of stimulating discussion."
	"You may be assured the problem will not be repeated."
VI.	"It is a practical truth of broadcasting that high commercial content is necessary to maintain high quality service to listeners."
VII.	"We have no obligation under Federal Communications Commission regulations to provide equal time . . ."

* This response was evoked by two complaints against the rudeness of a talk show host and by one complaint against the rudeness of a producer.

listeners feel different from you." A commitment to intellectual excellence and superior performance was the defense used in the comment that a talk show host is "among the best in the country." A charge of bias or racism on the part of a talk show host (Topic V) was countered by an invocation of the principle of diverse and free-flowing ideas. And a complaint against too many commercials (Topic VI) was met by a categorical statement about the need to recognize the connection between good business and good service. Interestingly, when a feedback letter invoked a rule—the Equal Time rule, for example—the station countered by saying that the writer had misunderstood its meaning and applicability: "Until [one of two men who are both obviously running for public office] announces his candidacy, we have no obligation under Federal Communications Commission regulations to provide equal time to either man."

PRODUCERS AND PUBLIC ADVOCACY ORGANIZATIONS

It is very likely that in the great majority of cases production organizations do not have to go beyond this kind of containment when dealing with critical comments and demands. For one thing, it probably works most of the time. In the study just described, analysis of questionnaires that were sent to, and answered by, the letter writers indicated that the stations' pattern of reply was quite successful at accomplishing the station manager's objective of not alienating members of the audience. For another thing, the little evidence that exists regarding people's knowledgeability regarding the way mass media operate suggests that, barring issues that reach to the core of people's beliefs about themselves and their society, most individuals will not take the time or trouble to find out what further steps they might take toward successfully consummating their demands.[12]

When individuals do pursue their complaints and demands, it is often because they have found strength and ammunition in other individuals who have an interest in the issues they raise. They might tap established organizations with broad-ranging activities—for example, the NAACP, the American Civil Liberties Union, the Ku Klux Klan. They might seek organizations that pursue specific interests or deal with specific media—for example, Morality in Media, the National Citizens Committee for Broadcasting. Or they might start their own organization. Whichever the case, it might result in concerted action directed toward one or more mass media production organizations. Sometimes, the demands and perspectives of the individuals develop a groundswell of support, if only in a localized area. When that happens, the phenomenon can be said to have developed into *collective behavior*.

Collective behavior is an umbrella term sociologists use for "relatively unstructured, temporary, emotion-laden and keenly interpersonal social situations, such as crowds, riots, rumors, public opinion, and social movements."[13] Neil Smelser suggested that there are a number of determinants that must be present for any kind of collective behavior to occur. He outlined those determinants as value-added stages, each stage being a necessary but not sufficent prerequisite to the next and, ultimately, to the emergence of the collective behavior. The states are: (1) *structural conductiveness* (the form of collective behavior must be physically and socially possible); (2) *structural strain* (within the context of the conductiveness there must be some social or social psychological disequilibrium, inconsistency, or conflict); (3) *growth and spread of a generalized belief* (the strain must be articulated, and its source identified and labeled); (4) *precipitating factors* (an event or situation must focus the generalized belief more clearly, or give evidence that the source of the strain is correctly identified and labeled); (5) *mobilization of participants for action* (events and/or the leader[s] must develop and implement a course of action based on the generalized belief—that is, a course seen to be able to alleviate the strain); and (4) *the operation of social control* (counterdeterminants to the first five stages must be activated that shape the form, direction, and intensity of the collective behavior).[14]

Of all collective behavior, the social movement is considered the most organized. Louis Zurcher, Jr. and his colleagues define a social movement as "a large scale, informal, but solidly collective effort supported by an ideology and intended to correct, supplement, or in some way influence the social order by direct action"[15] Drawing on Smelsner's work, they focus on the *norm-oriented social movement*. That is the kind of collective behavior that would seem to characterize many of the most vociferous public advocacy demands on mass media organizations. The norm-oriented social movement aims at restoring, protecting, modifying, or creating norms in the name of a generalized belief. That attempt, they say, is "carried out by an organization of some sort which tries to influence norms directly or induce some constituted authority to do so." Certainly, groups such as the Moral Majority, the National Organization for Women, and the National Gay Task Force can be seen as touchstones or foci of norm-oriented social movements when they militate for changes in the portrayals of certain groups or lifestyles on television or in other media.

Using Smelser's value-added stages, it is not very difficult to envision a scenario whereby a particular production firm or a class of production firms could become the target of organized animosity, on a local or national level. Producers of sexually explicit material have long been targets that groups concerned with society's morals have marked for eradication. Much milder material in society's most widespread medium—today that is broadcast TV—also stands a good chance of being picked on in a nationwide campaign. The typical justification for this tactic is that the medium is crucial in forming public attitudes, particularly among children.[16] A more politically tuned reason based on Smelsner's scheme is that the most pervasive medium allows the social movement's leaders to choose a powerful symbol of structural strain that most potential followers can identify, label as such, talk about, and mobilize around. In other words, the medium becomes a key rallying point with which to recruit new members and keep old ones.

Unfortunately there is little concrete evidence to draw upon when trying to come to conclusions about the influence public advocacy organizations can have on mass media producers when they approach those producers directly with their demands. Production firm executives are loath to discuss these situations publicly, and advocacy group leaders are likely to sound as if their challenges were more successful than they really were in order to hold on to their followers. It would seem that a large number of organized protesters would be in a better situation than would individual plaintiffs, if only because production personnel might be cowed somewhat by the potential havoc that large numbers of people can wreak on their public relations images. This would be particularly true for an organization not used to such protests, since executives might be shocked at the insistent demands for action and at an initial uncertainty about how to preserve their autonomy. At the same time, we would expect executives in an organization familiar with and expecting protests to have a fairly routine procedure to evaluate and handle complaints and demands. To them protecting organizational autonomy in content production while maintaining the flow of desired resources needed to continue production is likely to be a paramount aim. Entering into these calculations will be (1) the extent to which the group's demands depart from the producer's basic approaches: (2) the extent to which the demands militate against fundamental economic constraints and opportunities of the producer-patron relationship or other interorganizational exigencies; (3) the power of the group to mobilize resources against the firm, and the importance of those resources; and (4) the availability of those resources, or substitutible ones, through other avenues.

Briefly comparing the outcome of two producer-directed activities to change mass media material will be a start toward illustrating these points. The cases involve different special interest publics, blacks and homosexuals. The earlier one, the "Amos 'n' Andy" crusade of 1931, was a large wave of protests by black citizens throughout the United States against an extremely popular radio program.[17] "Amos 'n' Andy" premiered on the National Broadcasting Company's Red network in 1929 and quickly climbed to the top of program popularity charts. A situation comedy about two black men who had moved from Atlanta to Chicago to seek their fortunes, it was created by whites and performed by whites in a mangled dialect that was typical of blackface vaudeville and minstrel acts. In 1931, Robert Vann, the black editor of an influential black newspaper, the Pittsburgh *Courier*, launched a campaign to remove the show from the airwaves. In an editorial aimed at blacks ignorant of the "evils" of "Amos 'n' Andy," he pointed out that whites assumed the program fairly represented the lifestyle and aspirations of the typical Negro. "It is now a common thing," Vann asserted, "for [white] salesmen to enter a Negro business place and begin by asking, 'Did you hear "Amos 'n' Andy" last night?' " Often, Negro laborers were called Amos or Andy, and whites assumed that their Afro-American employees would be as carefree and lazy as the two radio characters. Only Negroes, the editor lamented, "would stand for th[is exploitation]." Hoping to prove that blacks did not enjoy the program and did not relish being called Amos or Andy, Vann asked his readers to write the *Courier* and express their opinions about the most popular program on the air.

Response was enthusiastic. Scores of readers agreed that "Amos 'n' Andy" was a disgrace to the Negro race; their letters "flooded the *Courier* office." Catalyzed by Vann, nearly 750,000 blacks signed their names to petitions demanding that the Federal Radio Commission remove the program from the air. Too, at Vann's request, hundreds of black ministers around the country delivered "self-respect" sermons to their congregations. Yet the efforts to get rid of "Amos 'n' Andy" were unsuccessful. The program lasted on radio through the mid-1950s. Protesting blacks were simply not important enough to NBC, sponsor Pepsodent toothpaste, or the Federal Radio Commission to pull off a program that at its most popular attracted two-thirds of the entire U.S. radio audience. A Pepsodent boycott that a *Courier* letter to the editor proposed showed no evidence of taking hold or scaring the firm. Moreover, the series' producers marshaled alternative resources to support their intransigence. They claimed that before the first "Amos 'n' Andy" was broadcast, representatives of WMAQ (the originating station) and the Chicago Urban League consulted 150 prominent blacks in the city about the show, and they reacted favorably. Too, the program's defenders pointed out that many blacks were avid fans of "Amos 'n' Andy." In Harlem, they noted, loudspeakers broadcast the show to passing pedestrians, meeting few, if any, objections.

Place this episode next to a very different kind of confrontation between broadcasters and public advocacy groups—the attempts by gay activist organizations to change the portrayal of homosexuals on television during the 1970s. Kathryn Montgomery points out in her study of gay activists and the TV networks that in the 1970s and early 1980s the portrayal of homosexuals was one of the most problematic areas for treatment by commercial television.[18] Gay activists complained that mass media tended either to ignore their existence or to present them in ways that reinforced rather than challenged prevailing stereotypes. Network executives, however, could not simply accede to gay demands for fuller representation. The reason was that in an era marked by strong societal and network sensitivity to demeaning social stereotypes, gays remained exceptions. "While few people would come out openly against more positive portrayals of blacks or women, regardless of their own privately held prejudices, opposition to gays has been public and vocal as well as political." Too, "since discussions of homosexuality often involve the corollary of sex, a topic which in and of itself [has created] heated debates over television content, the work of gay activitists [has posed] a particularly difficult set of problems for network organizations."

According to Montgomery, organized pressure activity directed at television network treatment of homosexuality began in 1973, when gay activitists joined in protest over an episode of the "Marcus Welby, M. D." dramatic series. While several groups were involved in that campaign, the primary job of pressuring network television was assumed soon after by the National Gay Task Force. This organization remained the principal media activist group to represent the gay community to the networks. It employed a staff member to lobby the television networks. Activity by the Task Force and affiliate groups was consistent through the decade. In fact, Montgomery notes, "spokespersons from all three networks reported that gays were the most effective and well-organized of the special interests groups who lobby the television entertainment industry."

Several interrelated factors seem to explain this effectiveness, limited as it will be seen to be. The factors relate to tactics that contrast starkly with the protest tactics of the "Amos 'n' Andy" crusade. First, gay activists evolved a very detailed, systematic approach to their activity, organizing themselves "in a way that [paralleled], both geographically and operationally, the structure of network television." Principal homosexual advocacy groups located themselves close to network headquarters on both the East and West coasts, with "affiliates" in other cities that stood ready to apply pressure to the network TV affiliates during cases of extreme protest. Generally, the strategy was to concentrate on influencing the networks' broadcast standards departments, since they set policy for the treatment of controversial and sensitive issues in programming and have the power to censor scripts and even completed programs. This approach, which presupposed a sophisticated understanding of network operations, was combined with a dogged determination to keep in touch with network executives on a continual basis, feeding them ideas, sharing complaints from gays around the country, and offering themselves as program consultants.

Overall, gay representatives presented themselves as "an educational lobby" that was seeking to educate media decision makers. The advocates employed two key tactics in their relations with network officials: monitoring and feedback. Monitoring involved watching television and anticipating upcoming programs that contained what they felt were derogatory portrayals of homosexuals. Often, the advance information came from a well-developed "underground network" of homosexuals working within the TV industry. Feedback involved consistent and immediate forwarding of positive or negative reactions to network executives, particularly the vice-president of broadcast standards, regarding a gay portrayal or theme. Because of their frequent contacts, the relationships between gay media activists and important network officials became institutionalized and informal. This routine, day-to-day communication between the National Gay Task Force and the networks was, though, carried out against a backdrop of more heated exchanges "which [served] to ensure support from the networks lest the more serious instances happen again." Between 1973 and 1978, seven major protest campaigns flared. They involved national letter writing crusades, sit-ins, and pressures on affiliates. While the activists by no means won all of their demands, in six of the seven flare-ups the network involved did concede some major points.

Montgomery suggests that the key reason this highly organized carrot and stick approach resulted in effective compromises over content during that period was that the demands gay activists made did not really require fundamental reorientations in network and producer approaches to programming or, even in their use of gay program motifs. The advocates accepted "the rules of the game for network television." The agreed with their network counterparts that certain compromises had to be made when dealing with "sensitive" and "controversial" material in network entertainment programming. Consequently, the decisions affecting the portrayal of homosexual lifestyle were influenced by the constraints that both parties agreed were necessarily part of commercial television's territory. For example:

> The fundamental goal of garnering the largest possible audience necessitated that (a) the program be placed in a familiar and successful television genre—the crime drama; (b) the story focus upon the heterosexual male lead character and his relations to gay characters rather than upon the homosexual characters themselves; and (c) the film avoid any overt display of affection which might be offensive to certain segments of the audience. These requirements served as a filter through which the issue of homosexuality was processed, resulting in a televised picture of gay life designed to be acceptable to the gay community and still palatable to a mass public.[19]

Clearly, the reasons for the different outcomes of the "Amos 'n' Andy" crusade and the gay activist activities go beyond the differences in time period and general social milieu. Simply considering the cost-benefit criteria discussed earlier can explain why the networks were more malleable in their dealings with the gay activists. At base was the issue of organizational autonomy. While the black groups of 1931 forced NBC into an uncomfortably public all-or-nothing position with an extremely profitable program, the National Gay Task Force organized its activities essentially so as to integrate itself into the operations of the network broadcast standards departments. The first tactic did not work then, at least in the short run, and it has not worked since. It is difficult to think of a single program that a national television or radio network has removed from its schedule as a result of public advocacy group protest. Flare-ups in the 1970s and early 1980s over TV programs as diverse as "Playing For Time", "Beulah Land," "Bridget Loves Bernie," "Soap," and "Love, Sidney" indicate that when pressure to remove a show or its star becomes public, the networks will refuse, even when it is not clear that the program will be a money maker. Perhaps they feel that capitulating will invite an avalanche of similar protests. One network official confessed his exasperation that pressure groups' many, often conflicting, demands regarding TV content could lead to an unprofitable "balkanization of the audience" if followed.[30]

That does not mean that direct pressure by such movements on TV networks will always fail. As Zurcher and his colleagues point out, to a social movement success often means the organized venting of anger about certain aspects of the world and the taking of a stand regarding social change, even if the activities do not produce the desired tangible results.[21] Too, the possibility must be considered that a succession of advocacy group protests will cause network executives to pause before airing material that will bring another storm of petitions. They might fear that continual protest by powerful constituencies can ultimately embarrass them publicly, cause advertisers to hesitate in their sponsorship of material, and invite agencies of the federal government to hold regulatory hearings.

Compromises can sometimes be worked out. In the cases of "Soap" and "Love, Sidney," for example, network executives, in an environment of general rising advocacy group protest about the acceptance of sexual titillation and homosexuality on TV (protests relevant to these shows), agreed to modify the programs' most objectionable aspects. Still, it seems clear that ABC, NBC, the CBS would rather witness the more "helpful" pressure involved in the routine relationships between the National Gay Task Force and the networks. Of course, the strategy gay activists followed was a pragmatic trade-off. In return for guidelines and suggestions about the portrayal of homosexuals that network officials would not find difficult to accept, the activists agreed to limit their public denunciations so the networks would not have to expend boundary personnel resources trying to quell sophisticated nationwide protest flare-ups.

The difficulty public advocacy groups have influencing production decisions in broadcasting is compounded when they deal with other media. The reason, noted earlier, is that TV broadcasters, unlike other media producers, operate as public trustees and must renew their licenses every five years. While the networks technically do not fall under government regulation, the valuable stations they own do, as do the stations of their affiliates. No station has ever lost its license in a scuffle solely over content. Nonetheless, station owners remain skittish about the possibility that in-place regulators might interpret rules and license renewal petitions in ways that reflect tides of public indignation they see directed at broadcasters. These concerns ripple to record companies that need radio stations as promotional outlets. However, other record companies, as well as book, newspaper, billboard, magazine, and film producers, have no such standing watchdogs. Actually, even people demanding action from radio and television executives often feel that the possibility that government regulators will hear of their arguments and get involved is not a great enough threat to broadcasters to force them toward an accommodation. Consequently, individuals and advocacy organizations often turn to potentially powerful intermediaries—legislatures, regulatory agencies, courts, and advertisers.

PRESSURING PRODUCERS THROUGH AUTHORITIES

Individuals and organizations have a straightforward purpose for turning to legislatures, regulatory agencies, and courts in bids to reform mass media material. Lacking the leverage to influence producers directly, they hope to convince the authorities to join forces with them and, through the increased leverage that they would achieve, carry out their goals. Two major assumptions underlie this advocacy activity—(1) that authorities truly do have substantial leverage with producers, and (2) that the public advocacy organizations can convince the authorities to use the leverage toward certain ends. The following discussion will show that these assumptions are not always warranted.

First, some preliminary observations about the process are relevant. If one wanted to cast the largest net possible over government-related activities that influence the production of mass media material, one could argue that virtually any legislative, regulatory, and judicial decision affecting the structure of a mass media industry or the industry's relation to other industries would be fair game. Thus, rulings affecting the number of distributors in the movie industry, the viability of newspapers in middle-sized cities, the right of book publishers to demand copyright fees from libraries, and the right of cable companies to "import" distant TV signals all ultimately influence the kind of material released to the public. These kinds of rules, which adjust or create the boundaries in which mass media industries operate, are some of the most important activities authorities carry out regarding the media. Because of the activities' importance, factions from the potentially affected industries will converge on the authorities to defend their interests. When stakes are high, large businesses and business associations pour money and lobbying energy into all-out efforts to win for their side. Most times, that kind of wide-ranging fray is not initiated by public advocacy organizations, though they may feel a stake in its outcome. In that situation, faced with a battle of giants, advocacy group representatives often have little choice but to stop to the side of the giants they like, cheer them on in front of authorities, and hope that makes a difference.

The situation is different when a public advocacy organization has initiated the battle. Steering the debate at its start has some advantages, particularly when it takes place in a courtroom. The motive idea behind lawsuits is that, left alone, producers, and sometimes even government decision makers, will not be sufficiently responsible to the advocacy organization's constituency. When lawsuits are not the best vehicle, strong pressure through legislative and regulatory channels becomes the preferred government route. Mark Nadel, in his study of "the politics of consumer protection," notes that a public advocacy group's success relates to its ability to broaden politicians' conceptions of the group's constituency during its attack. The successful advocacy organization, he says, "takes phenomena defined as problems and lifts them to the point where they become political issues—a larger public becomes aware of the problems and governmental participants feel pressure to take action on the problem."[22]

Nadel emphasizes the role "the press," broadly defined, plays in constituency expansion. "The public's knowledge of government hearings and records comes from the media; determination of which parts of the public record are truly public is made by the press."[23] Nadel does not deal with mass media except in this agenda-setting context. So, he fails to see that difficulties in successful advocacy pressure on government are compounded when mass media industries are the targets. Two areas of difficulty stand out. One involves the possibility that the vested interests of media executives might dramatically oppose a group's constituency expansion. Media executives might perceive that reporting advocacy demands and government hearings to the public could encourage public activity that would hinder the autonomy of people in their very organizations.[24] The second difficulty is that attempts to change media activities through the government are often stifled due to a force that is usually inapplicable in other kinds of consumer movements. The ironic culprit in these logjams is the First Amendment to the United States Constitution, which guarantees freedom of speech and the press from government control and thus strongly limits the ability of authorities to act.

These difficulties, together with the problems that have traditionally plagued all public advocacy organizations in dealings with authorities, make advocacy influence on mass media material through government pressure complex and limited. Room does not permit going down the many eddies and rivulets of this issue. Here, general tendencies of the two most intentional kinds of attempts to shape material will be sketched—(1)

pressuring authorities to provide access to a producer's medium; and (2) pressuring authorities to eliminate certain materials created by the producers.

Pressuring Authorities to Provide Access

A.J. Liebling, the writer and journalism critic, once quipped that in America there is freedom of the press for the man who owns one.[25] As already noted, the First Amendment protects the rights of most producers of mass media material, including the right in the great majority of situations to withhold from citizens access to content production. Regarding access, however, an important distinction must again be made between the unregulated "press"—that is, print media, discs, movies, and other circulating paraphernalia—and the regulated "press," that is, broadcasting and cable television. In the former group, citizen petitioning of authorities for access is futile. The United States Supreme Court essentially said as much when, in the Tornillo case of 1974, it declared that laws requiring newspapers to allow individuals they attack to reply are unconstitutional. Writing for the Court, Chief Justice Warren Burger's position was uncompromising: "A responsible press is undoubtedly a desirable goal, but press responsibility is not mandated by the Constitution and like many other virtues cannot be legislated."[26]

A few years earlier, however, the High Court had ruled that responsibility in radio and television broadcasting *can* be legislated. In deciding a suit that challenged the constitutionality of the Fairness Doctrine, the justices ruled unanimously that the FCC edict does not violate the First Amendment. The difference between print and broadcasting hinged for the justices on the idea that broadcast frequencies comprise a "scarce resource." While there is no law of nature that prevents anyone from starting a newspaper, they said, there are simply not enough frequencies to go around. That being the case, it is permissible for the federal government to regulate the use of the airwaves by issuing licenses. The airwaves belong to the people, not the licensees, the Court asserted, and "it is the right of the viewers and listeners, not the right of the broadcasters, which is paramount." Consequently, "there is no sanctuary in the First Amendment for unlimited private censorship operating in a medium not open to all."[27]

Note, however, that while the Supreme Court used this, the Red Lion decision, to validate citizens' right to demand "fairness," it developed a line of reasoning in later cases that made successful demands for access to the broadcast medium for reasons other than achieving fairness extremely difficult. In two 1973 decisions, *CBS* v. *Democratic National Committee* and *Business Executive Movement for Vietnam Peace* v. *FCC*, the High Court set down a barrage of arguments against the more general notion of access. The arguments had two major themes. The first was that the imposition of an access right would necessarily lead to an unwanted increase in governmental control over the media, because it would require FCC policing of disputes over access time. The second was that in the case of controversial issues, the requirement that broadcasters adhere to the Fairness Doctrine's mandate to present adequate coverage and opposing viewpoints was enough to deal with the problem of access. Related to both these themes was the fear, expressed most clearly by Justice William O. Douglas, that forcing access on broadcasters would make the medium a public forum for legal purposes. It would assume the same status as a park, municipal theater, or thoroughfare, which when made available at all for speech purposes must be made available without regard to content, and subject only to reasonable regulations of time and manner. Douglas said that a commercial radio or television station run in that way would find it difficult, if not impossible, to obtain sponsors, and would probably cease to function. Since the purpose of the First Amendment is not to interfere with but to encourage speech, he said, any such result would be abhorrent. This position by the Court led one communication lawyer involved in access struggles to assert that "it can no longer be cogently argued that the Constitution, in and of itself, guarantees any person a right of access to a particular medium."[28]

Still, one might say that regarding the narrower area of fairness relating to access, the FCC does have the High Court's support. But despite this support, the FCC has not worked hard for the fairness cause. Its stance should not come as a surprise to anyone familiar with the pressures that tend to guide government regulatory agencies. Barry Cole and Mal Oettinger are only two among many observers who agree that the Federal Communications Commission has been the classic case of a regulatory agency that is captive of the industry it regulates.[29] Just a few hard numbers are telling. According to a staff study by the House of Representatives Subcommittee on Oversights and Investigation, ten of the nineteen commissioners and chairmen appointed and confirmed to the FCC from the mid-1960s to mid-1976 have been employed in a business or law practice that furthered industry interests. Only one of the nineteen commissioners had demonstrated "consumer sensitivity" prior to commission appointment, through involvement in a consumer, environmental, or conservationist cause.[30] A strong incentive toward an industry orientation is also reflected in commissioners' tracks upon leaving the agency. Between 1945 and 1977, twenty-six of the forty-two commissioners who departed became affiliated with the communications industry, either as employees of companies regulated by the FCC or as lawyers practicing before the agency.[31]

Important staff members of the commission, too, have moved on to lucrative legal positions, very often representing clients before their former employer. And, if occupational backgrounds and future occupational incentives have not been enough to guide FCC members toward industry rather than consumer concerns, their daily dealings with representatives of the regulated firms have served to crystallize that perspective. Every industry the FCC oversees—whether it be telephone, broadcasting, or cable television—mounts extensive, continual lobbying efforts that are "both subtle and meat-ax."[32] When big issues arise that might place one industry in a more powerful position than another, the commissioners usually try to find a middle line between them. As Dean Krugman and Leonard Reid point out, in the FCC balancing various powerful interests may at times be more important than the merits of an argument. The two also note, as others have, that the FCC chooses issues to confront according to the strongest pressures of the moment. The process, they say, "relies on participating groups to initiate actions and vie for positions in an advocacy system."[33]

In this kind of regulatory environment, public advocacy organizations and individual advocates not affiliated with powerful firms have had to wage an uphill battle for access to the airwaves. Historically, in fact, it has been the courts that have forced the commission to admit advocacy groups to license renewal hearings and to consider the impact of station format changes on the community when such changes are part of license transfers. So, not surprisingly, license renewal challenges and format change appeals have, along with reliance on the fairness and equal time edicts, been used by activists to play a role in shaping radio and TV programming.

The fairness and equal time notions have been the most straightforwardly accepted by the commission. And, indeed, some important avenues to the airwaves have been carved by individuals or groups using those provisions. For example, John Banzhaf, a law professor who formed Action on Smoking and Health (ASH) in 1968, persuaded the FCC that out of fairness considerations antismoking ads should be carried by broadcasters who aired cigarette commercials.[34] In general, though, the commission has made the odds that people filing fairness or equal time complaints will get a chance to present their views on the air very small. In many cases, plaintiffs have a nearly impossible task to establish that the issue they raise is a controversial issue of public importance. Again, there is room here only for some statistics that reflect the lopsided nature of this situation: In 1973 and 1974, a high period of media activism, the FCC received 4300 complaints dealing with fairness and equal time. Of these, only 19 (.4% of the total) were eventually resolved against a station to the point that citizens got access to airwaves.[35]

For reasons just suggested, the Fairness and Equal Time rules are recognized by most public advocacy groups and broadcasters as narrowly defined edicts realistically applying under unusual, even rare, circumstances. A more powerful weapon in the arsenal of a citizen group would, on the surface, appear to be a petition to the FCC asking the agency to deny renewal or transfer (that is, sale) of a broadcast license. Since 1966, when the United States Court of Appeals forced the commission to include public advocacy groups in license renewal hearings, hundreds of groups with as many goals have filed "petitions to deny." By far the largest numer of filings have been introduced by organizations representing blacks, Latinos, and women. The typical reasons have been inadequate ascertainment of community needs, discrimination in employment, and inadequate programming for a segment of the community.[36] However, while citizen groups have spent much energy in these fights, delaying and confusing tactics by both broadcasters and the commission have made success extremely rare, despite support advocacy groups have received from the courts. Unsuccessful outcomes are virtually assured when an advocacy group petitions to deny a license or its transfer because of programming inadequacies. Longtime FCC observers Barry Cole and Mal Oettinger conclude as much in a book aptly titled *The Reluctant Regulators*: "When petitioners have alleged that a station has not been meeting its public service obligations in programming, but no question of racial discrimination has been raised, the Commission usually cites its philosophy of leaving program judgments to the licensee's discretion."[37]

For a while during the late 1960s and early 1970s, it appeared that public advocacy groups interested in shaping a radio or television station's programming had found one surefire method toward their goal: the citizen-licensee agreement. Such agreements, not carried out under FCC auspices, essentially entailed an assurance by activists not to challenge the station's license renewal or transfer if the licensee would promise in writing to implement certain station practices. Unless the citizen groups' requests were outrageous, the broadcasters often had strong reasons for reaching a truce with them. Even if the station management were sure it would win a license challenge, the process would be extremely expensive in monetary terms as well as in terms of station public relations with its community. As scores of public advocacy groups jumped on the citizen-licensee agreement bandwagon, though, broadcast executives and FCC commissioners became nervous that managers were abdicating too much of their programming autonomy. Moreover, the broadcasters could not see a way to placate several license challengers with contradictory aims. Thus, when WXYZ Detroit signed an agreement with the National Organization for Women (NOW) to devote a minimum ninety minutes to women's programming each year during prime time hours, a number of antifeminist organizations objected strongly to the FCC. The station's general manager observed, "We're damned if we do, and damned if we don't."[38]

The commission's solution to this difficult problem was in consonance with everything else the FCC has done with respect to access: It came fully to the rescue of the broadcasters. In a 1975 policy statement, the commission stated that it would sanction no agreement in which a licensee delegated programming and public service decisions, even voluntarily. Ronald Garay, reviewing the history of the citizen agreement in 1978, saw that the FCC had taken away a great deal of the leverage citizen groups had used when they associated themselves with federal power. The 1975 Policy Statement on Agreements, he said, "all but erased many gains that citizen groups had made in terms of citizen-broadcaster negotiations."[39]

Pressuring Authorities to Eliminate Materials

While United States regulatory authorities have been reluctant to provide public advocacy organizations with access to mass media material except in certain narrow situations, over the years they have been willing to accede to requests by certain activist groups to try to help eliminate certain mass media material. Perhaps this willingness to censor and to narrow the boundaries of acceptable content has to do with the emotional and political load of the topics often involved—sex and violence. Whatever the reason, the rhetoric on all sides has often been high-pitched, the battles have often been rough and tumble. Often, too, pressure through authorities has been carried out in tandem with direct pressures on producers or other organizations in the targeted industry. And, a good many times the consequences have been quite significant. Fascinating to note, however, that because of the need by courts to define terms clearly, because of First Amendment considerations, and because of straightforward business considerations, even the most significant results of activists' pressures through authorities to eliminate mass media materials have not always been the ones activists have expected.

Take militancy against sexually explicit literature as one example. Although in America laws that made "obscene libel" illegal date to the early 1700s, active public advocacy group opposition to this kind of publishing first surfaced in the nineteenth century.[40] The 1821 Massachusetts court decision banning *Memoirs of a Woman of Pleasure* (*Fanny Hill*) was the first United States judicial case in which sexual content was the sole issue. While court cases were few before the last quarter of the nineteenth century, there seems to have been at least enough social consciousness of obscenity as an issue to cause several states to enact restrictive legislation, beginning with Vermont in 1821. About twenty years later, Congress empowered the Customs Department to seize "indecent" materials, and in 1865 Congress adopted a law declaring that mailing obscene publications as a criminal offense. In spite of federal and state laws, the relative infrequency of obscenity cases on record before 1870 indicates that little attention was paid to the issue prior to that time. But in the last quarter of the nineteenth century groups of citizens began calling for censorship. They targeted fiction of all types, classics as well as dime novels.[41] According to Felice Flanery Lewis, whose *Literature, Obscenity, and Law* is a comprehensive treatment of the subject, this rise of public advocacy groups against literary obscenity did not result from any actual greater frankness in the main body of literature circulated in the United States after the Civil War. It did, instead, result from a confluence of social forces that crystallized in the success one Anthony Comstock had in mobilizing various censorship forces. "With Comstock's whirlwind assault on material and activities that he considered immoral, the country entered a period of turmoil from which it has not yet emerged."[42]

Clearly, space does not permit even the briefest exposition of the ways such advocacy organizations as the Watch and Ward Society, the New York Society for the Suppression of Vice, and the National Organization for Decent Literature have tried to use federal and state courts, as well as legislatures and police, to prohibit the publication or sale of sexually explicit material throughout the country. Here the purpose is much narrower: to point out that while those organizations scored some impressive victories, particularly during the first half of the twentieth century, the ironic lasting product of their labors has been elimination of the threat of being censored as "obscene" from the great majority of books with sexual themes. The sequence of events that started the ball rolling in this direction was a series of court challenges between about 1910 and 1930 by antipornography organizations against the importation and American publication of Greek, Roman, and French classics with erotic overtones or motifs. It was assumed by most judges (and upheld by the Supreme Court in 1957) that obscene publications are not protected by the First Amendment. The difficulty, however, was in defining "obscene." Vigorous defenses by publishers and importers as to the historic importance and enduring qualities of the classic works targeted for censorship brought various judges to evolve specific criteria for "obscenity." Those criteria, when logically extended, pointed to much greater leeway for newer books that at the time were being called obscene. Lewis captures the point well: "In challenging the classics, censors ironically precipitated the birth, in a very restricted form, of the concept that literature with social value was outside the scope of censorship laws, a concept that would eventually do much to defeat the banning of literature."[43]

Ironic outcomes like this weave through history of movies and television in the United States as well. Of course, in saying that, our level of generalization has changed. "Attempts to eliminate sexually explicit literature" relates to one broad topic on one medium, but "pressure against movies and television" subsumes a multitude of controversial issues, each with its own particular history and rate of evolution. While sex and sexual innuendo in movies and television have ignited advocacy groups, many other subjects have also led to confrontations. Violence has been the second major inciter, followed by racial, ethnic, and gender stereotyping, and the quality and nature of children's material. A key difference between battles over obscenity and battles over other aspects of movie and television content has been use of the courts. While lawsuits have been used often to try to force elimination of obscenity, they have not been nearly as frequent regarding the other content areas. With a few very important exceptions, the advocacy group tactic has been to apply pressure to government regulatory or legislative officials who, in turn, have bullied ("jawboned") producers of content into making changes.

Generally, sensitivity to pressure at each step of this process is based on the kinds of evaluations of resources and leverages discussed earlier. Politicians not personally seized by the issue will likely try to gauge the size of the advocacy group's constituency, the sophistication of its public relations apparatus, and the ways the group can help them. Then they might place their perceptions of the group's power against that of the industry they are being urged to attack. Industry leaders, too, are likely to conduct a formal or informal cost-benefit analysis. In doing so, they will consider not just the pressure group and the potential revenues the company will realize from the targeted material. They will also consider the possibility that key politicians might be persuaded to drop their crusade or, failing that, the potential damage that flouting government calls for content changes can bring.

In certain situations, the producers might well conclude the damage would be great. It was, in fact, fear by early movie executives that government reprisals against uninhibited films were likely to include strict censorship that led them down a path of self-regulation in Hollywood's early days. During the decade before the 1920s, several states began to create censorship boards to fight what many public advocacy groups around the country insisted were excessively sexy, violent, and generally immoral films. A challenge to state censorship on free speech grounds said the motion picture was "business pure and simple" and that therefore First Amendment rights did not apply.[44] This perspective was overturned by the High Court in 1952. However, in 1922 the movie moguls, fearing a bewildering maze of film rules from forty-eight states and the federal level, decided to nip government control in the bud by joining forces to create the Motion Picture Producers and Distributors of America. Headed by Will Hays, the MPPDA was given two tasks: to fight off national censorship and to set up a policy of self-censorship that would convince public advocacy organizations, legislatures, and state censorship boards of the producers' good faith.[45]

Hays succeeded remarkably well at his mission. He homogenized and codified state censor complaints into the MPPDA Code, a document that received the imprimateur of no less an advocacy group than the powerful Legion of Decency. This code, modified and expanded over the years, became a model for the National Association of Broadcasters Code when television executives in the early 1950s moved to head off government and public advocacy pressures. The movie industry, for its part, was then moving in the other direction. Competition with television for viewers was driving film producers toward subjects the home tube could not touch, and which were against the film industry code as well. With the 1952 Supreme Court "free speech" decision liberating movie makers from the most direct form of government reprisal, and with economic concerns driving even the major studios toward desperation, production code barriers shattered as the 1960s passed. Besides, now the main target of advocacy group concern was TV, and broadcasters had picked up the code gauntlet. The networks, going further, had set up "broadcast standards" departments with staffs instructed to eliminate objectionable scenes from scripts and completed shows. The movie producers replaced their code with a rating system to warn the public about—and just possiby lure it to—violence and sex in particular films.[46]

The saga of public advocacy pressure joined to government pressure against the movie and TV industries is complex and convoluted. Some issues have been raised, dealt with, and dropped, only to be raised and dealt with in much the same way several years later. Other issues have been brought to the public agenda at different times and treated differently. In both kinds of situations, pressures to excise material generally have been brought when production firms have been making a good deal of money for themselves and their patrons from that material. The popularity of certain plot lines or themes, and their repetition in various movies or TV shows, is generally what has led to crescendos of public, and legislative, uproar. Not wanting to relinquish their profits, production executives expreiencing this kind of pressure have tried to (1) pacify the legislators while making them look good to their constituents; (2) calm the legislators and advocacy groups by assurance of change in the direction they have demanded; and (3) impose actual changes in content that bow somewhat to the pressures but still contain the essence of the controversial elements (or substitutible ones) that are believed to draw the profitable audiences.

One brief example of this general "performance program" can be presented here. It is a movie case that harks to the early days of the MPPDA (often called "the Hays office") when the first code was being established. As a result of the code, organized voices of protest were beginning to fade. With state and federal legislators calmed, film executives began to see Will Hays and his associates as instruments by which they could test—and define and slowly expand—the outer limits of movie respectability. And, indeed, the mechanical morality that the Hays office promulgated among its producers through its widely heralded code tempted those looking for a way to subvert the code's spirit while remaining true to its letters. Weaving through the moral dicta of the MPPDA was the notion of *compensating values*. It meant that "if virtue were always rewarded and sin punished, if good eventually triumphed and evil doers perished miserably, the laws of God, man, and the drama would be simultaneously satisfied."[47] Arthur Knight notes the ironic consequences of this approach:

> The studios were quick to perceive that what this meant, in effect, was that they could present six reels of ticket-selling sinfulness if, in the seventh reel, all the sinners came to a bad end, and that they could go through all the motions of vice if, at the last moment, virtue triumphed. Censors around the country might continue their snipping of occasional scenes, but who could object to movies in which "morality" was so eagerly espoused?[48]

Certainly, public advocacy groups did not expect the Motion Picture Code to lead to such films when they pushed the industry toward self-regulation. Such, however, was the unanticipated consequence. Similar patterns of response can be cited regarding the many episodes of legislative and FCC jawboning of network officials over the years in response to advocacy group outcries over violence; sexual innuendo; racial, ethnic, and gender stereotyping; and the need to eliminate objectional plot lines and characterizations in children's television. Violence has been replaced by sexual innuendo and "action comedy." Sexual innuendo has been replaced by violence. Clearly "unfavorable" racial, ethnic, and gender stereotypes have been replaced by more subtle stereotypes of the same groups, or by stereotypes of other groups that might evoke similar audience responses. And children's television has incorporated elements that mollify some advocacy groups while not really changing the fundamental plot lines and characterizations that stirred the groups in the first place.

All this implies that when advocacy groups have been powerful enough to pressure legislators and regulators toward action, production executives have moved to alter the content, sometimes greatly. The point to underscore, however, is that what has emerged as a result of the altercation has often not been what the advocacy group members or the government officials anticipated. Sometimes, in fact, what was emerged has simply been another version of the same problem.

PRESSURING PRODUCERS THROUGH PATRONS

Advocacy group members who are frustrated with the runaround they get when they appeal directly to producers, and with the maddening snail's pace, hesitation, and unpredictability they find when they try to change material by working through legislatures or courts, have increasingly been turning their energies toward the organizations that sponsor the mass media content. Their reasoning is straightforward. Since the buying patterns of primary patrons are crucial to mass media producers' survival, successful advocacy pressure on the patrons would create a powerful leverage to eliminate or change the producers' material. In reality, though, the situation is not that straightforward. Organizations taking on the patron role, like producers and authorities, are continually faced with many competing interests from quarters that hold a variety of different resources. That makes their sensitivity to advocacy groups not at all clear-cut.

What we have, then, is the probability that leaders of patron organizations, like their counterparts in producer and authority organizations, will carry out cost-benefit analyses to decide whether, how, and to what extent they should accede to advocacy group demands. Of course, media patrons can be very different from one another, and it is impossible to make blanket statements about the outcome of such cost-benefit calculations. For example, one can argue that public organizations taking on the patron role factor their costs and benefits differently than do private organizations taking on the patron role. The reason is that public patrons must consider that in buying the material they are spending public funds, open to the light of public scrutiny. Private patrons, by contrast, are akin to private producers in placing at the forefront the protection of their profit-making activities. The difference suggests that public patrons on the whole might respond more sensitively than private patrons to advocacy pressures.

The difference should not be exaggerated, however. Certainly, private merchants that carry controversial materials exclusively (e.g., pornographic films or books) are unlikely to respond favorably to advocacy group attempts to stifle producers through them. Because those emporia exist specifically to sell, exhibit, or rent taboo products, advocacy organizations are not at all likely to persuade them to get their suppliers to mend their ways. But private patrons that sell a variety of products and are concerned with their public images will probably respond in a more complex manner to advocacy group attempts at influence. So, too, will cross-pressures on public patrons often lead them toward vacillating, drawn-out decisions that are not so clearly sensitive to one side.

As one example of public patrons, take the organizations that select and purchase textbooks for elementary and high schools. Those organizations are typically part of a multilayered political process open to input from various groups at both state and local levels. The formal balance between state and local control has been struck differently across the country. In so-called adoption states, major responsibility for selecting materials is lodged in state agencies. In nonadoption states, the main authority is vested in largely autonomous school districts or other local government units. However, selection decisions lie exclusively at one level in only a very few states. So, in some adoption states, the responsible state agency selects texts and other materials, leaving little or no discretion to local districts. In many others, the state agency approves a long list of texts, giving local districts discretion to choose from the list and to purchase supplementary materials chosen on their own with reimbursement from the state. Parallel differences also exist among nonadoption states.[49]

Since textbook selection is an activity conducted by state and local agencies and controlled by elected officials, it is an activity wide open to many pressures from public advocacy organizations. Moreover, the tradition in the United States is that parents have the right to help guide curriculum development in their children's schools.[50] Incidents of active public unrest regarding the texts that schools have chosen have, however, been rather uncommon and cyclical. In the late 1960s, for example, a Carnegie Corporation study of school materials selection concluded that "despite the publicity given to the attempts of organized interest groups to influence materials selection, such instances are extremely rare in the views of both materials producers and respondents to [a] ten-state survey."[51] The report went on to note that "in most states members of local school boards are the only nonprofessionals involved in materials selections and they indicate that they tend to rely on the recommendations and selections of other members of the system conveyed to them by the superintendent."[52]

During the mid-1970s, by contrast, a rash of textbook controversies flared. In fact, the chairperson of the American Library Association's Freedom to Read Foundation warned that "a nationwide, persuasive, antiintellectual movement is developing that can be compared to the McCarthy era."[53] The seventy-seven large and small "censorship attempts" reported by teachers and public librarians to the ALA's Office of Intellectual Freedom might not be considered high for fifty states. Still, it was certainly a huge jump from 1966, when the number was twenty-three.[54] Moreover, such advocacy groups as the Citizens for Decent Literature, the Hard Core Parents of Louisiana, the Ku Klux Klan, the John Birch Society, the National Parents League, and numerous others raised basic objections to textbook contents that created a general climate of fear among book selection committees around the country.[55]

A centerpiece of protest was a large-scale book selection conflict in Kanawha County, West Virginia, during 1974. The conflict was instigated by a single member of the Kanawha School Board, the wife of a fundamentalist minister, who objected to the method of textbook selection. She said that the "board should have stronger control over selection.[56] She was joined by thousands of protesters against the board's adoption of 325 books they felt "denounced traditional institutions," promulgated the notion of cultural relativism, and in general subscribed to an ideology of secular humanism as a substitute for orthodox conceptions of the rule of God and the Bible. Tempers flared. The antitextbook protesters organized their ranks and developed strategies. They held marches, rallies, circulated petitions, appealed to elected officials, and boycotted the school system. Violence erupted; vandals destroyed school property, and a picketing protester was shot. After the majority of a special citizen review committee recommended that all but thirty-five of the books remain in the classroom (a minority report recommended many more be banned), the board of education building was bombed and partially destroyed.

By the end of 1974, the protesters initially appeared to win a number of concessions from the county school board. The board issued strict new guidelines for textbook selection and content. In addition, parents were to be placed on text selection committees. However, these new guidelines were declared illegal by the state superintendent of schools. In the meantime, many parents had begun to send their children to newly created private Christian schools. This activity siphoned off much of the core of the protest movement, and the situation calmed a bit. Sociologists Ann Page and Donald Clelland, commenting on the situation four years later, noted that "although the vehemence of the protest has subsided, the anger lingers on."[57]

It seems, then, that in Kanawha County the more politically powerful "modernists" held the "cultural fundamentalists" at bay. The modernists cast the issue in terms of censorship, academic freedom, and the importance of instilling in youngsters an appreciation of rational, creative approaches to reality. Moreover, the Kanawha conflict and others like it mobilized teachers and librarians around the country in preparation for further "textbook battles." Professional publications such as the *American School Board Journal* and *Library Journal* suggested performance programs that its readers could follow so as to minimize the damage created by fiery groups. "Don't *you* get scalded," warned one article.[58]

Nevertheless, books in several communities were changed in response to public protests and renewed interest in school board elections. More important, a climate of fear and caution spread over many textbook selection committees that were not embroiled in controversies and did not want to be. In fact, legal scholar Paul Goldstein contends that "the public's greatest influence [in textbook selection] lies in its silence, and in [school professionals'] decisions to reject materials that will spark controversy and rouse the public from this silence."[59] Book salespeople and their editors know that, says Goldstein, and they create textbooks that are likely to fit the least controversial common denominator of acceptance among relevant school systems. As one textbook company executive noted, the dominant concern of a supervising editor has become

> to achieve a compromise between the controls necessary for national acceptance and the originality of the author's contribution to education. In the el-hi field, particularly, he must balance skillfully the demands of contradictory curricular material, of "progressive educators" and traditional, or exponents of the science-centered culture and the humanists, and above all of the majority and minority pressure groups.[60]

We tend to conclude, then, that on a nationwide level and in a complex manner the textbook controversies of the mid and late 1970s led to timidity on the part of important producers. One manifestation of this influence was the guidesheet that a major publisher of texts for elementary schools gave to its authors in 1981. The stapled pages advised against depiction of several specific activities, from death to divorce to games of chance. In addition, they cautioned that authors best "avoid topics considered by some to be antireligious, e.g., evolution, witchcraft, and secular humanism."

We move from an example of advocacy group pressures on large public patrons to one relating to large private patrons, TV advertisers. The biggest threat advocacy groups seem to hold over TV advertisers is a widespread boycott of their products. Big companies that turn out a multitude of consumer goods seem particularly skittish about getting on a major advocacy movement's "hit list." Perhaps because well-organized threats of boycotts over media sponsorship are relatively new to them, perhaps for other reasons, these advertisers have been much more vulnerable to advocacy pressure than have media producers and networks accustomed to direct threats from these quarters.

In fact, one can make a strong argument that it was advertisers' fear of boycott—a fear legitimized by research reports from giant ad agency J. Walter Thompson—that finally forced the United States television networks away from a cycle of violence-oriented action programs around 1977. Similarly, it seems that threats by the Coalition for Better Television and the Moral Majority to finger sponsors that support sexually and ideological "immoral" programs in the early 1980s created a climate of fear among advertisers that influenced ad agencies' time buying habits and began to lead network programmers in more compliant directions. Of particular significance to the coalition's cause was the public endorsement of its aim to "improve" television by the chairman of the giant consumer goods firm and largest TV advertiser, Procter and Gamble. Word in the trade press was that Procter and Gamble executives had been nervous over reports that the Coalition was going to list it among companies that sponsored unacceptable prime time programs. They were even more worried that the Coalition might later move to attack Procter and Gamble's ownership of six sultry daytime soap operas, a huge and important investment for the manufacturer. "P & G was afraid the soaps would be a problem down the line," said a television network executive. "By focusing [the Coalition's] attention on prime time, I guess they figured they'd get them off their backs."[61]

This comment reflects an awareness of the intricate strategies sometimes involved when patrons and advocacy groups meet head-on over network TV. The role of the television networks and their producers in this tug of war is generally to try to convince advertisers and ad agencies that the advocacy organization or movement is unrepresentative of the public at large and that, in any case, product boycotts tend to be ineffective. In fact, ABC and NBC commissioned separate studies to show just these points in response to fundamentalist threats in the early 1980s.[62] At the same time, Norman Lear and other TV producers and performers attempted to garner moral support and public sympathy for sponsor resistance of those pressures by invoking the First Amendment and decrying censorship.[63] Also pushing the sponsors in the direction of the networks was a goal they share: reaching a receptive audience in an efficient manner. Advertisers and their agencies have found that certain forms of programs—violence-oriented action shows, for example—induce higher viewer recall of commercials than do more placid shows.[64] Since many advertisers measure the effectiveness of an aired commercial by the number of people who can recall it, the firms' media buyers sometimes feel obliged to sponsor as many violent programs as they can.

In the case of advocacy group pressures against TV violence in the mid-1970s and against "immoral" values in the early 1980s, the consequence of the battle seems to have been to initiate change, though not of the magnitude that public advocacy groups probably wanted. For example, with respect to the response by Procter and Gamble and other firms to the Coalition For Better Television, there is evidence that shifts in sponsorship policies and procedures were significant, though less drastic than some executives' rhetoric implied. What seems to have happened is that companies revitalized program sponsorship guidelines that had always existed but had lain dormant for some time. The guidelines still allowed sponsorship of borderline cases with high audience ratings and strong commercial recall scores, if the shows were toned down a bit. The change began to get communicated through the advertising agencies to the networks and the producers. After Procter and Gamble's conciliation with the Coalition, several other large companies began to give in. One ad agency executive noted that "advertisers are going to pay through the nose" for spots on so-called clean programs, while racier though high-rated shows "may be a tougher sell" for the networks.[65]

For their parts, network leaders still maintained a tough stance toward advocacy groups. But at the same time they began to insist to advertisers that they have always chosen programs not simply because of ratings but because of a "desirability index" sensitive to public attitudes as well.[66] In fact, the future programs they showcased for advertisers in the spring of 1981 reflected advertiser concern. "There are few programs our clients object to in the new season," an advertising agency executive said. "Just take a look at a publicity photo for ABC's [series] 'It's a Living' and compare it to one from last year. Then the girls were standing around in the brief costumes with everything hanging out. Now they're dressed in high-necked French maid outfits with little, if anything, showing."[67]

Of course, the degree and substance of change is often in the eye of the beholder. While the agency executives indicated satisfaction with the networks' efforts to tone down immorality on television, Moral Majority and Coalition leaders continued to rail against ABC, CBS, and NBC. Their targets were not just the remnants of sexual titillation but also a spectrum of presentations which, they felt, demeaned traditional American values. Clearly, though, despite the rather frightened reactions of some corporate sponsors, the networks and their producers held the ultimate card: the ability to decide *how* to vary the programming with as little disruption of their basic programming perspectives as possible. In 1981 and 1982, it seemed that programming decision makers had decided to respond only to the most obvious and superficial demands for change on the part of fundamentalist groups, those relating to sex and an absence of conservative political values.

The result was an updated reinstatement of programming that had lain dormant for a number of years. Leering, sex-oriented comedies began to fade while a clutch of new action-packed police dramas emerged on the scene with explicitly conservative orientations. "Strike Force", "T. J. Hooker, "Cagney and Lacey," "Hill Street Blues," "Simon and Simon," "Magnum P. I.," and others used violence to hammer home some extremely conservative themes about the rights of citizens and the police in an urban (and international) jungle ruled by criminals. A new cycle of programming seemed to have begun. It might not have been the kind the protesters had demanded, or expected. But, as this chapter has shown, the demands of the public are constantly refracted in mass media production firms by organizational and interorganizational imperatives that receive higher priority. The bridge that sometimes connects producers and the public is long, and fraught with holes, broken planks, and tortuous passageways.

REFERENCES

1. Kalman Siegel, *Talking Back to The New York Times* New York: Quadrangle Books, 1974), p. 8.

2. Herbert Gans, "Letters to an Anchorman," *Journal of Communication*, vol. 27 (Summer 1977), pp. 86–91.

3. See David Leroy and Wenmouth Williams, "Citizen Feedback: A Review of the Literature," (Tallahassee; University of Florida, Department of Communications, 1974; Mimeograph). Joseph Turow, "Talk Show Radio and Interpersonal Communication," *Journal of Broadcasting*, vol. 18 (Spring 1974), pp. 171–179; Bernadette McGuire and David Leroy, "Audience Mail: Letters to a Broadcaster," *Journal of Communication*, vol. 27 (Summer 1977), pp. 79–85.

4. James March and Herbert Simon, *Organizations* (New York: John Wiley, 1958), p. 141.

5. Siegel, p. 8.

6. Siegel, p. 8.

7. Siegel, p. 7.

8. Siegel, p. 8.

9. Sidney Head, *Broadcasting in America* (New York: Houghton Mifflin, 1972), pp. 347–350.

10. Manny Lucoff, "The Rise and Fall of the Third Rewrite," *Journal of Communication*, vol. 30 (Summer 1980), pp. 47–53.

11. The following paragraphs in this section are based closely on Joseph Turow, "Another View of Citizen Feedback to the Mass Media," *Public Opinion Quarterly*, vol. 41 (Winter 1977–78), pp. 534–543.

12. See Turow, "Another View of Citizen Feedback to the Mass Media." Also see Lee Becker, D. Charles Whitney, and E. Collins, "Public Understanding of How the News Operates," *Journalism Quarterly*, vol. 57 (Autumn 1979), pp. 571–575.

13. L. A. Zurcher, R. G. Kirkpatrick, R. G. Cushing, and C. K. Bowman, "The Anti-Pornography Crusade: A Symbolic Crusade," *Social Problems*, vol. 19 (Fall 1971), pp. 217–237.

14. Neil Smelser, *Theory of Collective Behavior* (New York: The Free Press, 1962).

15. Zurcher, et. al., p. 217.

16. See Joseph Turow, *Education, Entertainment and the Hard Sell: Three Decades of Network Children's Television* (New York: Praeger, 1981), pp. 1–5.

17. This discussion draws from Arnold Shankman, "Black Pride and Protest: The Amos 'n' Andy Crusade of 1931," *Journal of Popular Culture*, vol. 12 (Fall, 1979), pp. 236–253.

18. Kathryn Montgomery, "Gay Activists and the Networks," *Journal of Communication*, vol. 31 (Summer 1981), pp. 49–57.

19. Montgomery, pp. 56–57.

20. Montgomery, p. 50.

21. Zurcher, et. al., p. 217.

22. Mark Nadel, *The Politics of Consumer Protection* (Indianapolis: Bobbs Merrill, 1971), p. 211.

23. Nadel, p. 213.

24. Barry Cole and Mal Oettinger, *Reluctant Regulators* (Reading, Massachusetts: Addison-Wesley, 1978), pp. 56–57.

25. Quoted in Jethro K. Lieberman, *Free Speech, Free Press, and the Law* (New York: Lothrop, 1980).

26. Lieberman, p. 123.

27. Lieberman, p. 126.

28. Oscar G. Chase, "Broadcast Regulation and the First Amendment," in Michael Botein and David M. Rice, (eds.), *Network Television and the Public Interest* (Lexington, Massachusetts: Lexington Books, 1980), p. 143.

29. Barry Cole and Mal Oettinger, pp. 1–22.

30. Cole and Oettinger, p. 5.

31. Cole and Oettinger, p. 8.

32. Cole and Oettinger, p. 37.

33. Dean Krugman and Leonard Reid, "The 'Public Interest' as Defined

by FCC Policy Makers," *Journal of Broadcasting*, vol. 24 (Summer 1980), pp. 381–399.

34. Cole and Oettinger, p. 69.

35. Cole and Oettinger, p. 123.

36. Cole and Oettinger, pp. 204–225.

37. Cole and Oettinger, p. 220. See also John Pennybacker, "The Format Change Issue: FCC vs. U.S. Court of Appeals," *Journal of Broadcasting*, vol. 22 (Fall 1978), pp. 411–424.

38. Cole and Oettinger, pp. 228–229.

39. Ronald Garay, "Access: Evolution of the Citizen Agreement," *Journal of Broadcasting*, vol. 22 (Winter 1978), p. 103.

40. Felice Flanery Lewis, *Literature, Obscenity and Law* (Carbondale, Illinois: Southern Illinois University Press, 1976), pp. 4–5.

41. Lewis, p. 7.

42. Lewis, p. 9.

43. Lewis, p. 45.

44. Garth Jowett, *Film: The Democratic Art* (New York: Little Brown, 1976), p. 120.

45. Jowett, pp. 164–182.

46. Jowett, pp. 440–443.

47. Arthur Knight, *The Liveliest Art* (New York: Signet, 1958), p. 112. In 1982, the United States Justice Department brought a suit against the National Association of Broadcasters, the main lobbying organization for over-the-air radio and TV stations. The target was the NAB Code's limits to hourly advertising time. The Justice Department contended that the code's rules about advertising time were a restraint to trade, that stations ought to be allowed to sell as much time as their market allowed. In response to the suit, the NAB dismantled its entire code system, including programming rules that were borrowed from the old movie code. Some observers speculated that by getting rid of a written code of "good conduct," the NAB was allowing its members more flexibility to compete for audiences with risque and violent programming on (unregulated) cable channels.

48. Knight, pp. 112–13.

49. Paul Goldstein, *Changing the American Schoolbook* (Lexington, Massachusetts: Lexington Books, 1978), p. 39.

50. "Textbook Battles," *American School Board Journal*, July 1975, p. 25.

51. Institute for Educational Development, *Selection of Educational Materials in the United States Public Schools* (New York: Carnegie Corporation, 1969), p. 303. (Also available through Resources in Education—ERIC—system).

52. Institute for Educational Development, p. 303.

53. *American School Board Journal*, July 1975, p. 21.

54. L. E. Woods. "For Sex: See Librarian," *Library Journal*, vol. 103 (September 1, 1978), p. 1562.

55. *American School Board Journal*, July 1975, p. 21.

56. Ann Page and Donald Clelland, "The Kanawha County Textbook Controversy: A Study of the Politics of Life Style Concern," *Social Forces*, vol. 57 (September 1978), p. 268.

57. Page and Clelland, p. 278.

58. *American School Board Journal*, July 1975, p. 21.

59. Goldstein, p. 38.

60. Goldstein, p. 57.

61. Colby Coates and Bob Marich. "P & G's Rap at TV Laid to Fear of Boycott," *Advertising Age*, vol. 52 (June 22, 1981), p. 85.

62. Coates and Marich, p. 85.

63. See, for example, Colby Coates, "Coalition May Not Call Boycott," *Advertising Age*, vol. 52, p. 79; and "Boycott: Pro and Con," *Emmy Magazine*, vol. 3 (Summer 1981), pp. 39–41.

64. Interview with Seymour Banks, vice-president of Leo Burnett Advertising, Chicago, 1978.

65. Coates, p. 79.

66. Coates, p. 79.

67. Coates, p. 79.

Four

The Organization of Production

By this point in the book, the crucial importance of a mass media organization's environment to shaping the material it creates should be clear. Chapters One, Two, and Three have gone into some detail about the kinds of organizations—patrons, authorities, distributors, and more—that control valuable production resources and, as a result of this leverage, play important roles in determining the product. The chapters have also noted the relative powerlessness of some forces, notably publics, in influencing mass media content. Putting the pieces together leads to two general conclusions: (1) that the structure of a mass media industry reflects the overall power relations of the society in which it emerges and develops; and (2) that a mass media production firm tends to bend to the interests and perspectives of socially powerful organizations and movements that act upon it.

What the previous chapters have not underscored in a systematic way, however, it that many mass media production organizations go a far bit beyond bending in response to demands by organizations and groups with valuable resources. They continually produce mass media materials that actually reflect and validate the right of those organizations and groups to remain powerful, to control resources and hold leverage. The realization that this occurs is shared by a large number of writers from a variety of backgrounds. Gaye Tuchman, for example, has argued that "news both draws upon and reproduces institutional structure." Phillip Tichenor, George Donahue, and Clarice Olien have observed that "where there is diversity in social power, media tend to reflect the orientations of those segments that are higher up on the power scale." And, George Gerbner has described entertainment as "the celebration of conventional morality" and dubbed media producers "the cultural arms of the industrial order from which they spring."[1]

Reflecting social power, celebrating conventional morality, and acting as cultural arms of the industrial order can collectively be taken to mean legitimating—that is, upholding the authority of—the established economic, political, educational, cultural, religious, and military institutions of the society. To take this position does not mean that one believes that mass media material is unquestioning and bland. Certainly, glancing through newspapers and magazines, watching television dramas, or listening to news on radio, we often come across arguments on various political issues, articles describing social injustice, or stories depicting social problems. Moreover, we note that intellectual and material fashions change, that social divisions and ideological contradictions occur, and that these and other tensions find their way into the media. It seems clear, too, that facets of media material often displease members of the elite (for example, business leaders) as well as other portions of the public.

Recognizing that media materials often reflect social tensions and conflicts does not, however, sweep away the argument that mass media content tends to legitimize the establishment. Despite depictions of social problems, most mass media in a society rarely use their portrayals as platforms to explicitly challenge the fundamental legitimacy of the nation's dominant institutions and raise realistic alternatives. Rarely, for example, do United States television programs hold extended discussions about solving the nation's economic problems by doing away with the capitalist system, about reducing the nation's armament problems by completely dismantling the military establishment, or about reducing personal monetary difficulties by stealing and then flouting the police. To the contrary, in all but the most unstable societies, the essentially legitimate entrenchment of the establishment and its values is an implicit theme weaving through the bulk of mass media culture.

Certainly, nothing in the previous chapters contradicts such an assessment. In fact, the basis for it was set chapters ago, when the resource dependence perspective was introduced. As noted, the interactions of organizations taking on various power roles within a mass media industry set up crucial boundaries for a production firm's activities and make crucial demands on the firm, even to the point of defining its audiences. And, also as noted, displeasure by primary patrons, authorities, and other powerful entities with mass media content that runs counter to their basic interests can result in severe harm to the production firm. That awareness typically leads production firm executives to orient their activities in the "proper" direction from the standpoint of the audience targeted, the kind of material created, and the social values portrayed.[2]

The resource dependence perspective also leads to an awareness that certain kinds of mass media firms are more likely than others to be concerned about pleasing the establishment. Production firms that rely on getting a great many of their most important resources (money, authority, personnel, services, and the like) from the mainstream of society (governments, giant advertisers, powerful advocacy organizations, necessarily huge audiences) will likely arrange their activities so as to offend as few of these entities as possible. Conversely, production firms that can rely on resources from areas of society that are outside the mainstream (e.g., nongovernmental bodies, atypical advertisers, specialty distributors and exhibitors, rather homogeneous audiences) might not have fears about attacking the mainstream. The difference is between what we will call "mainstream" and "peripheral" media output. So, for example, in the United States it is possible to produce novels extolling Communist ideologies as a solution to social problems; the First Amendment to the United States Constitution prohibits government interference. However, it is extremely doubtful that such peripheral material would be highlighted on network television or considered attractive by major movie studios.

Having said all this, however, we have not detailed how the people in firms oriented toward mainstream media output go about generating and continually reproducing portrayals that legitimize the social structure. Filling in the details is particularly difficult in a society such as the United States where political and economic governance is under mixed private and public control and where mass media are neither agencies of the state nor responsible to centralized private interests. In this kind of decentralized situation, the direct filtering and coordination of mass media material to match the needs and nuances of ideology is impossible. Nor does such coordination take place simply through the contemporary struggles of organizations in various power roles to gain what they need on a daily basis (e.g., audiences, the removal of false advertising, the removal of "sex" from television). These interactions of industry forces helps all parties adjust to environmental change day to day and year to year. However, they are not the primary factors ensuring that production organizations keep fundamentally in tune with the establishment. That function is rooted in the very development of mass media production firms' approaches to the world. It is to this issue that we now turn.

A CONTEXT FOR LEGITIMATION

The question boils down to this: In the absence of direct coordination by the government or the private sector, what is the mechanism by which mass media content comes to mirror the legitimacy of institutional power? The best way to begin an answer is to look carefully at the circumstances that gave rise to the mass media in question, at the factors that encouraged the entry and success of leaders of those media, and at the routines that the leaders and their followers developed in attempts to continue that success. Unfortunately these are extremely difficult points to tackle, particularly since for most United States media not enough historical groundwork has been tilled to allow meaningful analysis. Perhaps the most work to these ends has been carried out on the development of the daily newspaper. A very brief overview of the context that gave rise to, and perpetuates, modern journalistic practices will hint at the promise, and complexity, of this kind of analysis.

The Case of News

Ask a journalist what the most important concept guiding reporting is, and he or she is likely to answer "objectivity." Objectivity is, in fact, such a key concept in late twentieth century news reporting that during the past several years a number of studies have been published that inquire into its historical origin and contemporary meaning. Michael Schudson and Dan Schiller, writing separately on the subject, agree that present-day requirements that news reports be objective trace their origins to the emergence of the American penny press in the late 1830s.[3] Schiller, particularly, attributes the rise of those papers to profound changes taking place in United States society as a new, restless population of urban workers ("artisans" and "mechanics") emerged on the scene. These city laborers became increasingly angry with what they saw as the control the established mercantile elite held over the entire spectrum of American institutions. They could not draw moral and intellectual support for their anger from the mainstream daily newspapers of the big cities. Those "six-penny" papers, supported as they were by the dominant political parties and by expensive subscriptions, adhered firmly to the status quo. Instead, the artists and mechanics turned during the 1820s and 1830s to a trade union supported labor press that reached a substantial segment of the wage earning population. Foremost among the labor papers' positions were the ideas of equal voting rights for all white men, equal access to property, respect for individual property rights, the sweeping away of elite monopolies over knowledge and other resources, and the demand that the government stand above class interests in order to promote equality. The labor press saw the dominant daily newspapers as agents and reflections of the corruption in high places. The feeling was that, like medicine, law, and religion, which, in the 1830s, were objects of suspicion and animosity by working people, mainstream journalism "shared a direct interest in preventing the article they deal[t] in [i.e. knowledge] from becoming common and cheap."[4]

The labor press did not survive the Panic of 1837, which threw thousands of artisans and mechanics out of work and crippled the nascent unions. One-third of the work force of New York City, for example, is estimated to have been out of work. Yet what the labor papers initiated through their declaration of independence from monopolists and elite factions invited imitation from a different, more entrepreneurial breed of journalism. Note that the ideology the labor press had spread among the urban working class was actually in turn with core American beliefs, particularly the celebration of entrepreneurial spirit and the legitimacy of individual ownership of property. United States working men did not want to tear down the political structures of their nation. Rather, they wanted to be involved in shaping them. In this environment, then, newspapers that extolled the basic social-political values, insisted upon their applicability to working men, and, at the same time, pursued the profit motive would seem to have been acceptable successors to the labor press for the growing and increasingly literate urban labor population.

That, in fact, is precisely the approach the people who started the early successful penny press operations used. Benjamin Day of the *New York Sun*, James Gordon Bennett of the *New York Herald*, George Wilkes of the *National Police Gazette*, and others were embarking upon journalistic enterprises at just the time that the economics of producing a paper accessible to "the masses" were favorable. Improved print technology made it possible to reach large numbers of people at low cost, while a large number of advertisers stood ready to help support papers that delivered to them large segments of the population that the elite dailies did not reach. When Benjamin Day hit upon the notion of selling his paper not by subscription but on the streets, a penny at a time, that made the daily newspaper all the more accessible to the great majority of the public.

The penny press publishers positioned their products toward "the great masses of the community," not just toward the laborers.[5] While excoriating the sixpennies for their alliances with "cliques and parties" and not with the general public's good, the penny paper entrepreneurs claimed to speak—"to shine," the *New York Sun* put it—for all, worker *and* merchant. A newspaper costing only a penny would give all citizens equal access to knowledge, they argued, and the "commonsense" reports the paper would present, controlled by no party and no class, would benefit democracy.

The business spirit was viewed as an ally of this cause. Financing an extravagantly expensive courier system to beat the sixpennies with the news, James Gordon Bennett said he did it because "speculators should not have the advantage of earlier news than the public at large."[6] An additional advantage would follow, of course, if businessmen and merchants would look to the *New York Herald* for timely commercial news. In the same vein, the penny press also welcomed all advertisers as contributing to the new democratic spirit. The rationale was that, as pioneer adman Volney Palmer put it, impartially sought advertising revenue released the press "from pecuniary dependence upon cliques and monopolies."[7]

So, started by struggling entrepreneurs whose sympathies could reach out to the laboring population while simultaneously embracing the business community, the penny press managed to blend an insistence on entrepreneurial equal rights in commercial journalism and a more general respect for individual property rights, the market system, and the state with a vocal concern for the rights of workers to move upward in the society. This approach proved an appropriate one for United States journalism to carry into the twentieth century, an era when the legitimacy of individual property rights and equal access to entrepreneurial risks and rewards became crucial rhetorical principles (and defenses) underlying American institutions. It was also this approach, Schiller shows, that led to the development of objectivity as the key criterion of good journalism. Plugging into a general belief in science and a widespread interest in photographic realism, penny press editors and publishers adopted the idea that it was possible to reveal the world impartially, to separate fact from fiction. Their most comfortable rationale was that once truth was revealed, men of good sense would know which path to follow. Schiller has noted, however, that entrepreneurial designs also underlay the reach toward objectivity:

> Objectivity...was an *ideal*—and it was acceptance of the newspaper's right and capacity to pursue this ideal that was essential. Such acceptance allowed the press to cultivate and to accumulate a modern mass public by appearing to present simply *facts*, in such a form and temper as to "lead men of all parties to rely upon its statements," as the *New York Times* (22 March 1860) put it.[8]

Of course, believing in the objective reproducibility of the world and carrying it out are different matters. In carrying out their mission, editors and reporters were forced to place together a variety of facts, and to arbitrate between conflicting versions of the same situation. They were, in short, compelled to develop definitions of objectivity that all newsworkers could share so that stories could be predictably accurate. What is most relevant here is that doing that, publishers, editors, and reporters created strategies for "gathering the facts" that implicitly incorporated, reflected, and upheld the established power hierarchy of the society, even when the subjects they dealt with were chosen to reveal problems of that society. In his close analysis of the popular *National Police Gazette*, Schiller shows that as early as the 1840s, journalists had developed routine reporting methods which, for reasons of efficient access to reliable information, tagged police and other officials from dominant institutions as standard sources for crime news. The result of stories so constructed, says Schiller, was that "the legitimacy of the American state was presumed [even] as the particular corruptions of its officers were assailed."[9]

Both Schiller and Schudson show that the rationale for news reporting underwent important changes from the 1890s through the 1920s. During the turmoil of strikes and riots at the start of that period, social critics accused many newspapers of clearly and systematically slanting stories and headlines to favor employers rather than workers. In an effort to restore their credibility among all readers, newspaper industry leaders sought to return their function to grounds acceptable to as many parties to the national unrest as possible. By that time, thinking journalists realized that a simple reliance on facts alone could not ensure news objectivity. It was too easy for a nonneutral observer to choose facts that best suited his or her biases. So, in the spirit of early twentieth century science, journalists such as Walter Lippmann invoked the importance of common, professionally instilled methods to gather facts. In order to keep journalists objective in an atmosphere of social polarization, Lippmann and others believed that it was crucial that journalism "become a specifically trained profession, for in schools of journalism there is an opportunity to train that sense of reality and perspective which great reporting requires. . . . There is an opportunity to create a morale [among journalists] as disinterested and interesting as that of the scientists who are the reporters of natural phenomena."[10]

Dan Schiller asserts that by explicitly stressing professional methods as the basis for objective reporting, editors, publishers, and liberal intellectuals of the 1920s and 1930s hoped to reclaim "the commercial newspaper's earlier role of the defense of public good by demonstrating that the century-old ideals of the commercial press were being adhered to."[11] We have already seen that not only were those ideals of "responsible capitalism" (as Herbert Gans calls them) trumpeted by penny press pioneers, they were built into the very routine that the penny press journalists created and modified over time. By the mid-twentieth century, those routines had developed into a full-blown professional approach to defining the world.

A number of writers have carefully described the mosaic of activities and perspectives that journalists use to create the news. For the most part, says Herbert Gans. "the news reports on those at or near the top of the [economic, political, social, and cultural] hierarchies and on those, particularly at the bottom, who threaten them."[12] Objective news routines generally emphasize reliance on accredited sources and, in this way, permit elites to help manage the news. Objective news perspectives generally maintain a nineteenth century distinction between public and private sectors of the economy and stress freedom to investigate the former more than the latter. The routines and perspectives narrow the frame of storytelling to yield atheoretic, ahistoric accounts of actions by specific individuals or organizations. And, they emphasize a posture of technical neutrality through the use of conventions(e.g., concentration on verifiable facts, quotes from those involved, and presentation of more than one side of the study).[13]

One result of this approach is that in routinely describing conflicts as separate incidents removed from historical frames of reference and disconnected from larger insitutional issues, journalists disguise situations that might represent systemwide tensions and contradictions. Doing so, they quietly protect the dominance of established institutions. The following examples by Gaye Tuchman illustrate the way in which journalistic routines flowing directly from the entrepreneurial basis of the United States press serve implicitly to protect national economic, political, and military institutions from fundamental public challenge and disillusionment:

> In 1968, I observed reporters attending a news conference of five anti-Vietnam war activitists, including Dr. Benjamin Spock, who had been accused of conspiracy. The reporters were dismayed when one activist introduced the topic of an American ship, the *Pueblo*, seized by the North Koreans earlier that day. They insisted that the Vietnamese war and America's relationship to North Korea were not interrelated, and that the activist was spouting off. The American journalists' reaction resembled that of...British reporters who saw picket signs decrying inflation at an antiwar rally.... In the same vein, daily news reports associating fluctuations in the stock market with traders' views of the day's political events obscure the structure of our economic system even as they claim to elucidate it. In the case of the news conference, the event orientation of reporters prevented them from recognizing the validity of drawing connections between international events. The connections drawn by the financial reporters represent "the logic of the concrete, a present time orientation, and an emphasis on contingent events" rather than economic structure. In both cases, newsworkers impose their professional understandings upon occurrences to shape a reality that legitimates the status quo.[14]

When Gaye Tuchman refers to the status quo, she does not mean that the press literally advocates a static social situation. Rather, she means that the practice of objective journalism leads newsworkers, knowingly or unknowingly, continually to weave their reports with the implicit theme that the institutions that lead the society ought to keep doing so, if only because there are no viable alternatives. It is true that many news organizations pride themselves on uncovering social problems that suggest that need for corrective modifications in the establishment. This role of the newspaper, has, in fact, become such a clear one that many writers refer to the press as "the fourth branch of government." Note, though, that the characterization of the press as a branch of government actually supports the larger point being made here. It reflects a clear understanding that journalism does not stand in opposition to the established order of things, but, to the contrary, exists to participate in the growth of that order.

Formalizing this idea, George Donahue, Phillip Tichenor, and Clarice Olien state that journalistic media—in fact, mass media in general—are agencies that regularly help manage social conflict in the interest of maintaining the established social system.[15] But managing conflict, they point out, need not mean ignoring social strains or smoothing them over. Conflict management may include the *generation* of conflict as well as the direct dissipation of tension. The latter approach may simply mean avoiding or withholding news that might reflect badly on certain elements of the community's power structure. Or, it may mean selecting facts and adjectives about certain tension-filled situations in such a way as to assure the public that there really is no problem. Donahue, Tichenor, and Olien cite research suggesting that newspapers in small communities are likely to stress this approach to conflict management when reporting about their areas' governments and businesses. For example, Morris Janowitz found in the early 1950s that local inhabitants, including community leaders, expected the local press to "put the town's best foot forward."[16] Years later, Olien, Donahue, and Tichenor similarly discovered that publishers and editors of small town papers were more likely to stress that they exist to promote community stability and less likely to stress arousal of public interest in local issues as crucial parts of their jobs. The researchers also found when they studied weekly newspapers that the press's reluctance to deal with conflict in an open fashion was greatest when the editor "was very closely aligned with the local power structure."[17]

The other way to manage conflict—trying to reflect and even seek out societal tensions—is typically done under the banner of the fourth estate or watchdog role of the press. Newspapers in the largest cities tend to initiate this kind of reporting; their stories of national significance are often picked up by smaller papers via the wire services. In carrying out this watchdog role, journalists typically approach specific incidents or types of incidents as individual problems and describe institutional attempts to deal with them. However, at the same time they often depict groups working toward solutions to the problems outside accepted institutional bound-aries, particularly groups that hold extremist solutions, as illegitimate alternatives. That is, they depict them as neither holding nor deserving the right to exercise political or moral authority. Gaye Tuchman has shown this in reviewing the women's movement's coverage by the press, Todd Gitlin has shown it in his analysis of a 1960s left wing political movement's relationship with the press, and J. D. Barber has noted it in discussing media portrayal of political candidates. The assumptions and techniques of contemporary journalism are sufficiently robust to allow the framing of an individual, an organization, or a social movement as illegitimate, trivial, or marginal while still following the cannons of objectivity.[18]

Everything discussed until now points to the idea that the mainstream press in a society grows out of, and is at its very core imbued with, established values and perspectives to the extent that it becomes itself a powerful social institution. The political power that comes with setting an agenda for public discussion and the economic power that follows when patrons (in the United States, advertisers) perceive that the press can help fulfill their aims is attractive to individual and corporate owners. Note, too that individuals or companies wanting to successfully start or take over substantial journalistic enterprises in the United States pretty much have to be part of the establishment to begin with. Gone are the days when near indigent entrepreneurs could found daily newspapers aimed at "the masses" and succeed. The costs of technology and labor for the industrialized production and distribution of messages are such that financing even mid-sized newspapers can cost millions of dollars. For example, the American Newspaper Publishers Association indicated that 425 papers responding to a survey spent an estimated outlay of $249 million for new equipment and plant modernization in 1977 alone.[19] Price tags of major newspaper acquisitions in the 1970s also reflect the wealth needed to manage the descendants of the penny press. Rupert Murdoch acquired the *New York Post* in 1976 for $30 million. Newhouse Newspapers acquired Booth Newspapers (eight dailies in Michigan along with the *Parade* Sunday supplement) in 1977 for $300 million. Capital Cities Communications acquired the *Kansas City Star* and *Times* in 1977 for $125 million. The Gannett Company acquired Speidel newspapers (thirteen papers in the West and Midwest) in 1977 for more than $170 million. And Time, Inc. acquired the *Washington Star* in 1978 for $20 million. Such costs tend to limit entry to the daily newspaper industry to the already well heeled, to people and companies with vested interests in the establishment and, by extension, in the established ways of depicting institutional reality.[20]

Legitimation in Non-News Material

Many of the same points that we have suggested about mainstream journalism in the United States can also be suggested about mainstream mass media that are not primarily journalistic. Certainly, a large number of analysts have shown that widespread fictional material tends to accept the basic political and social relationships of the society as given. They show that even when the material portrays tensions that exist as a result of those relationships, whether the portrayals are comedic, satiric, or serious, the enactment typically tends to uphold the legitimacy of the social order—or at least not to point toward realistic alternatives. In fact, as George

Gerbner points out, fiction can often assuage important societal tensions more effectively than can news, if only because journalists must be guided by "the facts" and cannot make up endings to the story.[21] Ethnic, racial, sexual, and other stereotypes portray power relations of society more clearly in fiction than they can in news.[22] Too, when violence is manipulated for fictional purposes, it can emphasize the need for law enforcement to protect society's basic values, even if the enforcer has to be the lone arm of the law (Marshal Dillon or James Bond), a vigilante cop (Dirty Harry), a private detective (Mike Hammer), or Superman.[23]

Unfortunately, no one has traced the historical roots of organizational mechanisms that lead the wide range of entertainment in United States media to continually trumpet the legitimacy of institutional power. Part of the difficulty of this kind of investigation is knowing how far back in time to go. Storytelling is as old as humankind. And folklore from around the world contains themes of institutional legitimacy and the celebration of social values that presage some of those in mass media material.[24] Moreoever, even supposedly "indigenous" American mass media forms have important roots in other societies. Research on the Western, for example, indicates its origin in folklore of early Colonial settlers, in published memoirs of Indian captivity and movement west, and in the very popular books of knights in shining armor that Walter Scott was writing in the early nineteenth century.[25] Tracing the historic creation, perpetuation, transformations, and interconnections of a large number of entertainment forms in much the same way that people have traced the development of objectivity in American journalism would be a prodigious undertaking.

Part of the answer, though, must surely lie in that basic starting point for fiction-making in many mass media production firms—the formula. The next chapter will explore some broad implications the concept of formula holds for understanding continuity and change in mass media material. Here the focus is narrower, on the way formulas might incorporate portrayals of the status quo in much the same manner that objectivity does it for news organizations.

To start, we might observe that both objectivity and formula imply routines. A formula, John Cawelti states, is a "conventional system for structuring cultural products. It can be distinguished from invented structures, which are new ways of organizing art."[26] Formulas represent widely recognized principles for selecting and organizing material. In nonfiction, a formula is characterized by the subject, the point of view, and the sequence in which the argument is developed. As examples, consider how-to books, Hollywood biographies, and magazine articles on the latest trends. In fiction, which is the area Cawelti discusses, formulas consist of certain plots, characters, and settings. Every fiction formula implies an array of plot types, character types, and locales. Combining these in different ways can yield a multitude of stories. Combining elements from two or more formulas may yield new formulas that may appear more creative and sophisticated than traditional ones.

To John Cawelti, a formula "is a culture's way" of reaffirming its values as well as "simultaneously entertaining itself and...creating an acceptable pattern of temporary escape from the serious restrictions and limitations of human life."[27] Cawelti examines the rise of the Western (scout and cowboy) formula in response to nineteenth century social tensions in a way that echoes Dan Schiller and Michael Schudson's probes of objectivity. The Western, he concludes, "is effective as social ritual because within its basic structure of resolution and affirmation, it indirectly confronts those uncertainties and conflicts of values which have always existed in American culture but which have become increasingly strong in the twentieth century."[28]

It seems clear, then, that the objective approach to journalism has an important counterpart in the use of formulas for the production of fiction and other nonjournalistic material. Formulas that are popular at a certain time provide media production firms with easily discoverable models for output to large numbers of people. At the same time, formulas guide the creators implicitly to structure the symbolic world so as to protect national institutions from fundamental public disillusionment. Too, as Robert Sklar points out, formulas can serve to protect *producers* in the face of outcries by powerful public advocacy movements and their allies.

His example comes from the early history of the United States movie industry.[29] After World War I, the nascent industry became the target of assaults by groups in the society that feared that movies were against them in a battle they were waging over values in American life. To simplify for the purpose of this brief discussion, their aim was to maintain a conservative, "small town" perspective in the face of an increasingly urban, industrial, and ethnically diverse society. They saw American movies, with their vivid portrayals of crime and salacious behavior, as standing in direct opposition to this goal. To those spokespersons for the traditional middle and upper classes, the direction of the movies was particularly worrisome because power over the photoplay rested largely in the hands of foreign born Jewish producers who, they felt, could not be trusted to promote traditional American values.

The producers' response, Sklar says, was to steer a middle course through the warring factions in American society. The film executives did present new lifestyles on the screen, but in such a way as to "clearly avoid breaking away from the fundamental economic and social mold."[30] A major way they protected themselves, notes Sklar, was to base their films on time-tested formulas but to vary them in style and minor detail to suit the period:

Faced with an audience more divided, more defensive, and yet increasingly avid for visions of alternative styles and behavior, moviemakers not unnaturally sought the subjects and treatments that pleased the most and alienated the fewest. The noisy and well-organized opposition and their own settled beliefs and filmmaking practices kept them from straying too far beyond the remaining stereotypes and formulas of the middle-class order. What they became adept at was reformulating older conventions; only when the need was obvious and overwhelming did they dare to generate a new formula. The results were not so different from traditional culture as reformists and censors sometimes made it appear.[31]

Sklar makes another point about the movie moguls that resonates with what we have said about journalist entrepreneurs. These men were, despite the fears of the defenders of middle class culture, "deeply committed to the capitalist values, attitudes and ambitions that were part of the dominant social order."[32] Surveying today's situation makes clear that, as in ownership of mainstream newspapers, controlling mainstream nonjournalistic mass media usually presupposes being part of at least the *economic* establishment. Television and radio licenses regularly trade for hundreds of thousands, even millions, of dollars; aliens and morally disreputable people cannot even obtain government licenses.[33] Too, as noted in Chapter Two, the cost of producing and distributing theatrical movies can easily shoot into the millions. Buying an ongoing film studio and its diverse holdings requires stratospheric sums; Coca Cola paid $750 million for Columbia Pictures Industries in 1982.[34] Even in the magazine business, where technology and labor expenditures need not be astronomical, publisher Leonard Mogel estimated that launching a periodical economically but wisely in 1981 would cost at least a couple of hundred thousand dollars.[35]

The reason is that in the magazine industry, as in the record and book industries, the key to success lies not just in producing material that will attract the public. If that were the case, magazines, records, and books could be produced at very low costs by just about anyone. The trick, rather, lies in also building distribution and exhibition channels for the product. With a magazine, that would require promoting the periodical strongly to advertisers, mail subscribers, and a viable number of distributors and exhibitors to get them to feel that supporting the product will bring them profit. This many-sided promotion can be very expensive, in money and in time. Being successful at it usually takes keen knowledge of the magazine business. Previous experience (a "track record") in the business is crucial, since that makes it easier to cultivate the trust of wholesalers, retailers, advertisers, investors, and banks.

It should come as no surprise, then, that the much-heralded entrepreneurs who successfully founded the magazines *Games, Runner,* and *Inc.* for relatively small sums in the 1970s already had solid reputations in periodical publishing or allied businesses.[36] Some writers have contended that such risk takers are the most efficient vehicles toward new magazine success. They point out that when giant magazine firms have developed new consumer "books," their costs of trying to ensure against failure through a lot of research, incentives to distributors, and strong promotion have propelled magazine startup costs to near unbelievable heights. Conde Nast, a subsidiary of Newhouse Newspapers, reportedly spent $20 million to launch *Self* in 1979.[37] In a similar vein, Readers Digest Association spent several years and, reportedly, many millions of dollars to develop its ill-fated *Families* in the early 1980s.[38]

Often, large firms have tried to skip the headaches of launching new magazines by purchasing them after their initial success. So, for example, Playboy Enterprises bought *Games* for a lot more than the $300,000 Milton Block and his syndicate used to start it.[39] And, in the biggest magazine publishing deal of the 1970s, CBS paid $50 million in cash to buy Fawcett Publications. Undoubtedly, a key factor in CBS's interest was that Fawcett not only stabled a valuable lineup of magazines (including *Women's Day*), it controlled a powerful magazine and paperback book distributing operation as well.[40]

JOINING THE ORGANIZATION

We have seen, then, that institutional legitimation through mainstream mass media material has deep roots in the history of production activities, roots that are reinforced by patterns of media ownership. Studies of the people who join mainstream United States production firms to help create material suggest that many of them, too, accept the values that underlie their production activities. That seems particularly true regarding newspeople. Studies of journalists consistently reflect what John W. C. Johnstone, Edward Slawski, and William Bowman have called "the fact that in virtually any society those in charge of mass communication tend to come from the same social strata as those in control of the economic and political systems."[41] During the 1970s, for example, Johnstone and his associates found United States journalists to be overwhelmingly from solidly middle class or upper middle class backgrounds.[42] The same tendency probably holds true with regard to non-news in the United States, though possibly not to as great an extent. Some sociologists point out that entertainers are likely to come from religions—particularly the Jewish and Catholic faiths—that have generally been considered socially disadvantaged.[43] As we have seen, the founders of the Hollywood movie industry fit this theme, and Jewish producers still maintain a Hollywood presence much out of proportion to the percentage of Jews in the population at large. Note, however, that the *class* background of producers seems to have changed quite a bit since the early days of film. In the late 1960s, a solid majority of the Hollywood television producers Muriel Cantor interviewed said they came from upper middle-class or upper class homes.[44]

It does appear that hiring throughout the mass media has tended to reflect sexual, racial, and class dominance patterns in U.S. society as a whole. Government agencies, women's groups, and labor guilds, for example, have presented a good deal of evidence of the low representation of women as directors, producers, and performers for television and the movies.[45] Women in key positions are also unusual in book publishing firms. In the late 1970s Michelle Caplette found that while one-half to one-third of the employees of book publishing firms were women, "with few exceptions women have remained at the bottom of the occupational hierarchy, dominating secretarial and assistant positions, service and staff departments such as publicity and advertising, and less prestigious departments such as children's books."[46] Socially disadvantaged races—red, oriental, and black—have found even greater difficulty getting creative jobs in mass media.[47] Surely one of the lowest areas of black representation in the early 1980s was writing for television. According to a 1980 report by the Writers' Guild of America, West, only 15 of the 2,746 Writers' Guild members working in television during the previous two years were black.[48]

Reflecting on the mainstream characteristics that describe mass media creators, some researchers have been tempted to suggest that the individuals involved perpetuate the theme of institutional legitimacy primarily through the imposition of their personal values—what Herbert Gans calls their "lay values"—on the content. Johnstone and his associates present this impression. After sketching the typical background of journalists, they conclude it is "perhaps more than accidental that. . .news in large measure reflects men's rather than women's definitions of newsworthiness . . .and that the establishment groups in the society are virtually always defined as more newsworthy than those of minority or disadvantaged groups."[49]

Herbert Gans, however, reaches more to the heart of the matter when he states that neither the lay values nor the upper middle-class status of most journalists really explain newswork. Surely, some personal likes and dislikes influence what appears in print or on the home screen. But, barring major societal changes, Gans asserts, the "basic shape of news" would not be different if a journalist came, for example, from a working class or a middle class home. The reason, as we have shown, is that the mainstream perspectives guiding newswork are built into the newswork activities; the work guides the person. Working class people, Gans suggests, would have a hard time filling the employment prerequisites for newswork. Even when they could, to act as journalists they "would likely have to shed their working class values and reality judgments."[50] Having a background that reflects dominant values, then, helps a recruit adapt to mainstream media work more easily than people without that background.

The way recruitment takes place and the way in which recruits adapt and move through production organizations have important consequences. For one thing, the system ensures that routine activities are well learned, even if not always well followed. And, for another, it ensures that the people given the most autonomy will not undermine the economic health of the production organization. Both these circumstances set upper limits on the deviation creators can make from mainstream, accepted viewpoints on the establishment. To understand how that happens, we must examine the subjects of recruitment and socialization to mass media production organizations.

Craft and Bureaucratic Recruitment

A good way to begin is to recall that creators are essential resources for mass media organizations. They provide production firms with talent to conceive and arrange mass media material. Once involved in the organization, creators both cooperate and compete with one another. Cooperation comes from needing to get a product that matches environmental demands out on time and at efficient costs. Competition comes from wanting to accumulate individual prestige and value to the organization so as to raise the person's own value as a resource. The two aims do not necessarily cancel each other out. Executives and consultants are constantly trying to find the proper mix of cooperation and conflict that will ignite greater organizational success.

Part of the value a recruit brings to a production organization lies in the kinds of creative activities he or she carries out. We can distinguish two broad roles creators may hold: the artist role and the selector role. Creators take on the artist role when they come up with ideas for a product or are involved directly in shaping it. Writers working on book manuscripts, actors playing movie parts, TV executives creating prime time schedules, and journalists creating news stories are all acting as artists. The role of selector, by contrast, involves decisions about whether the organization should accept or reject the work of certain artists.

We can talk about direct and indirect selectors. A person acting as a direct selector has direct power over the selection, timing, withholding, or repetition of a particular messages. A person acting as an indirect selector controls resources like information and money that direct selectors need to perform their duties. Examples of direct selectors are magazine editors who must choose among stories coming down the line, and network executives who deliberate about the TV shows they should pick for their schedule. Indirect selectors might be book salespeople who inform their publishing company's editors about the kinds of books that store representatives want, newspaper sales personnel whose information about the amount of advertising sold helps determine the size of the newspaper, and television network accountants who help provide program executives with information on the money available to test new series (pilot) ideas for the next season.

As these examples illustrate, the same people within a production firm might very well carry out both selector and artist roles in their jobs. However, in many production firms the responsibility for carrying out the actual writing or illustrating or photographing or acting is often delegated to people whose activities are heavily weighted toward those artistic responsibilities. One reason is simply the time it takes to follow through on a creative idea. Writing books or scripts, memorizing lines, acting as a professional photographer, or directing a movie takes a lot of time. It often means that personnel trying to ensure that enough right ideas are generated and carried out to keep the company successful simply don't have the necessary hours. So, one magazine editor may coordinate the work of many writers for the next issue, and one story editor might be the instrument for finding and coordinating writers for all thirteen episodes a TV series needs in a year.

Another reason for recruiting artists, of course, is that sometimes selectors in the firm do not have the know-how to carry out aspects of the creative effort. A related, but still different, reason speaks to the marketplace. "Marketplace" here means members of the public as well as people who write about or arrange the choice of material available to the public. They include, among others, critics, selectors in patron organizations, selectors in distribution organizations, and selectors in exhibition firms. Often, their expectation is that certain creative ventures will use individuals with special talents that surpass the abilities of those who selected them, even when the selectors could do serviceable work.

Note the accent on *certain* creative ventures. Mass media producers with different markets will face different expectations. For example, when critics, book store agents, and possibly members of the public evaluate hardback adult trade books from major publishing firms they typically expect that new titles were written not by the editors of the firms but by people the editors chose for their special writing abilities and ideas, or for their expertise on the subjects at hand. It is doubtful, however, that "the market" holds these criteria with respect to compilations of road maps or, for that matter, with respect to certain kinds of children's books. Recall from Chapter Two that editors in children's book publishing firms orienting books primarily to department stores and book stores had no qualms about writing the books themselves. The nature of their producer-patron relationship was such that mixing selector and artist roles was often the most successful way to produce the material. On the other hand, editors from children's book publishing companies that oriented books primarily to school and public libraries shuddered at the thought that they should routinely write the books their firms release. To them, and to their librarian-clients, quality books meant the best children's books they could find, no matter who wrote them.

In addition to the conditions that bring certain production organizations to recruit special artists, there are circumstances that lead many of those organizations to hire the artists for short periods at a time; this is an approach they tend not to use with other creators. One such circumstance applies when a firm's revenues simply cannot support a permanent lineup of artists. It may be that their specialties are infrequently used; another difficulty might be that the artists need a long time to complete their work. Both difficulties mean that those creators, unlike others in the firm, do not contribute to the firm's profitability on a day-to-day basis.

How serious a condition this is depends on the financial health of the firm, its tradition, and its executives' perceptions of their company's environment. For example, a daily newspaper organization typically uses its reporters' work every day. However, some papers find it prestigious and ultimately profitable to support a few bureaus and investigative reporting units even if they prepare publishable stories every few days or weeks. But a small scholarly publishing company, a struggling monthly magazine firm, or a new record company might not be able to afford that kind of delayed gratification; a different newspaper might not want to. So, circumstances would probably dictate that those firms recruit freelance artists when selectors feel they have something specific to contribute, and only for the length of time it takes them to contribute it.

Another condition making it likely that artists will be hired for short periods at a time is an industry where popularity and acclaim are unpredictable from one work to the next. Selectors in areas ranging from scholarly book publishing to network television know that the value of particular artists may rise while the value of certain others may plummet. They realize that in hiring artists for a short period of time they might be forced to pay more money to more highly desired recruits. In many cases, though, this added expense is more than made up by the selectors' ability to choose creators quickly and efficiently so as to meet current fashions and production workloads.

In many mass media production firms, then, artists are hired on very different terms than are other creators. Sociologist Arthur Stinchcombe would probably says that what we have in these situations is a mixture of two approaches to administering production.[51] One approach, which Stinchcombe calls a "bureaucratic" administration of production, involves the generation and development of material in house by regular members of the production organization. The second, which Stinchcombe calls a "craft" style of administration, involves management's hiring creative personnel to carry out specific tasks. They are relied upon to do the job according to their best knowledge, and they leave when they are finished.

It is not difficult to think of several examples where artists are recruited to an organization on a craft basis and other creators are not. A publishing company that has full-time editorial and production employees (type selectors, cover designers, and the like) and, at the same time, contracts with writers for specific manuscripts, with advances and royalties based only on those manuscripts, is mixing the two modes. So is a record company that, while hiring producers and artist and repertoire (A & R) personnel on a long-term basis, makes deals with most performers for a few records at a time. On the other hand, daily newspapers and broadcast news organizations tend to be mostly bureaucratic, although they do hire freelance reporters or camera handlers once in a while. A large greeting card company like Hallmark also generally hires both its artists and selectors in the bureaucratic mode. Television network program scheduling likewise tends toward a fully bureaucratic administrative style. However, TV production work in Hollywood tends to fit the craft description for artists. With important exceptions, actors, directors, composers, musicians, and even producers are hired by production firms to complete short run tasks and then let go.

The mode—craft or bureaucratic—by which a production firm hires its artists surely holds many implications for the creation of mass media material; the subject has hardly been studied. Lewis Coser, Charles Kadushin, and Walter Powell point out, for example, that one reason the book publishing industry stays so close to New York City (fourty per cent of all firms are based there, including the biggest ones) is the large pool of freelance artists the city holds who can do a multitude of chores from copy editing to jacket design.[52] The combination of dependency and influence such a craft-supported population might feel vis-a-vis production firms would seem to have a multitude of fascinating consequences.

Here we are concerned with only a very small part of this issue. We are interested in the extent to which recruitment through a craft or bureaucratic mode creates differences in the way artists learn about and deal with production rules that they find in the firms that hire them. A number of studies suggest that craft recruitment does differ from bureaucratic in the process by which such "socialization" takes place. The studies also suggest, however, that in both areas strong pressures operate to lead artists toward continuing the norms of the firms that employ them.

Craft Socialization

Right off, we will accept the approach Gaye Tuchman, among others, takes to socialization. Tuchman argues persuasively that socialization should be viewed as an active, creative process in which "people learn to use ... norms or rules as a resource for the construction of meaning."[53] The idea is that as people move through social situations, including organizations, they get involved in activities. Through these activities, they and the people they work with negotiate rules explicitly and implicitly about their interdependent behaviors (their roles). We should add that just as power is a key ingredient in directing, clarifying, and enforcing the interdependent behavior among organizations (see Chapter One), so power is important in helping to carry on and shape the norms of activity *within* production organizations. These ideas apply to both craft and bureaucratic production styles. However, socialization does take place differently if an artist is a full-time, long-term member of a particular production firm than if he or she works freelance, getting recruited stop-and-go by various organizations. It is possible to exaggerate the difference. Certainly, as we shall see, just as artists hired in the craft style need contacts in order to get recruited, so contacts are invaluable for bureaucratic artists to get a first job, to move up in the organization, and to move to another firm. Nor should we ignore the fact that some artists who work steadily within individual firms also moonlight as freelancers, thus plugging into both work styles.

At the same time, it is worth recognizing that a key difference between craft and bureaucratic artists is the major site of their competition over privilege and prestige. For bureaucratic artists, that site is the "home" organization, the firm in which they work. Daily, the continuation of their employment and their promotability are judged primarily by people within that firm. Freelance artists, on the other hand, must not only convince the companies they work for at any point in time to hire them again, they must also cultivate power bases outside those companies to continue to generate more work in other places. Doing that effectively generally requires admission to a community of similar artists. It is a community where a complex hierarchy, an elaborate system of contacts, and an often ritually prescribed gamut of competition strongly influence the artists' ability to enter production organizations, as well as the artists' market value.

Robert Faulkner refers to many of these issues when he writes about the Hollywood studio musician's search for freelance work:

> When he seeks to enter studio work, the unestablished recruit sees his career as contingent upon his ability to develop the proper web of contacts with those who control access to jobs. Sponsorship is the major social mechanism which brings him to their attention, allows him to establish a reputation as a solid and dependable performer, and prepares him to cope with the various pressures of the work itself. From the viewpoint of the sponsors, several important conditions must be attended to: (1) the young musician must be sponsored in such a way that established colleagues are not threatened with loss of power and prestige; (2) contractors and leaders [who recruit for and work for the studio, respectively] must be convinced that the recruit is competent and can be depended upon; (3) the appropriate timing and pacing of the candidate's introduction into the division of studio labor must be determined and implemented and (4) the candidate must learn the subtle etiquette of the referral system and, most importantly, that sponsorship is a process of reciprocal exchange.[54]

Sociological analyses of the book industry by Lewis Coser, Charles Kadushin, and Walter Powell, as well as an analysis that I carried out on the way actors are chosen for small television parts, suggest that the pattern Faulkner observed is generalizable to other recruitment situations.[55] Memoirs of artists from a variety of mass media industries further confirm this view. The accounts agree that the delicate power struggle that takes place over the recruitment of unknown freelance artists involves people in a variety of roles. Chief among them are neophyte artists themselves, who must learn to convince the right people of their talents; artist-sponsors, who already belong to an "inner circle" (there may be many) and who can help artists advance toward prominence; talent agents, whose job is to help artists make connections, and who often take up where artist-sponsors leave off; and selectors in the production organization, who are looking for talent to help get their company's work done.

The frequent pressure these people feel to meet one another typically makes social and business occasions indistinguishable for them. A sense of community—with its overtones of both comradeship and social control—develops. Ideas are shared, stolen, exchanged; rules are articulated, changed, reformulated; expensive deals are initiated by the shake of a hand. Through it all, there is a strong awareness that at the end what counts is satisfying the relevant selectors in specific production firms. Of course, those selectors are very much involved in the artistic community. Thus, the relationship between them and the artists is likely two-way: Just as the selectors set the requirements for the artists, so the community of artists can sometimes influence the selectors' perceptions of potential, quality, and success.

The requirements selectors bring with them to artistic communities are set within their production organizations. Especially when their firms operate in industries where the popularity of artists is volatile, selectors will win kudos only if the new faces truly prove talented in their work, and then only if their talent comes without disruption in organizational routines and profitability. Highly talented people who will not recoup the costs of recruiting them may not be worth it. In some mass media industries, in fact, selectors may reject even geniuses if they cannot deliver material that can be used efficiently. As a member of the Hollywood television community told Thomas Baldwin and Colby Lewis in the late 1960s, "a script by a genius may contain a scene twenty-five minutes long that can't be edited." So, to avoid this trouble, a producer or story editor who recruits writers will look not for geniuses but for people "who can meet their deadlines and give him material that he can shoot in six and a half days, within his budget, and without any trouble [from network censors]."[56]

The members of artistic communities make it their business to discern the needs of selectors in various production firms, and the pressures upon them. Thoughts of the audience—those people "out there" whose relevant characteristics have been defined by the producer-patron relationship—fade in daily importance for the artists since the desires of production firm gatekeepers become more immediately crucial. The need for new talent differs across mass media industries and across sectors of those industries. Similarly, the nature and level of cautions that selectors follow in hiring artists varies. (The editor of a "little magazine" might be willing to take a chance on a writer who has never published a story before, but the editor of a large circulation magazine might not.) Established artists and agents in an artistic community assimilate these criteria, and they approach new artists with them in mind. As Robert Faulkner suggests, the members of an artistic community's inner circle are likely to feel ambivalent about suggesting new names. On the one hand, selectors want to learn about good new faces, and they are likely to be grateful to artists who help them in their search. On the other hand, suggesting artists who fail can be worse than not suggesting someone at all. Note, too, that established artists and agents see newcomers partly as threats. Artists might feel that too many people are reaching for their jobs. Agents might feel that newcomers not affiliated with them may take jobs away from current clients.

Fear of competition, then, combined with an awareness of the needs and cautions that selectors face in their production organizations, leads the various inner circles of many an artistic community to coordinate an artist sponsorship system that both minimizes threats to established artists and protects artist-sponsors and agents from selectors' wrath. A common way to do that is to promote the idea that artists should not be suggested to selectors unless they have "paid their dues" in related endeavors and begun to establish track records. Someone establishing a track record is someone who, in paying dues by creating perhaps less widespread or expensive material, has shown that he or she is reliable, talented, and ready for more responsibility. Note that this approach ensures that a relatively small number of newcomers will move through the recruitment gauntlet, thereby protecting most members of the inner circles. More important for our purpose, however, the approach also tends to weed out artists who might disrupt the chain of a production organization's typical activities and profits. Newcomers who want to move upward must prove themselves reliable to their artistic community. Doing that means performing activities in such a way as fundamentally not to rock the boat. Too, it means negotiating an image that resonates with the image that at least one of the community's inner circles holds of itself. It means, in short, becoming part of that community's establishment.

Often, of course, the products artists are working on can be classified as mainstream mass media material. Recall that the material is mainstream in the sense that production firms derive their most important resources from society's largest or most powerful sectors (the government, giant advertisers, powerful advocacy organizations, and the like). When that is the case, the craft system of artist recruitment tends to act as yet another influence helping to perpetuate portrayals that do not fundamentally challenge the legitimacy of the dominant institutions that often make up those sectors. A good way to illustrate this mechanism is to sketch the position black writers find themselves in when they want to help create those most mainstream of mass media materials, network television programs.

We have already seen from Baldwin and Lewis's informant that producers and story editors who recruit writers are not interested in geniuses. They are, rather, interested in hiring efficient workers who can turn out usable material in the requisite amount of time without getting the firm in trouble with network censors over unacceptably controversial words, actions, and ideas. According to several industry sources, a large number of black writers are interested in applying their skills to this lucrative field, but their efforts have been stymied. As noted earlier, in 1980 only 15 of 2,746 members of the Writers Guild, West, who found TV work in the previous two years were black. Another startling statistic is that in 1980 only 65 certified members of the Writers Guild, West, were black.[57] Putting the two findings together yields the conclusion that at least 50 supposedly qualified black writers had not worked in TV for two years.

Undoubtedly, some of this exclusion of black writers comes from out-and-out bigotry on the part of people doing the hiring. However, as Len Riley found when he investigated the subject for *Emmy Magazine*, an important contributor to this situation is the craft system of recruitment with its key requirements of connections, paying dues, and track record.[58] These points are closely interwoven. As Riley notes, television producers must create a new product each week, and this pressure of time can be relieved by experienced people they trust. A new writer's lack of experience might cause costly rewrite time. That makes it difficult for all writers to break into the business. However, the situation is more difficult for black writers, since they are very likely to find it harder to develop trusting contacts in the overwhelmingly white TV community. As Riley notes, the doors to employment may be declared open to minorities, but "the buddy system transforms them into revolving doors."[59]

The few writers who do make it through the doors to write for TV pose no threat to the United States economic or political system, the United States TV system, or its time-tested formulas. Comparing black writers and white writers, Riley found that "the two groups have similar educations, speak the same language with the same idioms, swing in the same economic and social mainstream...[and are] all products of the television generation."[60] Still, even those people cannot get the widespread work they want because they are associated with writing only about the black experience. Having paid their dues in that area and developed track records for writing about blacks, the writers are then pigeonholed by artist-sponsors, talent agents, and production firm selectors. As literary agent Rick Ray puts it, "They gain their reputations and credit getting the only assignments available [on ethnic shows]. Then an agent's told those writers are too ethnic for a project that doesn't require that background."[61] Ray's solution is a straightforward one:

> A dramatic writer is a dramatic writer, and it doesn't matter if he's green. If I were to encourage a new black writer, I'd say, "Sit down and write a good script that doesn't have a single black man in the damn thing. Make it a totally non-color oriented experience.[62]

It turns out that in the early 1980s several organizations within the television industry were moving slowly to initiate minority writer training programs. The Writers Guild's set-up was typical in approach. It gave a minority writer a chance to work with an established writer who had been recommended by a producer "as someone in tune with that producer's series."[63] According to a Writers Guild executive, the program allowed an inexperienced writer to be "shepherded through the system—from initial story conference through finished script—while deriving inside knowledge about the particular show."[64] Clearly, such a program is designed to help new writers with talent find jobs by plugging them into the inner circles and operations of the artistic community. Clearly, too, the program is not designed to bring out any new perspectives about life that minority writers might be able to contribute to the artistic community. Rather, it is set up to help them shed from their work any ethnic background that might fundamentally change formulas and activities that people in the industry share as standard. Certainly, this kind of education system ends up ensuring the usefulness of those writers to production organizations. It also makes it quite unlikely that writers will generate stories that expose un-exposable tensions in society and seriously challenge the right of society's establishment to rule.

Bureaucratic Socialization

The same statement could be made about writers recruited to a bureaucratic style of work, though the process by which their socialization takes place is likely to be different from the one craft writers follow. As noted earlier, a key difference between craft and bureaucratic artists is the major site of their competition over privilege and prestige. Freelance artists fight their subtle battles both as temporary members of production organizations and as full-time members of artistic communities. On the other hand, bureaucratic artists, by the very nature of their positions, need to direct a much clearer loyalty to one source, the production organization that hires them on a long-term basis.

This difference suggests that learning "the company line" of routines and perspectives is much more straightforward in bureaucratic than in craft situations. We do not mean to imply, though, that the two types belong on opposite ends of a long continuum. Bureaucratically employed artists—for example, permanently employed magazine writers, public relations practitioners, advertising copywriters, and journalists—are by no means hermits confined to firms. On the contrary, many of them get involved actively with counterparts from other organizations. Moreover, from the standpoint of occupational socialization these involvements influence their work in ways that parallel the influences that communities of craft artists exert on their members.

We can identify four particularly important avenues of involvement outside the firm by bureaucratically employed artists: (1) school training; (2) job mobility; (3) on-the-job contacts; and (4) participation in professional associations and subscriptions to professional media. Not every avenue holds equal importance in every mass media industry. Take United States journalists in the 1970s, for example. For them school training seems to have been not nearly as important as it might appear when one considers the large number of universities that had journalism programs with swollen enrollments at the time. It turns out, though, that only one in four journalism majors in the early 1970s actually went on to a journalism career.[65] Moreover, John W. C. Johnstone and his associates found in the mid-1970s that while the great majority of that generation of journalists was college-educated (unlike those who started careers before World War II), only about a quarter of those with undergraduate or graduate training majored in journalism.[66] It may well be, of course, that even nonmajors took journalism courses here and there. And, surely just living in a society where objective journalism is practiced everywhere constitutes training for people who end up working for newspapers.

Another mechanism for sharing journalistic values and routines across news organizations is undoubtedly job switching. We might suspect that newspeople who work in different organizations tend to carry some of the practices and perspectives of their previous employment to their new situation. From this standpoint, the findings by Johnstone and his associates about job mobility tend to support the idea that it is a vehicle for sharing norms. In their sample of over 11,000 journalists of all kinds throughout the United States, the researchers found that sixty percent reported working previously for one or more different news organizations. Slightly over a third of the sample reported two or more previous employers, and one in five reported three or more. Johnstone and colleagues also found that journalists tend to conform to general trends of the labor force at large in terms of the timing of their job switches. That is, they more commonly change jobs during the early rather than late stages of their careers.[67] Therefore, as a journalist grows older he or she is likely to be involved with counterparts from other organizations less through job switches and more through on-the-job contacts and participation in professional associations.

On-the-job contacts are very common among working reporters. Journalists from different papers meet each other often in the course of assignments. They file similar stories after viewing the same events, speaking to the same sources, reading the same press releases, and sharing ideas about it all. The phenomenon has been called "pack journalism," and it has been cited as a key reason for the similar subjects and angles that the many reporters covering the same event tend to use.[68] Often, too, reporters get ideas of what is important by reading the same elite newspapers and tuning to the same wire services. Journalist Robert MacNeil made this point through an anecdote from his tenure at NBC television:

> In 1963, when Governor George Wallace tried to prevent the integration of Alabama's schools with his "stand in the schoolhouse door," NBC correspondent Tom Pettit, covering the story there, phoned a producer in New York, who started telling Pettit how to handle the story.
> "There's a good story in the *New York Times* this morning," he said.
> "We don't get the *New York Times* down here," Pettit said.
> "Well, the night lead of the AP says—"
> "We don't have the AP."
> "Never mind. The UP's got a pretty good angle on it—"
> "We don't have the UP either," Pettit said.
> The producer said, "You don't have the UP?"
> "No."
> "You don't have the AP?"
> "No."
> "You don't have the *New York Times*?"
> "No."
> "Then how do you guys know what's going on down there?"[69]

Professional associations (such as the American Newspaper Association and the Association for Education in Journalism) and professional media (e.g., *Editor and Publisher*, the *Columbia Journalism Review*, and the *Washington Journalism Review*) also tend to bring journalistic heads together on both large and small issues—from gossip about people in the field to canons of journalist ethics to the proper way to cover certain types of events. Doing so, they provide umbrellas of public precedent to protect journalists who might feel forced by their organizations to carry out activities they consider unprofessional. And, by singling out practices that deviate from journalistic norms ("The Failure of Network News," reveals the *Washington Journalism Review*), by showing how new problems can be corrected through accepted routines ("Sex in the News: Some Guidelines," suggests the *AP Log*), and by celebrating the accomplishments of those designated the best and brightest (through, for example, the Pulitzer Prizes), the professional activities can go far to reinforce the principles of objective journalism among the corps of journalists in mainstream news organizations throughout the country.[70]

It warrants saying, though, that while involvement in professional activities and the other forms of contact with the field help reinforce work routines, the primary training ground for reporters—in fact, the primary training ground for all bureaucratically employed artists—is the organization in which they work. Sociologists and social psychologists have written much about the processes by which individuals learn to use the norms and routines of their workplace.[71] Whatever the specific social psychological path, learning what to do and how to do it correctly is often the result of explicit instruction, learning by example, and learning through mistakes.

Organizational resources serve as incentives. Superiors control resources—permission, salary increases, company perquisites, authority to make decisions independently—which they can release to artists carrying out "good" work. Colleagues, too, control resources. They are likely to be more friendly and helpful to artists who do good work than to those who do not. An artist learns that good work means activities that fit nicely with superiors' policy regarding what the organization should create and how it should create it. As we have noted, the norms that make up the most basic aspects of a production firm's mass media policy necessarily carry with them perspectives on the domains of legitimate social power, authority, and justice—and on the limits to questioning them. By extension, then, an artist who does good work perpetuates those perspectives at the core of his or her material.

DEALING WITH VALUE CONFLICTS

In his classic study of the way journalists learn their organization's policy, Warren Breed calls what he saw "social control in the newsroom."[72] By invoking the notion of social control, Breed raises another idea—the possibility of clashes between creators' personal values and the values of the organization. We ought to note that Breed's approach to the idea of journalistic policy is very different from the one used in this chapter. The approaches do not contradict one another. They simply get at two different aspects of an organization's policy. One aspect, the one this chapter has been dealing with, is the organization's *core policy*. Core policy represents the fundamental perspective an organization follows regarding the legitimacy of dominant institutions in the society. The second aspect, the one Breed deals with, is the organization's *general policy*. General policy is built on top of core policy. It represents perspectives the organization follows in portraying areas of life about which executives have set guidelines.

An example might be in order. Take two newspaper firms that conduct their creative activities so as to fundamentally legitimate society's dominant institutions; they have common core policies. But, at the same time, say one paper reflects a Democratic point of view, the other a Republican viewpoint. Also, one encourages investigative reporting, and the other does not. Beyond their core policies, then, the news organizations diverge in approaching the world. As noted in Chapter Two, such variability among mass media producers is typical. It stems from differences in the firms' environments and from differences in executives' perceptions of the environments. On the other hand, in this chapter we have observed that many firms are likely to share the same mainstream core policies, even when they draw on different resources. One reason, we showed, is that different as the resources are, they still come from mainstream sectors of the society. A related reason is that in using the resources, the organizations often follow similar production routines—for example, routines that carry out the ideas of objectivity and formula. Because the development of those routines is tied closely to the development of mass media industries and society, they are likely to reflect mainstream core values.

Not much is known about the nature of value conflicts among creators in mass media organizations. It is probably safe to suggest, though, that most conflicts that occur relate to general policy, not to core policy. That conclusion seems logical in view of the high degree of selectivity that goes into the recruitment of artists and other creative personnel in any sector of the mass media, whether mainstream or peripheral. The selectivity ensures that creators who are admitted to responsible positions have paid their dues, carved out track records, and plugged themselves into social circles that make acceptance of their production firms' core values simply part of their lives. Herbert Gans was reflecting this idea when he wrote about the essentially middle class core values of the mainstream news organizations he studied. Gans noted that "relatively few journalists came from working-class homes, and those who did lost touch with their origins long ago."[73] Similarly, when William Bowman interviewed journalists from nonmainstream publications in the United States during the early 1970s, he found that they shared notions regarding the legitimacy of dominant social institutions. They welcomed radical change in the society at large. They viewed mainstream news media as "centralized managers of public consciousness...devoted to the preservation of the present order." And, consequently, they saw their role as "opposition to the status quo, with a readiness to question the legitimacy of any social institution and a commitment to involvement rather than detachment as journalists."[74]

Regarding the nature and extent of value conflicts that are presumably more common—those involving a production organization's general policy—there is also little known. John W. C. Johnstone and his colleagues did survey the distribution of certain kinds of criticisms of the press by journalists—criticisms such as lack of objectivity, superficial handling of material, and failure to cover enough stories.[75] However, similar surveys of other industries are lacking.[76] It *is* clear that value conflicts exist throughout the mass media. Virtually every interview with a creator and every study of a mass media organization uncovers at least some clash between what a person thinks the production organization should be creating and what it actually is creating. As Warren Breed notes, the most common resolution is simply to find enough justification for the policy so that person can continue working. Failing that, there are other routes to reducing value conflict. Breed's concise summary of the options available is worth quoting:

> At the extremes, the pure conformist can deny the conflict, the confirmed deviate can quit.... Otherwise, the adaptations seem to run this way: (1) Keep on the job but blunt the corners of policy when possible ("If I wasn't here the next guy would let *all* that crap get through..."); (2) Attempt to repress the conflict morally and anti-intellectually ("What the hell, it's only a job; take your pay and forget it..."); (3) Attempt to compensate, by "taking it out" in other contexts: drinking, writing "the truth" for liberal publications, working with action programs, the Guild, and otherwise.[77]

What interests us most here are the implications those options hold for mass media material. It would seem that option two would lead to a near-apathetic approach to symbol creation. Take a TV writer disenchanted with the refusal by series producers to accept scripts that revolve around certain psychological conflicts of his characters. The writer may give up on that unusual theme and simply pitch ideas that fit time-tested action-adventure or situation comedy formulas. If he followed option three, he would carry out work apathetically part of the time, but he might also contribute to organizations holding policies more consistent with his values. So, for example, while proposing very traditional notions to most producers, the writer might also try to persuade a prestige-oriented TV production firm that the networks would be attracted to a special based on his "special" notion. Failing that, he might get a novel or a magazine short story out of his idea.

Only option one would seem to encourage attempts to get around the expressed policy of a production organization. If he followed that line, the disenchanted TV writer would propose plots according to accepted formulas. However, in the scripts he might include one or two scenes where characters reflect the issues he really wanted to highlight. Of course, if he failed consistently to get scenes like that accepted, the frustration that comes from frequent failure might lead the writer to fall back on options two or three. In general, we can suggest that the more powerful a creator is within an organization, the greater will be that creator's ability to get around general policy.

Discussing the circumvention of policy should alert us to the idea that production firm executives do sometimes allow aboveboard changes in organizational guidelines. Sometimes, too, the executives encourage changes in approach that use existing mass media policy in new ways. Raising these points here underscores the notion that, in a large sense, this chapter has mapped the forces that militate against basic changes in the production of mass media material. Particularly in the case of mainstream material, those forces are powerful and deeply rooted, and they generally ensure that creators will shape material that legitimizes fundamental perspectives on society. Many changes do occur *within* these fundamental boundaries, however, and they sometimes constitute important shifts in the way mass media portray the world. The way creators cope with pressures toward change and continuity in mass media material is a subject for the next chapter.

REFERENCES

1. Gaye Tuchman, *Making News* (New York: The Free Press, 1978), p. 210; Phillip Tichenor, George Donahue, and Clarice Olien, *Community Conflict and the Press* (Beverly Hills: Sage Publications, 1980), p. 224; and George Gerbner, "Communication and Social Environment," *Scientific American*, Vol. 227 (1972), p. 153.

2. The manner in which the dominant forces of production in a society (the "material base") relate to the symbolic environment (the "superstructure") has provoked intense discussion among Marxist cultural critics. It is called the "base/superstructure" question, and it involves such important thinkers as Antonio Gramsci, Raymond Williams, Louis Althusser, and Frederick Jameson. For a summary of the issue, see Frederick Jameson, *The Political Unconscious* (Ithaca, New York: Cornell University Press, 1982), pp. 1–58; and Raymond Williams, *Marxism and Literature* (New York: Oxford University Press, 1977), pp. 108–114.

3. Michael Schudson, *Discovering the News: A Social History of American Newspapers* (New York: Basic Books, 1978); and Dan Schiller, *Objectivity and the News: The Public and the Rise of Commercial Journalism* (Philadelphia: University of Pennsylvania, 1981).

4. Schiller, p. 46.

5. Schiller, p. 48.

6. Schiller, p. 52.

7. Schiller, p. 48.

8. Schiller, p. 87.

9. Schiller, p. 121.

10. Schudson, pp. 193–194.

11. Schiller, p. 195.

12. Herbert Gans, *Deciding What's News* (New York: Vintage, 1979), p. 284.

13. See, for example, Gaye Tuchman, *Making News: A Study in the Construc-*

tion of Reality (New York: Basic Books, 1978); Harvey Moloch and Marilyn Lester, "Accidental News: The Great Oil Spill," *American Journal of Sociology*, vol. 49 (1974), pp. 235–260; and Mark Fishman, *Manufacturing the News* (Austin: University of Texas, 1980). Although this discussion focuses on United States journalism, an important tradition of research in Britain on the sociology of news should not go unmentioned. See, for example, Jeremy Tunstall, *Journalists at Work* (London: Constable, 1971); Stanley Cohen and Jack Young, *The Manufacture of News* (Beverly Hills: Sage, 1973); and Philip Schlessinger, *Putting Reality Together* (London: Constable, 1978).

14. Tuchman, pp. 164–165.

15. George Donahue, Phillip Tichenor, and Clarice Olien, "Gatekeeping: Mass Media Systems and Information Control," in F. Gerald Kline and Phillip J. Tichenor, eds., *Current Perspectives in Mass Communication Research* (Beverly Hills: Sage, 1972).

16. Morris Janowitz, *The Community Press in an Urban Setting* (New York: The Free Press, 1952).

17. Clarice Olien, George Donahue, and Philip Tichenor, "The Community Editor's Power and the Reporting of Conflict," *Journalism Quarterly*, vol. 33 (1968), pp. 243–252.

18. Tuchman, pp. 133–155; Todd Gitlin, *The Whole World is Watching* (Berkeley: University of California Press, 1980); and J. D. Barber, "Characters in the Campaign: The Literary Problem," in J. D. Barber, ed., *Race for the Presidency: The Media and the Nominating Process* (Englewood Cliffs, New Jersey: Prentice Hall, 1978).

19. Ernest Hynds, *American Newspapers in the 1980s* (New York: Hastings House, 1975), pp. 136–137.

20. Hynds, pp. 136–137.

21. George Gerbner, "Teacher Image in Mass Culture: Symbolic Functions in the 'Hidden Curriculum,' " in David Olsen, ed., *Media and Symbols*, part 1 (Chicago: National Society for the Study of Education, 1974), p. 474.

22. Studies in this area are numerous. For examples, see George Gerbner and Nancy Signorielli, *Women and Minorities in Television Drama, 1969–1978* (Philadelphia: Annenberg School of Communications, 1979); Gaye Tuchman, Arlene Kaplan Daniels, and James Benet eds., *Hearth and Home: Images of Women in the Mass Media* (New York: Oxford, 1978); Molly Haskell, *From Reverence to Rape: The Treatment of Women in the Movies* (New York: Holt, Rinehart, and Winston, 1974); Robert F. Berkhofer, *The White Man's Indian* (New York: Vintage, 1978); Donald Bogel, *Toms, Coons, Mulattoes, Mammies, and Bucks* (New York: Vintage, 1973); Allen L. Woll, "Hollywood's Good Neighbor Policy: The Latin Image in American Film, 1939–1946," *Journal of Popular Film*, vol. 3 (1974), pp. 278–293; and Randall M. Miller, ed., *Ethnic Images in American Film and Television* (Philadelphia: The Balch Institute, 1978).

23. See George Gerbner, Larry Gross, Michael Morgan and Nancy Signorielli, "The 'Mainstreaming' of America: Violence Profile No. 11," *Journal of Communication*, vol. 30 (Summer, 1980), pp. 10–29. Also see Russell Nye, *The Unembarrassed Muse* (New York: Dial, 1970), especially part four.

24. Among the many relevant works are Stith Thompson, *The Folktale* (New York: Holt, Rinehart and Winston, 1946); Hugh Dalziel Duncan, "The Search for

a Social Theory of Communication," in Frank Dance, ed., *Human Communication Theory* (New York: Holt, Rinehart, and Winston, 1967); J. L. Fischer, "The Sociopsychological Analysis of Folktales," *Current Anthropology*, vol. 4 (June 1963), pp. 235–272; and Jerome Mintz, introduction to *Legends of the Hassidim* (Bloomington: Indiana University, 1968).

25. John Cawelti, *The Six Gun Mystique* (Bowling Green, Ohio: Popular Press, 1975); and Nye, 280–304.

26. Cawelti, p. 29.

27. Cawelti, p. 32.

28. Cawelti, p. 73.

29. Robert Sklar, *Movie-Made America* (New York: Random, 1975), p. 29.

30. Sklar, p. 30.

31. Sklar, p. 91.

32. Sklar, p. 91.

33. Sidney Head, *Broadcasting in America*, 2d ed. (Boston: Houghton Mifflin, 1972), p. 371.

34. *Variety*, May 19, 1982, p. 2.

35. Leonard Mogel, *The Magazine* (Englewood Cliffs, New Jersey: Prentice Hall, 1979), pp. 140–147.

36. *Advertising Age*, October 19, 1981, p. S-72.

37. *Advertising Age*, October 19, 1981, p. S-14.

38. *Advertising Age*, October 19, 1981, p. S-14.

39. *Advertising Age*, October 19, 1981, p. S-72.

40. Mogel, p. 156.

41. John W. C. Johnstone, Edward Slawski, and William Bowman, *The News People* (Urbana: University of Illinois Press, 1976), p. 26.

42. Johnstone, et. al., p. 28.

43. Muriel Cantor, *The Hollywood TV Producer* (New York: Basic Books, 1971), p. 234; and Sidney Willhelm and Gideon Sjoberg. "The Social Characteristics of Entertainers," *Social Forces*, vol. 37 (1958), pp. 71–76.

44. Cantor, pp. 233–241.

45. See, for example, United States Commission on Civil Rights, *Window Dressing on the Set: Women and Minorities in Television* (Washington, D.C.: United States Commission on Civil Rights, 1977).

46. Michelle Caplette, "Women in Book Publishing: A Qualified Success Story," in Lewis Coser, Charles Kadushin, and Walter Powell, *Books: The Culture and Commerce of Publishing* (New York: Basic Books, 1981), p. 173.

47. Mary Cassata and Molefi Asante, *Mass Communication* (New York: Macmillan, 1979), p. 200–202.

48. Len Riley, "Writing for Television: All White or All-American," *Emmy Magazine*, Spring 1980, p. 34.

49. Johnstone et al., p. 100.

50. Gans, p. 213.

51. Arthur Stinchcombe, "Bureacratic and Craft Administration of Production: A Comparative Study," *Administrative Science*, vol. 4 (1959), pp. 168–187.

52. Coser, Kadushin, and Powell, p. 40.

53. Tuchman, p. 206.

54. Robert Faulkner, "Hollywood Studio Musicians: Making it in the Los

Angeles Film and Recording Industry," in Charles Nanry, ed., *American Music: From Storyville to Woodstock* (East Brunswick, New Jersey: Transaction Books, 1972), pp. 205–206. Also of interest to this subject is Robert Stebbins, "A Theory of Jazz Community," in the same volume. For a helpful approach to the ways artistic communities both limit and encourage competition, see Richard A. Peterson and Howard G. White, "Elements of a Simplex Structure," *Urban Life* 10 (April 1981), pp. 3–24.

55. Coser, Kadushin, and Powell, pp. 70–147; and Joseph Turow, "Unconventional Perspectives on Commercial Television: An Organizational Perspective," in James Ettema and D. Charles Whitney, *Individuals in Mass Media Organizations: Creativity and Constraint* (Beverly Hills: Sage, 1982).

56. Thomas Baldwin and Colby Lewis. "Violence in Television: The Industry Looks at Itself," in George Comstock and Eli Rubinstein, eds., *Television and Social Behavior*, vol. 1 (Washington, D.C.: United States Government Printing Office, 1972), p. 362.

57. Riley, p. 34.

58. Riley, p. 34.

59. Riley, p. 39.

60. Riley, p. 54.

61. Riley, p. 54.

62. Riley, p. 54.

63. Riley, p. 56.

64. Riley, p. 56.

65. Johnstone et. al., p. 36.

66. Johnstone et. al., p. 36.

67. Johnstone et. al., p. 56.

68. Timothy Crouse, *The Boys on the Bus* (New York: Random House, 1972).

69. Robert MacNeil, *The People Machine: The Influence of Television on American Politics* (New York: Harper and Row, 1968), p. 30.

70. David Altheide, "The Failure of Network News," *Washington Journalism Review*, vol. 3 (May 1981), pp. 28–29; and Lou Boccardi, "Sex in the News: Some Guidelines," *AP Log*, June 28, 1976, p. 1.

71. See, for example, Daniel Katz and Robert Kahn, *The Social Psychology of Organizing* (New York: John Wiley, 1966).

72. Warren Breed, "Social Control in the Newsroom," in Wilbur Schramm, ed., *Mass Communications*, 2d Ed. (Urbana, Illinois: University of Illinois Press, 1972), pp. 178–194.

73. Gans, p. 210.

74. Johnstone et. al., pp. 176–177.

75. Johnstone et. al., p. 170.

76. An important exception is Muriel Cantor, *The Hollywood TV Producer* (New York: Basic Books, 1971).

77. Breed, p. 193.

Five

The Risks of Continuity and Change

How do people in a mass media production organization get their everyday tasks done in ways that fit the many demands of forces in their organization's environment? Consider the large number of activities executives in a production firm and the personnel below them must complete successfully when they create their company's output. A foremost imperative is to cultivate good relationships with organizations that provide crucial resources for generating materials efficiently, getting them to the right marketplaces, and displaying them to consumers. These forces often represent many of the power roles discussed in earlier chapters, from investors to exhibitors to public advocacy organizations and authorities. Another crucial requirement is to attract an audience to the material once it is displayed in the marketplace. Audience purchases (or audience attendance) must take place at a rate and in amounts that make all the parties bringing resources to bear on production and distribution feel the venture is economically justifiable. To further ensure economic justifiability, production personnel must carry out their activities within time periods that both satisfy the needs of the environment and maximize the efficiency of the production firm itself. For example, a daily newspaper must go to press at the same time each day because of tight printing and distribution deadlines; a television production firm must produce episodes of a network series in only a number of days to satisfy network needs and make the most efficient use of company personnel; and a book publishing firm must move manuscripts through the editorial process quickly enough to make room for other books coming down the line and to ensure that there will be enough titles for the firm's upcoming list.

Of course, whenever they try to carry out these interrelated requirements, the members of a mass media production organization run the risk of not being able to succeed. The risk of failure is individual as well as collective. For every direct selector, indirect selector, and artist, the need to produce successful material regularly within specified time periods, translates most directly into a requirement to satisfy members of the firm who can affect their status in the firm and industry. Filling that requirement means helping to coordinate the continual development of cultural products. Those products must be different from one another in order to keep attracting the interest of the same distributors, exhibitors, and audiences. So, every new book a publishing firm releases must be different from other books that have come out. Every day's newspaper must have stories different from those of the day before. And, every episode of a television series must be recognizably different from other episodes of the series.

Continually searching for ways to vary mass media material is an integral part of a creator's daily activity. Yet, there's the key rub. While the search for novelty is a necessity for the people who coordinate the industrialized production of cultural materials, it also poses a gamut of difficulties and possibilities for failure. Three broad sets of problems come to mind. One relates to the need to satisfy forces in the environment that are crucial to getting material out to the public. Exhibitors, distributors, patrons, investors, and public advocacy organizations might have welcomed the firm's previous creations, but that alone is no assurance they will feel the same way about the new product. The second set of problems relates to pleasing the targeted audience. Simply put, there is no guarantee the audience will respond to new products as it responded to the old ones. And third, there are potential problems that relate to the functioning of the organization itself. Recall the requirement that production personnel carry out their activities in the space of time that both satisfies the needs of the environment and maximizes the efficiency of the production firm. That can be hard to do when novelty becomes an important part of the equation. New ideas might bombard selectors from all sides; new ways of doing work might constantly pop into artists' minds; and new perspectives on the meaning of the creative process might intrude into the minds of the people involved. Creators facing time constraints must be able to control these possibilities in such a way that the material they release is both novel and efficient—and ultimately successful.

All three sets of difficulties boil down to a kind of balancing act between the need by creators to search for novelty and their need to limit that search in the interests of predictability and efficiency. Paul DiMaggio and Paul Hirsch express this point in another way. "Cultural production systems," they say, "are characterized by a constant and pervasive tension between innovation and control."[1] Part of the risk of failure that accompanies this tension can be alleviated by the leverage a production firm exerts over its environment. So, for example, creators in an organization that also owns distribution channels and exhibition outlets will likely feel confident about the chance their ideas will get in the marketplace. And, as we noted in Chapter One, even creators from firms without direct control over the market's spectrum of choice might rest easier knowing that management has adopted strategies to cope with environmental uncertainty—for example, deploying contact personnel to organizational boundaries, over-producing and differentially promoting new items, coopting mass media gatekeepers, and using direct mail (or video) marketing.

Despite the success of tactics aimed at reducing risk by controlling the environment, some concerns creators hold about the acceptability and limits of novelty are bound to remain. For one thing, a production firm will always face some kind of competition, if only from a different media form. So, for example, advertisers dissatisfied with recent issues of the only newspaper in a town might very well turn to local TV and radio instead. Another concern creators are bound to hold is that in searching vigorously for the "best" new ideas, they might lose the efficiency that keeps that organization both filling the environment's demand for output and bringing in the management's desired level of profits. It seems, then, that creators inevitably risk failure when they try to balance their search for novelty against the need for control and predictability. Understanding the way they deal with this fact of organizational life will help us go a long way toward understanding how creators approach continuity and change in mass media material. That is the aim of this chapter.

COPING WITH RISK THROUGH ROUTINES

Gaye Tuchman pointed out most emphatically that the major way creators cope with risks of failure when they search for novelty is to control that search by using routines.[2] Routines are patterned activities that people learn to use in carrying out certain tasks. As Tuchman notes, the control of work has been a dominant theme in the sociology of organizations. Writers in this area have stressed that individuals in organizations routinize their tasks if possible, since using routines makes predictability and control over work possible. Other writers have noted that people in an organization often have too much work to do. To cope with this problem, they try to control the flow of work and the amount of work to be done. Picking up on these ideas, Everett Hughes suggested that the need for routines is particularly acute among physicians, fire crews, and other rescue personnel who deal regularly with what we would generally call emergencies. Hughes suggests that when several unexpected events happen at the same time, those workers must be prepared to call quickly upon certain routines for getting the job done efficiently and in some order of accepted priorities. For example, "the physician plays one emergency off against the other; the reason he can't run up to see Johnny who may have the measles is that he is, unfortunately, right at that moment, treating a case of the black plague."[3]

Tuchman observes that newsworkers confront emergency situations all the time. Dealing with unexpected events is a large part of their job. Every day journalists are required to go out into the world, confront a wide variety of ongoing activities, pay special attention to some of them, and write stories about them in time for deadlines. Clearly, there are risks involved in this kind of work. Say the journalist covered a riot. One danger is that the journalist might focus on the wrong aspect of the riot. That is, the journalist's editor might not consider that facet of the riot news, or the editor might not consider it to be interesting news. Another potential difficulty is that the editor might not like the perspective the journalist used in writing about the disturbance. A third risk is that the journalist might write about someone taking part in the riot in a way that might place the newspaper in jeopardy of being sued for libel. Yet another risk is that the journalist might be so worried about these and other problems of depicting the riot that he or she might not get the story done in time to be placed in the next day's paper. That would mean one less story possibility for the editor, and one day of wasted salary from the standpoint of the organization's management. Multiply one reporter's problem by similar risks confronting all the journalists in the organization and it is clear that the difficulty of processing novelty can have a paralyzing effect on a news organization.

The answer, Tuchman points out, has been to shape newswork according to routines that guide journalists toward dealing with activities in ways that speed work along in an acceptable manner. Consider the problem of knowing what events make "interesting" news. Journalists are constantly involved in negotiating this point within their news organizations. As a result, when they decide to cover something, they invariably have a good idea that either (1) their colleagues and superiors would have done so too, or (2) they can persuade their colleagues and superiors that they would have done it. So, for example, a timely event taking place in the federal government would likely be recognized as news by everyone in the news organization. Whether the event deserves to be highlighted on the front page of the paper might be a subject of argument among selectors in the newsroom. For efficiency's sake, newsworkers set up a news "net" to make sure reporters are monitoring areas of society that are likely to yield interesting or important news. These areas with the most potential (e.g., the White House, the Congress) will get the most coverage. Other areas will have sparser coverage, sometimes only with a "stringer," hired when something newsworthy does happen. And many areas will simply not be covered at all.

Newsworkers approach the events that take place within their news nets in patterned ways, as well. They generate expectations ("typifications") of the way news events happen that allow them to decide immediately what human and technical resources to allocate to such events, and what difficulties they will face in doing so. Take an event that a reporter typifies as "spot" news, that is, news that is unscheduled and must be processed quickly. An example is the assassination of a national leader. Designating an event in this manner activates a performance program that places many other members of the news organization on special alert, calls for use of the fastest communication technologies possible, and allows for the immediate reallocation of resources (such as pulling reporters off other stories) if and as necessary.

A contrasting case is when a reporter and his (or her) newsroom superiors typify an event as continuing news—"series of stories on the same subject based on events occurring over a period of time."[4] An example is an account of the progress of a legislative bill through Congress. Because this chain of events is prescheduled, it allows the reporter to plan. That might mean researching specific topics relating to the bill, anticipating problems in covering various debates over the measure, and taking corrective action in advance to avoid those difficulties. Such continuing stories also assure editors that acceptable grist exists for the newspaper or news broadcast even if enough interesting spot news stories do not materialize. Moreoever, because of the relatively high predictability journalists feel they have when they cover continuing news, selectors believe they can plan the use of other resources for unexpected events. "At the very least, it enables a city editor to state, Joe Smith will not be available to cover spot news stories a week from Tuesday because he will be covering the Bergman trial!"[5]

Even when a journalist's place on a news net has reduced the problem of being where interesting news will happen, and even when the reporter and the news organization have mapped out priorities and alternatives regarding the coverage of certain events through typifications, the problem of actually reporting the event remains. Tuchman suggests that the most important strategy United States journalists have evolved to deal with the need to write acceptable stories by deadline is what they call "objectivity". There are many facets to the idea of telling a story objectively. Moreover, TV journalists follow some camera-related rules that their print counterparts need not consider. Perhaps the most well known of the techniques both use is the "inverted pyramid." That means summarizing the situation's basic facts concisely—the quick who, what, where, when and how of the story—in the first paragraph, and then unfolding other details in succeeding sections of greater breadth. Other conventions that denote objective journalism are reporting in the third person; not injecting personal opinions into the tale; concentrating on verifiable facts; quoting those who were involved; and presenting more than one side of the story.

Of course, it is quite possible for a reporter to intentionally place his or her personal biases into a story that uses these conventions. Journalists have learned, for example, to express their viewpoints by finding quotes they agree with from people who were involved in the event and placing those quotes at rhetorically appropriate points in their tales. Nevertheless, telling a story in an objective manner creates an aura of neutrality within the mainstream news business and throughout United States society. Consequently, a reporter using the objective method can be confident that his or her story will not run the risk of rejection by an editor as biased or libelous. More generally, in following the canons of objectivity, a reporter carries out an invaluable series of routines that help him or her frame events acceptably *and* in time for deadline.

It is not merely an interesting accident that the major routines that mainstream United States journalists find crucial to doing their work are the same ones that serve to legitimize the dominant institutions of the society. As noted in Chapter Four, the ideologies of the American elite were built into the very routines that penny press journalists created under the heading of objectivity and modified over time. By the mid-twentieth century, those routines had developed into a full-blown approach to defining the world. Recognizing this series of routines as both a strategy to accomplish daily work as well as a mechanism that legitimizes the Establishment should alert us to an important generalization: The routines all creators use to predictably manage the creation of novelty in mass media material ensure that the novelty will rarely run counter to the production organization's fundamental perspective on the legitimacy of dominant social institutions. In this way, the routines creators use not only protect them from failure at work, they protect their organization's basic approach to ideology as well.

COPING WITH DEGREES OF RISK

Gaye Tuchman's examination of the manner in which journalists cope with the risks of their occupation by using an elaborate set of routines provides the tools with which to be aware of the roles that routines and risks play in mass media production organizations, generally. Surveying a broad range of mass media operations, though, makes clear that to best understand the use of routines in several media contexts we must speak of the degree of risk creators face. *Degree of risk* means that for creators in certain media sectors the economic and political cost of failing at an individual product is greater than for creators in other media sectors. The higher the possible loss, the higher the risk. Potential for economic loss can be considered low when the amount of cash needed to generate an individual product is relatively small. The potential political loss is relatively low when the product is not likely to fall under the critical scrutiny of organizations that take on authority or public advocacy roles. Potential for relatively high economic and political loss—and thus high risk—can be found in situations where product development costs and public concern are high.

Contrasting the creation of prime time network television programs with the creation of scholarly monographs can illustrate these points. A television program is a relatively high risk venture both for its production company and for the network that orders the show. An hour of prime time typically costs about a million dollars; the fee the network pays the producer for two airings of the program often just barely covers stated expenses. Too, all expenses represent costs that cannot be altered whether the people who ultimately view the program in its first showing number ten million, thirty million, or fifty million. Production and network personnel get nervous when rating figures hover at the lower end of those numbers, since it means advertisers have not reached large enough audiences by prime time standards. Because the charges a network can demand of advertisers are based partly on the ability of the network's past and present shows to draw large audiences, a low rated program can cause network profits (and the production firm's reputation) to suffer. As noted in Chapter Two, bad ratings for one program might have a negative impact on a network's profit picture that goes beyond a single time slot. The reason is that low viewership at one point in a network's evening schedule might reduce the audience flow across all that network's programs that evening. Coupled to this high economic risk is the high political liability a prime time program can incur. Because of network television's ability consistently to reach an overwhelming percentage of United States households, the medium draws the special attention of groups sensitive to what they feel are improper depictions of parts of society. Prime time is at the center of United States media in the eyes of government and public advocacy organizations. Consequently, there is a good chance that a new prime time show would draw the scrutiny of these groups.

By contrast, the production of a scholarly monograph is an example of a low liability and risk venture when compared to activities in other sectors of the mass media.[6] Manuscript acquisition and book production costs for individual titles typically require thousands of dollars as opposed to tens of thousands, hundreds of thousands, and even millions in other media sectors. Moreover, unlike prime time TV shows, certain financial elements can be contained depending on the audience size that is projected. In addition, book marketing, aimed mostly at libraries through librarians and academics, can often be carried out through mail order ad campaigns that are inexpensive by media advertising standards. Book reviews (which cost the price of mailing review copies) also can help a title along. These rather low economic costs also seem to parallel low political liability since it appears that the output of scholarly publishers is generally considered by forces outside the academic world to be esoteric and beyond the day-to-day concerns of ordinary citizens. Few advocacy groups exert energy against narrowly distributed scholarly tomes.

The degree of risk that creators in mass media production firms confront seems to influence the way they orient their routines to cope with risk. In general, we can suggest that the greater the risk involved, the greater the chance that creators will both (1) structure their activities toward highly predictable, highly patterned mass media content, and (2) orient their routines toward certain "administrative" techniques of coping, techniques that are not so obviously reflected in the content itself. When risks are not so great, creators will tend to orient their routines *only* toward administrative techniques of coping.

Administrative Techniques of Coping

Administrative techniques of coping are routines designed to help creators seek out information or personnel that will maximize the chance of a particular product's success. Two broad forms of these techniques stand out—the use of *track record talent* and the use of *market research*. A track record talent is a creator who has a list of proven successes and a strong reputation in his or her field. Such people often join the organization on a craft basis—that is, they complete a particular project and leave. The manner in which production firm personnel use track record talents varies widely. Sometimes a "star" is the primary artist in a particular endeavor. In the 1970s and 1980s that happened, for example, when John Updike wrote a new novel for Knopf or when Paul McCartney recorded a new disc for Apple or another label. At other times, the track record talent works behind the main artist, is known to a much smaller population outside the artistic community, but still has the reputation for bringing the magic of success to a product. A case in point in the television industry is the team of producer Gary Smith and director Dwight Hemion, known for over two decades for putting together successful musical variety programs.[7] In the record industry, producers often develop reputations for eking out the greatest possible chance for success in a group's work through careful selecting, arranging, and editing of their material. At different times, John Hammond, Lieber and Stoller, Shadow Morton, Phil Spector, and George Martin were considered the ablest and most important record producers in the business.[8]

A variation on this kind of behind-the-scenes use of track record talent is the use of stars to search out and sponsor people with the potential for success. It happens all the time in scholarly book publishing. As Ann Orlov points out, academic publishing firms continually rely on "senior scholar-brokers" to point them toward new manuscripts or projects that the field will accept as quality work.[9] Sometimes, those academics give their advice free; sometimes, the firm provides a fee for evaluating manuscripts. Sometimes, too, publishing executives make the scholar-broker's role public through a series of books under his or her aegis. The executives' expectation is that a reputable scholar in search of manuscripts can plug into the various "artistic circles" discussed in Chapter Four better than can company editors, who generally have fewer long-term ties to the academic community. Publishing executives hope that the result will be the discovery of manuscripts that hold great chance for success. Too, they expect that the scholar's name on every cover in the series will help works by newer academics to sell better than if those works had to stand on their own.[10]

The second broad administrative technique for coping—market research—involves a very different approach to the problem of risk. While use of track record talents relies on the ability of people who had previous success in the marketplace to try to repeat their success (or to judge the ability of others to repeat it), this second technique aims at probing the market itself in attempts to ensure a product's salability. We can speak about two different kinds of market research—research to get ideas for the creation of a new product and research to evaluate and alter a product that already exists or is under development. Both types can involve surveying a broad gamut of forces in the organization's environment, including patrons, investors, distributors, exhibitors, audiences, and sometimes even powerful authorities and public advocacy organizations.

Getting ideas for the creation of a new product can involve examining the results of various national "lifestyle" surveys (such as those conducted by Daniel Yankelovich), surveying members of the firm's target audience regarding their interests, or hiring consulting firms to pinpoint trends in the target audience that neither that firm nor its competitors have exploited yet. Less costly approaches might involve checking with representatives from patron, exhibitor, and distributor organizations regarding the kinds of material they would like to carry but cannot find. The suggestions can spark creators in search of ideas with good chances for success. In the adult trade book business such advice is often received by marketing personnel, who are continually on the lookout for trends they can report to their editors. Particularly helpful is advice from major patrons, the large bookstore chains like B. Dalton and Walden Books. The stores' computerized sales lists indicate book-buying trends that can signal useful directions to follow or gaps to fill in creating new products.[11].

At times, adult trade publishing executives even ask the store executives' opinions regarding a title that is under consideration or under development. Lewis Coser, Charles Kadushin, and Walter Powell point out that publishers' representatives show key chain buyers manuscripts of forthcoming books even before they are set in type.[12] Most of this kind of activitiy is not directed toward changing the content of a book, but toward judging its marketability and honing in on the number of copies to print. However, in certain special cases, a book publisher will contact some of its major patrons to ask whether they would be interested in purchasing a title or "line" (a group of titles with a similar format) that is still only on the drawing board. Marketing executives in the large mass market children's book firm that I studied did just that when they considered creating a line of paperback picture books. Before proceding with production, the executives showed some prototypes to their counterparts in major book store chains. Only when they received enthusiastic reception and even a commitment to stock the books did the new "pictureback" line get the full go-ahead.[13]

This cautious checking of developing ideas that production personnel carry out with members of powerful organizations in their firm's environment goes on in virtually every sector of every mass media industry. The checking might not take place with respect to all products (for example, each issue of a newspaper or magazine, each book title, each TV show). It is likely, though, to take place when new ventures demand long-term organizational commitment. Recall the Reader's Digest Association's tryout of its new magazine, *Families*, on advertising agency executives before proceeding toward publication. That sort of activity is increasingly common in the magazine industry, where the risk in failure is climbing steadily higher. In college textbook publishing, combining research to get ideas with research to gauge the potential of ideas is standard operating procedure, as Coser, Kadushin, and Powell observe:

> Major text houses know which texts have leading positions in the market and which lag behind: that X has 6 percent of the relevant market, and that Y has only 2 percent. Close analysis of the successful texts and the laggards alerts the publishers to the topics and styles currently in or out of fashion. Then instructors are polled about any changes they would like to see in a particular text. These data are supplemented by information gathered by college travelers. The final result is a text that is usually bland and "safe," but profitable since it has been tailored to the demands of the market.[14]

Note that here assessing "demands of the market" does not include polling the ultimate audience, the students. In text publishing, as in other areas of mass media, production personnel understand that the all-important first step toward success is getting the material in front of the audience through organizational intermediaries. The college instructor serves as an agent for the book store. He or she decides on the titles students should buy and then presents the list to the store's purchasing manager. Students typically hold only a very indirect influence on the decision to change the required book in a course. If they find a text really boring or difficulty to comprehend, classroom feedback might sway the teacher away from assigning that book and toward another one. Generally, the students have no choice but to read what is required.

In many media situations, however, the spectrum of choice directly confronting the consumer is greater than that. Even without cable television, for example, most Americans have at least four viewing choices when they want to watch their home sets—the three commercial networks and public broadcasting. The spectrum of choice in a book store or a magazine stand is usually much larger. Too, the consumer's option to use another medium or do something else is always available. Consequently, beyond checking products under development with organizations acting as patrons, exhibitors and/or distributors, creators sometimes try to test audience reaction as well. Because this kind of market research can be extremely expensive and time consuming, it is most likely to be used when the political or economic cost of a new venture promises to be high.

There are many ways of testing audience reaction to a new concept or a nearly completed product. The techniques creators commission range from in-depth interviews of a few people to superficial surveys of large numbers of people. People might be asked questions on the street, through two-way cable TVs, or on the telephone. One method that has been used by the movie industry since its early days is the screening of a film in a typical theater before its general release. The director, producer, and other creative personnel sit in the theater gauging audience reaction, and they note parts they feel should be edited differently (or even reshot) to elicit better response. Sometimes, people are asked to write comments about the film on cards that are reviewed by the creative team.

A related approach is sometimes used to test television programs or TV commercials that have not yet aired. People fitting a broad profile are solicited on the streets of New York or Los Angeles to attend a special "preview house" screening. They are shown a program of commercials and are asked to register their like or dislike of scenes by pushing one of two buttons as the material unfolds. Through their responses analysts can try to note patterns of satisfaction or objection at specific points in the show. A question and answer period after the screening helps them to pinpoint further the reason some people like or dislike certain parts. Subsequently, network executives might ask the creators to redo certain sequences to accommodate the audience suggestions.[15] A variation on this method is used in the record industry. It supposedly gauges a listener's emotional reaction to a song by measuring galvanic skin response. One aim of record company executives in commissioning such research is to prove to radio station program directors that a record has hit potential.[16]

Measuring audience reaction does not always stop when a product is placed on the market. Magazines, newspapers, television shows and other long-term projects are ripe for research that tries to find ways to make the material more attractive. Sometimes that means asking the audience in one way or another. Take local broadcast news. News programs are crucial profit centers for TV stations, and competition between news programs in nearly every major market across the country is rabid. In their competitive fervor, station managers often hire consulting firms such as McHugh and Hoffman or Frank Magid to improve their local news ratings. The consultants bring advice based on their interpretations of various kinds of audience research. Their suggestions have included, among other things, making anchor people more friendly-looking, making the program graphics crisper, shortening the length of stories, adding a larger number of stories, and in general quickening the pace and drama of the show. The results have lent a new look, tone, and content to local news across the country. It is a change that has horrified many seasoned observers of United States journalism.[17]

The television networks also conduct a good deal of research on ongoing programs. Special research departments commission studies designed to indicate why a show is not attracting more of its target audience or to sustain or overrule a creator's suggestion for a major change in the program's direction. It was this kind of research that lead creators of the series "One Day at a Time" to conclude that one of the daughters, Barbara, should remain a virgin.[18] Similarly, audience testing led CBS officials to decree that "Cagney and Lacey," a cop show about two women detectives, be "softened." An initial step was the replacement of one of the stars, whose character in the show was unmarried. A CBS programmer said the show was being revised to make the main characters less aggressive. Ron Rosenbloom, producer of the series, said he had to overcome the feeling that two women who work in a male-dominated profession could be perceived as lesbians. "Two guys, Starsky and Hutch or Redford and Newman, aren't considered fags or homos,' said Rosebloom. "They are pals, buddies. It's strange, but if it is two women, people say, 'What's going on?' I think that is unfair and unfortunate and had nothing whatever to do with the show, but it seems that some of CBS's research picked this up."[19]

These examples typify audience research in the sense that the producers, not the consumers, set the objectives and guide the question and answer agenda. Recall from Chapter Two, in fact, that an "audience" is actually a construct that evolves as a result of the producer-patron relationship. That is, when production executives speak of their audience, they speak of consumer categories and concerns that those executives and their counterparts in patron firms (but not necessarily consumers) consider important. Audience research is designed to help creators fine tune products and product ideas with the aim of improving the popularity of those products among the spectrum of choice in the marketplace. The research does not, however, invite suggestions from the audience that demand radical changes in the current system of production. If such suggestions were offered, the creators would not be able to follow them. After all, production personnel are trying to lower the risks of their activity from all sides. If they pursue notions radical to their industry sector, that might put them in hot water with their patrons and other forces in their environment. It is in creators' best interest, therefore, to keep the advice they get from ultimate consumers confined to a limited range of workable choices. In this way, audience research becomes an administrative technique that helps creators truly minimize risk both to themselves and to their organizations.[20]

Content-Based Techniques of Coping

One particularly useful aspect of the administrative techniques creators use to cope with risk is that the techniques often allow quite a bit of leeway in creating the content. The reasons the leeway is useful is that in some sectors of the mass media "quality" is identified with material that reflects the voice of an individual and that emphasizes unusual approaches to the world. Using track record talent and audience research, creators can lessen their risk in responding to this kind of environment while still fulfilling its demands. So, for example, editors in a trade book publishing firm can confidently contract with a John Updike, Norman Miler, John Irving, or James Michener to write novels, fully expecting that the book will get substantial serious critical attention in addition to earning money in advance of release through sale of the paperback rights. Too, having reviewed research on the kinds of nonfiction books chain stores expect will become popular, the editors might persuade well-known personalities with expertise in those areas to write books on those subjects. The result will be sold to critics and the public as the writer's individual accomplishment. The editors, for their part, will breathe much easier through the whole process than if the books had been written by people whose popularity in the marketplace had not been tested. The intellectual and emotional security these kinds of commissions bring might even lead publishing executives to approve a couple of manuscripts that literary agents have suggested because of their strong artistic merit. Doing that, they might feel they are fulfilling a certain literary responsibility to society. It also helps company morale.

There are, however, areas of the mass media where creators do not expect that forces in the environment require them to speak through an individual voice or emphasize unusual approaches to the world. In many areas of the mass media, too, creators perceive their social responsibility to be a different one from discovering new artists. High risk products tend overwhelmingly to fit this description. The reason seems to be that patron organizations and other forces contributing a lot of money or political capital to the creation of a product are likely to be more interested in ensuring that the product fills their monetary or political objectives than in advancing the cause of art. Network television programs and Hollywood movies fall into this class. At the same time, areas of the mass media do exist where product costs are low and individual artistry still is not emphasized. Paperback romances, pornographic novels, and pornographic films fit this category. We can suggest, then, that in most high risk situations and in some low ones, creators find it possible to routinely generate highly patterned, predictable mass media material that itself has a record of success. In these situations, administrative techniques of coping become only first steps in trying to reduce the risk of a particular item's failure in the marketplace. Risk reduction through previously tested formulas and stereotypes plays an important role as well.

Recall from Chapter Four that formulas represent widely recognized principles for selecting and organizing material. One of the tasks creators in many media organizations set for themselves is, indeed, to recognize these principles and to utilize them more successfully than their competitors. Often, recognition comes from immersing oneself in a lot of mass media material. Often, too, awareness of a formula's components comes from being part of an artistic community and listening to people talk about the way they created certain movies, books, TV programs, magazine articles, or whatever.

It does not take much brilliance to uncover some of the basic aspects of a formula. Take, for example, a list of "the best" and "the worst" of just about anything that one can see just about anywhere. They reflect a popular formula that magazine and book editors, particularly, have been scrambling to copy and make more attractive through creative subject variations. *The Book of Lists, The People's Almanac, The Book Book,* and *Esquire* magazine's yearly Dubious Achievement Awards represent just the tip of a huge iceberg. Chapter Four suggested that a nonfiction formula is characterized by subject, point of view, and the sequence in which the argument is developed. Using these categories for orientation, we find that the basic concoction for nonfiction lists seems straightforward: Find a subject that many people confront every day—restaurants, the thought of moving to another city, the need for trivia in conversation, the need for hotels when traveling, entertainment, politics—and find items to represent the best and/or the worst manifestations of that subject. Quantify the results if possible; a numerical "index" for the best and worst American cities, for example, is preferable to a simple listing. Also, stir well with a point of view that bespeaks absolute certainty and, often, urbane cynicism regarding the matter at hand. Bruce Felton and Mark Fowler describe the

tone of many of these works when, in their introduction to *Felton &*
Fowler's Best, Worst, and Most Unusual, they admit that

> The judgments offered in this book are both subjective and objective, rational
> and hysterical, serious and sardonic. In assessing their validity, you should
> bear in mind the words of Leonardo da Vinci: "I take no more notice of the
> wind that comes out of the mouths of critics than of the wind expelled from
> their backsides."[21]

This same "knowing" cynicism and sarcasm seemed to be the standard
point of view writers took up in nonjournalistic magazine discussions of
political and social trends during the 1970s and early 1980s. The approach
did not apply, however, to nonfiction formulas that reflected more
personal aspects of the target audience's life. How-to articles on cooking,
building, repairing, gardening and articles on coping with divorce, unem-
ployment, sex, parenting, and dating seemed to require a more empathic
tone. A still different tone seemed to belong in another formula, the
Hollywood star's autobiography (often written with someone else).
Whether such works carried insight or just vanity, it seemed *de rigueur* for
them to fit the following mold: Start with a key incident from the height of
the star's career. Slowly ease back toward stories of birth and upbringing.
Then move the story along through tragedies and disasters to triumph-or,
at least, to a better world today. The point of view should appear honest
and frank and self-revealing, even when it is actually none of these.[22]

Fiction materials have clear-cut formulas as well. Recall that according to John Cawelti fiction formulas can be characterized in terms of
setting, character types, and patterns of action. Cawelti uses the United
States Western as an example. The Western, he points out, is a story that
takes place on or near a United States frontier, usually at a particular
moment in the past. The setting is portrayed as "the meeting point
between civilization and savagery," and the complex of characters reflects
this confrontation.[23] There are three central roles in the Western: the
townspeople, who are the agents of civilization; the savages or outlaws who
threaten this first group; and the heroes (often cowboys), who are above all
"men in the middle." That is, they possess many qualities and skills of the
savages but are fundamentally committed to the townspeople. "It is out of
the multiple variations possible on the relationships between these groups
that the various Western plots are concocted," Cawelti notes:

> For example, the simplest version of all has the hero protecting the towns-
> people from the savages, using his own savage skills against the denizens of the
> wilderness. A second more complex variation shows the hero initially indiffe-
> rent to the plight of the townspeople and more inclined to identify himself with
> the savages. However, in the course of the story his position changes and he
> become the ally of the townspeople. This variation can generate a number of

different plots. There is the revenge Western: hero seeks revenge against an outlaw or Indian who has wronged him. In order to accomplish his vengence, he rejects the pacifistic ideals of the townspeople, but in the end he discovers that he is really committed to their way of life (John Ford's *The Searchers*). Another plot based on this variation of the character relations is that of the hero who initially seeks his own selfish material gain, using his savage skills as a means to this end; but, as the story progresses, he discovers his moral involvement with the townspeople and becomes their champion (cf. Anthony Mann's film *The Far Country*). It is also possible, while maintaining this system of relationships, to reverse the conclusion of the plot as in those stories where the townspeople come to accept the hero's savage mode of action (cf. John Ford's *Stagecoach* or, to a certain extent, Wister's *The Virginian*). A third variation of the basic scheme of relationships has the hero caught in the middle between the townspeople's need for his savage skills and their rejection of his way of life. This third variation, common in recent Westerns, often ends in the destruction of the hero (cf. the films *The Gunfighter* or *Invitation to a Gunfighter*) or in his voluntary exile (*Shane, High Noon, Two Rode Together*).[24]

Clearly, combining the three elements of the Western in different ways can yield a multitude of stories. Clearly, too, Cawelti believes that the people producing the Western in any medium are quite conscious of the building blocks they should use to generate plots. He notes that Frank Gruber, a veteran writer of pulp magazine Westerns, argued that there are seven basic Western plots.[25] Interviews with other writers and with film directors of Westerns also reveal people who have tried hard to develop a strong understanding of the form. In some media organizations, though, selectors are not content to rely on artists to pick up the most effective approaches to certain kinds of material fully on their own. Instead, company executives draw up written guidelines. Here, from the mid-1970s, are some notations by a writer of pornographic novels on the approach his publisher expected him to take:

It [i.e., the pornography] is aimed at the male market and is written to formula. There are seven basic story categories: incest (the single most popular genre), lesbianism, Lolita plots, domination, older woman/younger man, career girl plots, and straying from the marriage.

The publisher's style sheet advises: "The plots of our stories should involve a sexual problem of some sort...the denouement, a solution. How the characters get there is what it's all about.... What this means is that we don't want detective stories with a lot of sex [or] westerns with a lot of sex.... We want explicitly written, highly erotic novels of real people's experiences.... We CANNOT consider the following themes: Male homosexuality, child molestation, bestiality, excretion, violent sadomasochism, or murder as part of the sex act. ALL CHARACTERS INVOLVED SEXUALLY MUST BE AT LEAST FIFTEEN YEARS OF AGE."[26]

The discussion of fiction formulas has revolved around books and movies until now. Note, however, that the use of formulas to reduce risk has fueled many different areas of mass communication. This was true, for example, regarding certain kinds of poetry back in the nineteenth century; it was likewise true about popular music of that day. Historian Russell Nye has pointed out that music publishers of the 1860s and 1870s tended to divide the types of songs they accepted into eight categories: love, family, reform or moral, religious, comedy, minstrel, tragedy, and topical.[27] Such a classification system proved useful since it allowed publishers to evaluate ups and downs of particular categories in the marketplace and thereby have an effective approach to dealing with songwriters. Nicholas Tawa's research on the nineteenth century love song suggests, too, that each song category implied certain settings, characterizations, and patterns of action that publishers should expect in evaluating new songs.[28]

Since that time, the mainstream music world has become much more stratified. Some areas—such as parts of the progressive rock scene—place greater emphasis than others on idiosyncratic artistry and unusual approaches to the world. We would expect that in areas where artistic departures from the norm hold rather significant sway, producers would turn primarily toward administrative routines (in particular, the consideration of track record), not formulas, to cope with risk. There are, however, many areas of the music industry where selectors and artists try to spring toward success with variations on tried and true approaches to words and music.

This is particularly the case with respect to singles. Singles are typically songs that are released with the hope they will get played on "Top 40" radio stations and, doing so, fuel the sales of albums. Because of the importance of singles for album sales in many cases, and because of the high risk of failure in getting airplay (most releases do not get significant exposure on radio), singles will often be the most formularized of all cuts on an album.[29] As R. Serge Denisoff notes, record producers are well aware that program directors and music hit predictors are sent enormous quantities of material. As a result, they sometimes listen to only the first three seconds of a song to decide whether they should select it as "hit bound."[30] Formulas are considered crucial. Here is part of the way Clive Davis, a powerful executive at CBS and then Arista Records during the 1960s, 1970s, and 1980s, described the general singles formula:

> A hit single is a question of musical ingredients—they've all got to be in place and they've got to complement each other. You start with the "hook," a basic, repetitive melody or lyric line that grabs hold of the listener. In lyrics, the safest theme, naturally, is love or lost love.... Ideally, the lyric *and* melody combine within the hook to make this line something nearly impossible to forget. But hooks come in all sorts of rhythmic, melodic and lyrical shapes and sizes. Think of hit instrumentals...

When I hear a song, my mind works like a computer. The "hit" ingredients register in it, and they are shunted off to various preprogrammed compartments for analysis. Voice is terribly important. Certain kinds of voices *don't* lend themselves to Top Forty play....[31]

One of the reasons the concept of formula is helpful for understanding the production of mass media material is that it reflects an approach that is clearly recognized and used by many creators. Note, through, that just because creators search out and follow previously successful formulas does not mean they cannot or do not develp their own artistic personalities or styles. Horace Newcomb and Robert Alley, for example, take pains to emphasize that commercial television producers "clearly aware of the limitations [the industry imposes on them], work within, around, and through them to achieve creative goals."[32] Certainly, artists and other creators who become successful members of their artistic community might develop reputations for working in a particular style or reflecting a particular view of life. In TV, Bruce Geller, Aaron Spelling, David Victor, Frank Glicksman, Gary Marshall, Quinn Martin, George Schlatter, Norman Lear, Herbert Brodkin, and David Wolper are just a few examples of executive producers whose programs reflect a certain "personality." These are individuals whose approaches resonated with the needs of their industry at the time in which they worked. Most, such as Victor ("Dr. Kildare," "Marcus Welby, M. D.," "Owen Marshall"), Webb ("Dragnet," "Adam 12"), Spelling ("Charlie's Angels," "Hart to Hart," "Starsky and Hutch"), Glicksman ("Medical Center," "Trapper John, M. D."), Martin ("The FBI," "Barnaby Jones"), Marshall ("Mork and Mindy," "Happy Days"), and Geller ("Mission Impossible," "Mannix") either helped to develop certain formulas as the industry developed or refurbished old approaches with highly successful sheens.[33] Others—Lear ("All in the Family," "Maude") and Schlatter ("Laugh-In," "That's Incredible")come to mind—had to battle network executives to get their ideas accepted. Because those ideas proved insightful, they ignited a rash of imitations. The presence of Wolper and Brodkin on the list underscores the notion that production companies exploit different niches in their industrial environments. Some TV production firm heads choose to mine the most popular areas of action, providing the networks with bread-and-butter material stamped with their track records and styles. Others, like Herbert Brodkin and David Wolper, have chosen to be more selective about their activities and contribute the "prestige" programming the networks need once in a while. Brodkin's "Holocaust" and "The Missiles of October" and Wolper's "Roots" are examples. All these people and their firms, however, are keenly aware of their industry and the nature of its acceptable forms.

Two ideas that creators generally recognize as related to the formula are the *series* and the *serial*. A series is a collection of individual products (books, magazines, movies, TV shows) that have the same key characters moving through separate adventures in each product. A bit different is the serial, wherein the same key characters move through continuing episodes of adventures across the products; the serial is a kind of chapter play. We see series and serials all the time. TV's "Star Trek" is a series, while the *Star Wars* movie odyssey is a serial. The "Peanuts" newspaper comic strip is a series, while the "Doonesbury" strip is a serial. Other examples are within easy reach.

It is also easy to discover why creators might consider series and serials useful to their work. For one thing, start-up costs of episodes in an ongoing series or serial are lower than those in a new product. Thinking up new heroes, new villains, and new ways to inject life into old formulas is more time-consuming than simply putting a few new ornaments on an established frame. In television, having the same actors, crew, locations, and props for every episode makes production a lot less expensive than producing a new program from scratch every week or every day. Moreover, if early episodes of a series or serial catch on, producers can rest more easily about the chances that other episodes will succeed. Sometimes, in fact, stand-alone products do so well that creators cannot resist the opportunity to convert them into series. For example, in 1950 Universal Pictures' *Francis the Talking Mule*, based on a book by David Stern, was a runaway success. That movie begat *Francis Goes to the Races* (1951) which begat *Francis Goes to West Point* (1952) which begat *Francis Joins the WAC* (1954) which begat *Francis in the Navy* (1955) which begat *Francis in the Haunted House* (1956). The first five films were directed by Arthur Lubin, who went on to create a similar series for TV called "Mr. Ed" about a talking horse.[34]

There is an ironic flip side to the efficiency and risk reduction possibilities in series and serials. When the cost of several episodes must be allocated in advance, failure might involve much greater cost than would any particular product that stood alone. That is the problem television program producers and their networks face on a continual basis. When a series "hits," it can be a huge, consistent moneymaker for many years, but when it fails the cash and airtime already committed to it can drain network resources badly. As a consequence, the commercial networks have evolved an elaborate chain of strategies to develop, test, and schedule series so as to maximize their chances for success.[35] In searching for a series idea, production executives and their network counterparts say they look for material they can call "refreshing," "exciting," and "different." At particularly honest moments, they also admit that the best ideas they find will echo material already popular on TV or in other media. This contradictory approach leads them to combine a strong reliance on popular formulas with attempts to find interesting variations on those formulas that

will stand up over many episodes. Consider, for example, the arrival on
NBC television in 1967 of a formularized police-detective series called
"Ironside". Its chief novelty (or gimmick) was that the title character was
confined to a wheelchair. "Ironsides"'s high popularity over the next few
years led other producers and networks to build police or detective series
about protagonists with other handicaps. "Longstreet" (1971) was a blind
insurance investigator; "Cannon" (1971) was a fat private eye; and
"Barnaby Jones" (1973) was an aging detective.

Note that the search for the right formula-based material with the
staying power to make a successful series is not new with television or the
movies. The series was a clear part of popular American theater from the
early 1800s, and it was used extensively in magazines and books of that
century.[36] Here, for example, is a fascinating letter that Ormond Smith,
head of the powerful Street and Smith publishing firm, wrote to Gilbert
Patten. At the time, the 1890s, Patten was a well-known writer of juvenile
dime novels. Smith's purpose was to hire Patten to write a new series (or
"library") of juvenile books for the company:

December 16, 1895

Gilbert Patten, Esq.,
Camden, Maine.

Dear Sir:

Replying to your favor of December 13, at hand today, we beg to state
that the material of which we wrote you in our last letter is intended for a
library which we propose issuing every week; something in the line of the Jack
Harkaway, Gay Dashleigh series which we are running in *Good News* and the
Island School Series, all of which are expressed to you under separate cover,
the idea being to issue a library containing a series of stories covering this class
of incident, in all of which will appear one prominent character surrounded by
suitable satellites. It would be an advantage to the series to have introduced
the Dutchman, the Negro, the Irishman, and any other dialect you are familiar
with. From what we know of your work, we believe you can give us what we
require, and would be pleased to have you write us one of these stories at once.
Upon receipt of it, if satisfactory, we will be prepared to make a contract with
you to cover twenty thousand words weekly for this library and a sufficient
number of *Good News* stories to keep them running in the columns of *Good
News*, if you believe you can turn out this amont of work.

It is important that the main character in the series should have a catchy
name, such as Dick Lightheart, Jack Harkaway, Gay Dashleigh, Don Kirk [a
character in two previous stories by Patten], as upon this name will depend the
title for the library.

The essential idea of this series is to interest young readers in the career of
a young man at a boarding school, preferably a military or a naval academy.
The stories should differ from the Jack Harkaways in being American and

thoroughly up to date. Our idea is to issue, say, twelve stories, each complete in itself, but like the links in a chain, all dealing with life at the academy. By this time the readers will have become sufficiently well acquainted with the hero and the author will also no doubt have exhausted most of the pranks and escapades that might naturally occur.

After the first twelve numbers, the hero is obliged to leave the academy, or takes it upon himself to leave. It is essential that he should come into a considerable amount of money at this period. When he leaves the academy he takes with him one of the professor's servants, a chum. In fact any of the characters you have introduced and made prominent in the story. A little love element would also not be amiss, though this is not particularly important.

When the hero is once projected on his travels there is an infinite variety of incidents to choose from. In the Island School Series, published by one of our London connections, you will find scenes of foreign travel, with color. This material you are at liberty to use freely, with our hero as the central character, of course, and up-to-date dialogue.

After we run through twenty or thirty numbers of this, we would bring the hero back and have him go to college—say, Yale University; thence we could take him on his travels again to the South Seas or anywhere.

If you can do the opening stories of school life, you will be able to do them all, as we shall assist you in the matter of local color for the stories of travel.

This letter will, of course, be held as confidential. After you have fully examined the Island School material, kindly return to us.

Yours truly,
Ormond Smith[37]

Smith's reference to "the Dutchman, the Negro and the Irishman" brings to the fore another content-based device creators of mass media material use to cope with risk: the stereotype. A stereotype is the portrayal of an identifiable social group in such a way that members of that group are consistently invested with certain personality characteristics and social activities. The Dutchman (actually, *Deutschman*, the German), the Negro, and the Irish man were butts of comedy in many turn-of-the-century novels, magazines, films, and records.[38] Much has been written of the invidious characterizations that ethnic, racial, or other groups in society have suffered in popular culture through the years. In Chapter Four, we noted that such portrayals pictorialize the groups' relationships to society's hierarchy from the perspective of elites. Here the purpose is to point to an important organizational basis for the perpetuation of stereotypes in mass media material. Simply put, stereotypes are vehicles for getting work done quickly, efficiently, and with a lower risk of individual failure than would otherwise be the case.

Of course, today's mass media creators often recognize that the sensitivity and clout of various public advocacy organizations have, along with other social changes, turned some kinds of stereotypes into political liabilities for their firms. In the commercial television networks, in fact, censors routinely review scripts and completed programs to guard against obvious and consistent negative portrayals of individuals belonging to particular groups. Blacks, Native Americans, homosexuals, older people, and women have made them especially sensitive to certain injustices during the past several years. Nevertheless, many studies show that stereotypes are alive and kicking on television and in other mass media for these and other social groups. In the case of depictions that have been challenged by the most vocal opponents of social typing, the activity is much more subtle than before. The stereotyping of these populations is sometimes indicated by their virtual absence from a medium except where a certain "ethnic" or "special" characterization (often a "positive" one) appears to be needed.[39] This approach seems particularly prevalent in prime time TV's portrayals of older people, Native Americans, Mexican Americans, and homosexuals. When a social group does not have a strong advocacy body—as, for example, in the case of Orientals, gypsies, and until recently Arabs— media do not tread so lightly.[40] Even producers with great qualms about political liabilities have borrowed from a storehouse of unfavorable cultural images—foreign, secretive, alluring, dangerous, deceptive—to evoke certain moods and accomplish certain symbolic tasks with those groups.

We should note that stereotyping is by no means limited to ethnic and racial groups. Certain physical characteristics and occupational labels are quite often associated with personality characteristics and social activities. Overweight people, short people, people with glasses, blue collar workers, private detectives, police, physicians, nurses, high school teachers, college professors—these and other labels often ignite standard characterizations on television, in movies, and in formula-based paperbacks. In the early 1980s, commercial network television's Saturday morning cartoons for children were brimming with physical, occupational, and voice-created stereotypes. Ironically, that situation prevailed even as the networks responded to advocacy group pressures aimed at eliminating racial and sex-linked prejudices and at injecting explicit educational messages into the programming.[41]

Writers concerned about stereotyped portrayals have tended to speculate that the images are due primarily to conscious or unconscious personal decisions made by those engaged in the creation of characters. In the mid-1970s, for example, Amy Leifer, Neal Gordon, and S. B. Graves stated that just as a woman aware of the need to assert herself at a business meeting "sometimes slips back into a more passive, stereotypically female role," so "stereotyped [TV] programming probably often occurs in an unconscious way" as a result of the biases of writers, producers, and directors.[42] What we have been leading to in the past few pages, however, is that while the unconscious biases of writers, producers, directors, editors, and other creative personnel may well support media stereotyping, industrial reasons are even more crucial for the perpetuation of these patterned images. When time is short, when costs of a creator's failure are high, and when organizational and interorganizational reward systems are such that unusual approaches that reflect idiosyncratic talents are not valued highly, we might expect that artists would welcome images that are easy to generate and work with. We might expect that they would feel that characterization is, after all, but one important task among many important tasks and that it has to be dealt with as efficiently as possible.

Consider, for example, the many steps that creators of a television drama series must carry out simply to choose actors for small parts.[43] Small parts are parts not involving more than a few scenes and a few pages of dialogue. Despite their brevity, these role are important to TV creators. They feel that the minor characters who surround major protagonists of television dramas form a large part of the landscape of people that unfolds daily on TV and helps anchor the dramas to "real life" locations. Choosing actors for small parts is particularly important since television writers generally introduce small parts with a minimum of physical description and the casting process is needed to paint the landscape. After the producer accepts the script, talent agents are allowed to search through it for roles that might be appropriate for their actor-clients. In the late 1970s, when I investigated this subject in detail, the script was also sent to a commercial "breakdown" service, which abstracted the character descriptions and circulated them among subscribing talent agents.

While the talent agent is getting the scripts or script encapsulations, the show's casting director is charged with composing a suggestion list of possible actors for every small part. The list is frequently formulated after consulting the on-line producer and the episode's director; the executive producer rarely interferes. They clarify their conceptions of each part and the type of person (sometimes even the particular person) they want for it. Upon completion, the casting director's list is presented to the on-line producer and director. They make some choices immediately and ask that a few candidates for other roles come to the studio to try out for the parts. Final selections are made after these readings.

At the base of guidelines for this operation is the reward system creators collectively perceive. The twenty-seven producers and directors I interviewed pointed out that their job in creating series dramas is to tell entertaining tales that will reach millions of people in a visually appealing manner. All agreed on the importance of small part casting to telling their stories. All could relate incidents where "improper" casting had ruined a scene by destroying its mood and sense of reality. Because of the importance of such casting, the selectors have evolved the procedure of measuring their choices against two general (often implicit) guidelines— *credibility* (a caster's perception of what most people think someone in a particular occupation or role looks like) and *visual balance* (the caster's perception of how well actors fit next to one another from an aesthetic standpoint). With regard to decisions of credibility, the people I interviewed admitted they really do not know what most people think. Most claimed others will believe a portrayal if they and their colleagues believe it. Some said that certain notions of credibility have been part of casting operations since the early days of film. All emphasized that choices based on credibility must reflect the nature of the scene, its location, and the character ("quality") of the actor needed for the small part. They noted that in many cases a small part is simply a propellant of plot activity and should not draw attention to itself. In such situations, the most common "clichés" (the term casters use for stereotypes) are desirable. The following comments by an on-line producer were representative of this subject in the late 1970s:

> You have to recognize what the audience can buy instantaneously. Unless it's a plot point. Because if you have somebody walk in as a police officer, the audience should [snap fingers] accept him as a police officer. Unless you're doing a whodunit where everybody is suspect. So you look for where he is walking. I mean, you could have a little more effeteness in a policeman in Beverly Hills than you could in Watts. By a damn sight, you would be far more likely to accept a white or Chicano policeman in Beverly Hills than a black policeman.... Why should I start arguments in a living room or den between husband and wife? I mean, why make a point out of something that's not a point? Carpenters are male. Telephone operators are female. Now, there are a lot of male telephone operators now. But not enough so that when you say "telephone operator," the immediate thought isn't female.

Visual balance was also perceived as necessary to carry forth basic dramatic premises most effectively. One producer commented that "if you have your hero fighting in a shootout, you'd better cast a guy who's a little bigger than your hero, not someone who's going to make the hero look like a bully." In the casting session that I attended, the producer and directors chose a stout woman to play a nurse because they felt her shape would supply a pleasing contrast to the short and heavy "maid" who had already been selected to play a scene with her. Other examples of visual balance that people I interviewed mentioned often included a caution against casting actors who look too much alike (barring a plot-related necessity) and a rule that at least one guest of the opposite sex should be a very attractive vehicle for the lead to "play off of."

The interviewees contended that when a small part is not simply a propellant of plot activity, a casting director can add depth or appropriate color to a scene by casting against the most obvious cliche. However, most admitted that the short time a casting director often has to compose a list, present it to his or her superiors, and choose people for the parts militates against such creativity. Casting directors lamented that while a series episode might have six or seven days of preparation time, script changes and problems of finding feature players before small roles can be cast often force last-minute casting decisions for small parts. Moreover, in one of the busiest Los Angeles studios a casting director often works on three programs at a time.

A general consequence of the need to cast against the clock and to produce a show within a tight budget is the reliance by directors and casting directors upon a pool of dependable actors for most small parts. Although the casters I interviewed use different personal filing systems, all those systems are aimed at associating actors with parts for which they were chosen or suggested in the past. This procedure ensures the caster's ability to choose quickly and credibly. It also results in patterned looks for certain parts.

Another procedure fostered by the need to save time that encourages stereotyped casting is the designation of every *program* by its "look" (its "storytelling style," in the words of one producer) so those involved in suggesting actors for parts will know quickly what types are needed. Casters spoke of "beautiful people," "real people," and "street people" shows and in those terms encompassed the different perspectives stressed in different story-telling styles. They agreed that "street people programs" like "Baretta" and "Kojak" required "grubby," "ethnic-looking" types for most parts while shows like "Quincy" and "Police Woman" have "real" people who are "a step above the grubbiness of 'Baretta'." Interestingly, several interviewees pointed out that a "beautiful people" show will often not cast beautiful people in the small parts. Speaking of shows like "Charlie's Angels" and "The Bionic Woman," they said the deliberate predominance of handsome actors in lead and feature roles often guided a decision to use "character" types in lesser roles to balance the program visually and give it a more believable appearance.

From a personal standpoint, this approach undoubtedly derives from sharing the same dominant societal perspectives, living in the same Los Angeles environment, and viewing television; five people I interviewed remarked that TV is an important source for their notions of credibility. However, ideas about the types of people suitable for certain roles and the circumstances in which departures from traditional notions are acceptable are further reinforced through the web of relationships in the Hollywood community—that is, through the continual interaction of production personnel and talent representatives with each other. Casting directors, for example, placed importance on knowing the preferences of producers and directors. All seemed to support one casting director's comment that "I'll always give them somebody they're happy with; I don't want any problems."

Talent agents evidenced a similar inclination in trying to get actors jobs. They understood that time pressures often cause casting directors to rely on their own "repertory companies" and ignore agent offers. Nevertheless, talent agents said they do submit suggestions to friendly casting directors and directors who respect their judgment. The following remarks by an agent about age considerations in casting show how adherence to generally perceived rules often discourages nontraditional suggestions:

> Oh, they list [age in the breakdown] and they sometimes stick to it and sometimes don't. What I do when I make up my list [to be sent to the casting director]—if they say 30, I'll give them anything from 25 to 35.
>
> DO YOU FIND MOST AGE REQUESTS STOP AT 35?
> For men, there are a great number of roles over 40. Women over 40—not many, obviously.
>
> WHY IS THAT?
> Well, there's just not that much call for them. Because of the story lines. The story lines are always dealing with heavies, with troubles in situations. It's always men involved. Whether he's a banker, a doctor, or a lawyer, a Mafia chief, whatever.
>
> UNDER WHAT CONDITIONS WOULD YOU SUGGEST A WOMAN IF THE BREAKDOWN SAID "BANKER?"
> I wouldn't, because it would say "he."
>
> DO YOU SEE "HE" AS NECESSARILY DENOTING A MALE?
> Oh sure, I even look down [the breakdown page] for the "he" or "she" to see which [part] starts with "he" or "she." They say "all roles will be considered regardless of ethnic group, sex, et cetera." That's baloney. Well, sometimes you can take a role and if it's not in the script you can turn it from white to black.
>
> WILL UNUSUAL CASTING NOTIONS AFFECT YOUR STANDING WITH CASTING DIRECTORS?
> You don't send them in. What I do, if I have an offbeat idea, to protect myself. You say, "you know, I got an idea; you probably won't even like it. It's really off, far out..." And you protect yourself. If they like it—"terrific!" If they don't, "Yeah, it really was offbeat."

INTEGRATING CHANGE INTO ROUTINES

The quote above implies that "offbeat" casting ideas do sometimes get accepted. In fact, throughout the discussion of administrative and content-based techniques for coping with risk, the idea that change occurs even in high risk material has been a strong undercurrent. Of course, in one sense change must always take place. Every time a new media product is generated, that product must be different from previous ones. Spelling-Goldberg Productions, for example, could not get away with making exactly the same episodes of "The Love Boat" for TV week after week during its run in the late 1970s and early 1980s. Even with a placid, predictable marketplace, creators must follow their routines to pursue the kind of novelty that falls within their boundaries of acceptability. Those boundaries may well be denoted by formulas and stereotypes.

But some formulas may be more popular with audiences at certain times that at other times. Creators try to keep abreast of such trends; the most aggressive try to set trends or at least catch up with them early. So, changes in production might ensue as a result of certain fads or cycles of popularity. Also, for the sake of novelty and audience interest creators pursue new wrinkles in the formulas. They use the formulas to examine current social tensions or public concerns. And, they explore new aspects of stereotypes and form new combinations of settings, characters, and plots. Even so formularized a show as "The Love Boat" set forth on a "new," albeit predictable, voyage with each episode.[44] Too, when Spelling-Goldberg created another series based on the same light comedy/anthology formula, the firm's creators did vary the elements on the recipe a little. Each week, "The Love Boat" told three disconnected stories of three couples who fell in love or back toward love while on a cruise under the solicitous eyes of the ship captain and his crew. "Fantasy Island," by contrast, told two disconnected stories of people who learned to understand themselves or their loved ones at a magical vacation resort under the solicitous eyes of a wizardlike host and his staff.

As we said, minimal changes are required by even a placid marketplace. It hardly needs mentioning, though, that marketplaces are often not placid. To the contrary, part of them are often quite stormy. Various sections of this book have described how environmental conditions or demands can sometimes lead to substantial changes in the material a mass media organization produces. Under such extreme circumstances, top-level production executives initiate decisions that often mean altering the entire direction of the organization, including the content it creates. When that happens, new creators are often hired, new general policies are set, and the organization starts down a very different path.

There are many other less momentous times, however, when changes in a production firm's relationships with exhibitors, distributors, patrons, experts, artists, authorities, auxiliaries, unions, linking pins, facilitators, public advocacy organizations, and members of the public raise the issue of injecting approaches to content the producer has not tried before. Desire to try the unconventional occasionally originates with creators themselves. The creators might perceive a world of changing values and shifting political positions. They might want to reflect these changes not just through typical channels but also in approaches to the creative process that neither they nor their competition have tried, or that the organization's top executives have previously vetoed. Too, some unusual artists in the firm might have "wacky" ideas they want the chance to "run with." And, sometimes these ideas might come up by accident in the course of creation.

For ever wary top production executives, through, the problem with accepting ideas that do not fit general policy is that they might upset a delicate equilibrium through which they have managed to satisfy the organization's many powerful constituencies to at least a livable extent. Unconventionally creative actions, they fear, might ignite a chain reaction in which all the major forces in the organization's environment might grow angry about some aspect of their project. Conflict and confusion might reign. From their point of view, then, it becomes imperative to minimize changes in organization routines so as to minimize the loss of their organization's ability to act efficiently and successfully. When pressures for change come from the outside, executives can sometimes block them by creating buffers between creators and the unconventional demands of external forces. Examples of various performance programs that are dispersed throughout earlier chapters illustrate this approach. Other times, however, the organizations that demand change are powerful enough to force top production executives to confront the need for actually altering some approaches to material they produce. In such situations, they and other creators tend to respond as cautiously as possible. They try to implement changes they feel are necessary to satisfy the demands, but in such a way as not to change the tried the true approaches they feel form the basis of past success.

As earlier chapters noted, the changes that ensue might not be the kinds of changes the organizations or individuals doing the pressuring expected. Even demands for changes that carry profound societal implications may get transformed and defused (coopted) to fit with the flow and perspective (and particularly the core policy) of the rest of the material. Here we can illustrate the way these unexpected changes happen by continuing the discussion of small part casting in the television industry. All casters were aware of vocal and consistent demands by advocacy organizations and unions for more minorities and women in acting jobs and for greater social visibility of these populations on television. Commenting on these demands, the interviewees evidenced strong ambivalence. On the one hand, they generally professed liberal political inclinations and a desire to help blacks, Mexican Americans, Orientals, the aging, and women to increase their numbers and status on TV; most contended that blacks have to a large degree already succeeded. On the other hand, casters lamented that pressure groups have made it more difficult for them to adhere to credibility and visual balance guidelines while coping with constraints of time in the confines of an established web of casting relationships and talent pools.

The interviewees' examples of submitting women or minority actors for roles typically played by white males reflected explicit or implicit rules that help them respond to pressures for "unusual" casting through their traditional routines. Many of the "offbeat" ideas were actually quite in conformance with visual balance. For example, two casting directors spoke of selecting a woman to play the small part of a judge if the defendant is a child and the implied maternal relationship can lend interest to the scene. When visual balance was not the reason for unusual selection, casters said their choices were motivated by the urge to "help out" minorities, to dampen criticism by pressure groups, or to find parts for favored individuals.

These reasons seemed to explain minority selections during the casting session I attended in 1977. The producer instructed his casting director that a (female) nurse should be "black or old—but not both." The casting director independently included a young, spectacled black actor he had recently met among the three men reading for a hospital technician part. The actor was chosen, but not before the director and producer questioned if the ratio of minority to majority players in the episodes—six nonwhites and twelve whites—were not too high.

These examples illustrate a key strategy casters mentioned regarding "offbeat" selection: the choice should fall *within popular conceptions of a group's possibilities* while not portraying the group in an explicitly negative fashion. One casting director, echoing the consensus on ethnic casting, said "you have to be careful if it's a mad racist, that you don't make it ethnic for its own sake, for shock value.... And, of course, if the ethnic actor would be in an inappropriate setting or if he would draw attention to the scene, then you tag it. You don't do it that way. But if there's no reason not to... then you go ahead and do it." Four interviewees noted that some initially unconventional and accidental decisions may become part of a caster's repertoire and spread throughout the industry, particularly if the choices are seen to fit emerging notions of credibility and can be used to forestall pressure group criticisms. In this way, new clichés are established. One director described the phenomenon this way:

> ... if I make the right choice [of an unusual looking actor] the conception of the character changes. And that actor has a new career. See, the thing is that whenever a producer or director—whoever makes the decision—breaks a mold, it suddenly becomes a new mold.

Risking the Unconventional

These casting examples illustrate the way in which organizational routines often help channel unconventional demands for content change into material that does not disrupt the production firm's approach to material. It also illustrates the way creators convert perceptions of change in their society into grist for their preset approaches to reality. There are, however, circumstances where substantially unusual material does emerge from a production organization. The material we are talking about may be unusual only in the context of that industry sector. Moreover, the changes it brings are not of the kind that immediately and traumatically alters a large spectrum of the organization's product. Nevertheless, the material does represent considerable risk for top executives and other creators who are involved.

A familiar example is the television series "All in the Family," which began its run on the CBS network in January 1971. Right from its start critics and viewers realized that here was a situation comedy that in several ways challenged the approaches they expected from "the most popular art." Here was a series in which the main character was a bigot, who every week was involved in situations that allowed him to go after a variety of racial and ethnic groups, using words previously forbidden by the Television Code: Hebe, coon, spade, wop, kike, Polack, and others. Critics and advocacy group spokespeople divided fiercely on the program's social value and social danger.[45] All, however, recognized that it had elements that were unconventional for United States television. Robert Lewis Shayon, the *Saturday Review*'s perceptive TV critic, called the series "a unique experience in television viewing."[46]

What are the conditions that impel creators in a television production firm and a network, essentially partners in the decisions and costs of production and distribution, to take such unconventional risks? Daniel Marquis, in the tradition of other sociologists, generalizes regarding the conditions leading to both conventional and unconventional novelty.[47] He states that a production firm's response to routine demands for innovation by forces in its environment typically results in a certain level of new products that is conventional for that firm in that industry. For example, in the television industry, where fierce competiton for ratings encourages at least two "seasons" a year with new fare, the three commercial networks have program development departments to help production firms design new shows along traditional lines. By contrast, says Marquis, unconventional innovations by a firm are produced in response to what, for that firm, is an extraordinary (that is, unpredicted and nonroutine) problem or development. An extraordinary problem might be a severe sales drop. An unusual development might be the appointment of an individual to an important position. Studies have shown that many times newly appointed leaders show a greater desire than older ones to accumulate or exhibit power by taking risks and succeeding.

Other factors related to unconventional innovation are the size of the firm and the degree to which the firm is in the mainstream of its industry. Marquis implies, and C. Johnson explicitly states, that large organizations tend to take a lot longer to consider and implement unconventional suggestions than they do to consider and implement mundane ones.[48]

Everett Rogers and R. Rogers argue that one important reason for this difference is an inflexibility and a hesitancy to take risks that often develops among executives who control the routine communication channels by which organizational policy is made.[49] They suggest that unusual ideas that find acceptance often have been moved through the organization by atypical agents, connections, and procedures. In the same vein, Marquis, in agreement with Charles Perrow and A. Downs, points out that relatively unestablished organizations have been more likely to come up with unconventional innovations than have large firms in the center of their industries.[50] The reason, Marquis suggests, is that "technical people within [the center of] industry are apt to be preoccupied by short-term concerns ...cost cutting, quality control, expanding the product line, and the like."[51] The staff of unestablished firms, with no large product lines to protect and expand, is more likely to concentrate on unusual problems and daring possibilities.

Recall that a production firm is ordinarily dependent upon outlets for presentation of its innovations to consumers. Outlet receptivity to innovation would likely be of special concern to production firms in an industry where a small number of powerful outlets purchase the great percentage of a producer's material. This situation holds true in the television industry, where three commercial networks license most of the shows that production firms create. Therefore, it is important to point out that although the factors just mentioned suggest reasons for the generation of program innovation within production firms, they need only be rephrased slightly to predict situations under which outlets would search for, and accept, innovations from those producers. For TV, then, it is likely that unexpected tension-inducing changes that affect networks, production firms, or the relationships between the two, will have crucial consequences for the inception, development, and release of unconventional innovations. Note that the argument here is not that all shows produced under such circumstances will be unconventional, or even that such circumstances are bound to lead to unconventional shows. Rather, the hypothesis is that when unconventional programs do arise, they will arise from those conditions.

A study I conducted to compare the genesis of 3 conventional network TV programs with the genesis of 3 unconventional ones released around the same time and on the same networks strongly supported most of these ideas.[52] A graduate student, Trice Buzzanell, and I chose 6 programs after an analysis of about 2,000 television reviews and many articles that appeared in the trade journal *Variety* from 1965 through 1980. Our objective was to determine the shows people in the TV industry described as unconventional or very innovative. Only 26 series and specials fit these labels. We selected 3—"All in the Family", "Rowan and Martin's Laugh-In", and "United States"—for study. We then paired each of these with a conventional series that appeared around the same time on the same network—"Kraft Music Hall," "Arnie," and "Facts of Life," respectively. Our hope was that the comparative case study would yield ideas that could be tested further with respect to television as well as with respect to other mass media industries. Rather than review the details of the investigation, which is available elsewhere, it might be more useful to convey the flavor of its findings regarding unconventional shows by recounting the emergence of "All in the Family."

In interviews, CBS programmers recalled their strong ambivalence about accepting and scheduling "All in the Family," which the network began to air in January, 1971. Indeed, at first glance CBS was, as Richard Adler has observed. "the network least likely to broadcast" the series, startling as it was in its direct confrontation with bigotry and its use of racial and ethnic slurs never before heard on television. The network had perennially led NBC and ABC in the ratings by striving for audience loyalty through a stable of proven stars in proven vehicles. In 1970, however, CBS sought a program that departed from its traditional style, for two related reasons. One was the presence of a new network president, Robert Wood. Wood, despite a very limited experience in programming (he had been station manager at KNXT), was ambitious to show his leadership in the most visible of network areas—the selection and scheduling of prime time series. The second reason was Wood's belief that while CBS was first in the overall ratings, it was falling behind NBC and ABC in reaching a population segment that was becoming increasingly important to advertisers: young (18- to 49-year-old) urban adults. In a speech to his west coast development staff, Wood let it be known that he was willing to take a chance on something different, something with "ruby dust" that would begin to redefine the network's image and audience.

It happened that around that time Norman Lear and Bud Yorkin already *had* something that people in the industry deemed different from anything on American TV—a show they called "All in the Family." Lear and Yorkin had worked successfully (as a writer and producer, respectively) in television during the 1950s, and in 1959 they had joined forces. Their firm's initial TV venture, a dramatic series called "Band of Gold," was a failure. However, they proved modestly successful through the decade with theatrical films (*Come Blow Your Horn, Divorce American Style, and The Night They Raided Minsky's*). In 1968, shortly after completing *Minsky's*, Lear came across an article in *Variety* about "Till Death Do Us Part," a hit British comedy series about a bigot constantly at odds with his family, especially his son-in-law. Intrigued by the idea, and energized with an identification of the bigot with his father, Lear acquired the American rights to develop a series based on the show. With his agent from Creative Management Associates (CMA), he proposed the idea to development executives at ABC. The network's president, Marty Starger, liked Lear's "treatment" (his general idea for the show and his notes describing the characters), and he gave it the go-ahead for a pilot. It was shot in January 1969. When ABC executives saw the pilot, however, they became concerned the program was too controversial to air. Eventually, they rejected a second pilot as well. Neither version had done well in audience tests, and the executives decided the overall concept was just too risky for commercial television.

After the ABC rejection, Lear and Yorkin went back to making movies. Lear, who was finishing direction of his first movie, *Cold Turkey*, was offered a three-picture deal with United Artists. A film version of "All in the Family" was under serious consideration as one of these films. In February, 1970, Bud Yorkin was visiting his agent, Sam Cohn, at CMA in New York. After Yorkin mentioned to Cohn that he and Lear would consider working in TV again if "All in the Family" were picked up, Cohn called Michael Dann, the program chief at CBS, and persuaded him to see the second of the pilots ABC had rejected. It so happened that before Robert Wood's appointment as network president, CBS program executives had rejected a property loosely based on "Till Death Do Us Part" called "Man in the Middle." Still, Dann screened the program, liked it, and recommended it enthusiastically to Wood. After conferring with an uncertain CBS chairman William Paley and a nervous CBS chief censor William Tankersly, Wood decided to buy the show. Perry Lafferty, then head of CBS programming on the west coast, was sure that Wood's novice status encouraged his risk taking. Wood, looking back, agrees and adds that his early years as network president "were the freshest." Afterward, "you learn the rules too well and don't think in new directions."

After Wood bought "All in the Family," however, his executives questioned the advisability of airing the pilot as it stood; they specifically urged less objectionable language. Lear, buttressed by his three-picture deal at United Artists, held firm. He had no desire to return to television if it were not on his terms. Debate within CBS about the show stretched through the early summer. Audience tests paralleled those at ABC and upheld those at CBS who wanted to change the pilot. Finally, Wood decided that despite its negative test results and its controversial material, the pilot should air without major script changes. "All in the Family" fit his youth oriented, urban image for the network; he hoped the controversy over the show would generate viewership. It was midsummer 1970 when he gave Lear the go-ahead to produce thirteen episodes. Somewhat later, Wood decided to begin airing this show in January.

Lear reshot the pilot in order to accommodate a recasting of the bigot's daughter and son-in-law, but he would brook few attempts by the local CBS censor or the programming department's liaison person to change words or ideas. Quickly, word spread that "All in the Family" was Wood's concern. Crucial problems of phrasing became a matter of discussion between the network president and chief censor Tankersly. Wood stood by Lear in maintaining the language and plot of the pilot. However, that the CBS president was less than fully secure in his conviction that the show would succeed is evidenced by his decision to slot it on Tuesday at 9:30 P.M. in place of the failed "To Rome with Love." In doing so, he scheduled the show against two very strong movie series—the ABC "Movie of the Week" and the NBC "Tuesday Night Movie." Moreover, it aired after CBS's own "Hee Haw," a rustic version of "Laugh-In" that, as a lead-in, cultivated the very audience that "All in the Family" was presumably purchased to counter. Lear and Yorkin argued against this "death slot" to no avail. But even more troubling to them was a decision by Wood and several other CBS executives that it would be more prudent to begin the series with what was to have been the second episode. The executives deemed that one to be less shocking (and to have fewer racial epithets) that the first. After conferring with Yorkin and director John Rich, Lear refused. He threatened to disband the "All in the Family" company if the network aired the second episode in place of the pilot. He prevailed.

This is not the place for a careful comparison of the conventional and unconventional programs. It might be useful, though, to examine the one hypothesis that was not supported, and to review some ideas about unconventionality that surfaced during the course of the investigation. With respect to the hypothesis, the literature on unconventional innovation suggests that firms are likely to come up with nontraditional novelties when they are experiencing extraordinary problems or developments. That held true for each of the networks. However, it was not supported regarding all the producers who generated the program ideas in the first place. In the case of producers Norman Lear ("All in the Family") and Larry Gelbart ("United States"), at least, the motivation for tenaciously pushing an unorthodox program idea was related to the producers' awareness of having a power base outside the television industry that allowed them attractive alternatives to television work if a network did not accept their proposals.

The lack of support for the hypothesis at the production end is perhaps understandable when one realizes that while the networks are large organizations, that characterization does not fit the Lear-Yorkin association in the pre-"All in the Family" days, Larry Gelbart's status as an individual writer-producer, or, for that matter, George Schlatter's position at the start of "Laugh-In." Independent creative individuals heading their own small firms would seem to be free to pursue unconventional program ideas whether or not unusual pressures or changes are affecting the firms. Perhaps the prediction that unusual organizational pressures are particularly conducive to the generation of unconventional program ideas would hold in the case of large firms (such as Disney and Universal) that begin to falter.[53] In this study, it seems that the hypothesis most relevant to the production firms is the suggestion that the members of unestablished firms are more likely than the staffs of established firms to encourage and generate unconventional innovations since the latter are much more likely than the former to be preoccupied with the need to protect and expand existing product lines.

Now to some ideas about unconventionality that surfaced *during* the investigation. Like the hypotheses regarding unconventional innovation, these notions might well be applicable to other areas of the mass media. In fact, some of them derive from ideas already discussed in this book. We might have expected, for example, that risk taking would go only so far even in unusual environment and organizational conditions. One recurrent theme in the investigation was that the network executives were reluctant to air unorthodox shows in favorable time slots. Larry Gelbart described NBC's scheduling of "United States" as "euthanasic." Norman Lear made similar comments about the slotting of "All in the Family," and George Schlatter echoed them while discussing his attempts to get "Laugh-In" on the air. The unconventional series, much more than the conventional ones, evoked strong ambivalences in network schedulers. The programs were clearly unorthodox, and while key executives had taken the risk of buying them, those same executives and their program committees were hesitant about risking attractive—and valuable—time slots when airing them.

More important with respect to network risk taking was a feature of network program acceptance that implied severe limits on the range of unfamiliar approaches likely in unconventional shows on commercial television. That feature was the relatively small web of interpersonal relationships that dominated the process. Even in this study of only six programs, certain names—Grant Tinker, Perry Lafferty, Sam Cohn, Norman Lear, and others—recurred across time and across networks. Past activities and past acquaintances were keys to membership in the web and to present potential. Friendships in the artistic community were often crucial to initiating or facilitating network interest or acceptance. It is, for example, important to note that for both the conventional and unconventional shows, all of the principals involved at the production and network levels had considerable experience in the entertainment industry, and most had known one another prior to that program involvement.

As in casting, the web of relationships serves an important function. Choosing producers from within it helps protect network executives form the ultimate risk—not having technically acceptable products delivered to them on time. Yet, while the web helps accomplish that goal, it also seems to function (intentionally or not) to limit even unconventional risk taking to producers who have developed at least some track record within the entertainment community. Implicitly, these producers have indicated that, despite their unconventionality, they understand and follow many of the commonly accepted values and procedures of popular entertainment. By choosing people whom they consider, in some sense at least, "safe" producers of "entertainment," the networks imply a rather severe limit on the range of experimentation and unorthodoxy they will accept even in their unconventional shows. Moreoever, by choosing people who are solidly ensconced in mainstream artistic communities network executives are also making it likely that their artists will not challenge the basic legitimacy of social institutions. Certainly, unconventional programs might turn some formulas around and critique aspects of society that had previously not come under attack. Still, as we noted in Chapter Four, the choice of familiar creators with track records in "entertainment" means that, at base, the core policy that fundamentally supports the establishment will continue even as substantial changes take place.

REFERENCES

1. Paul DiMaggio and Paul Hirsch, "Production Organizations in the Arts," *American Behavioral Scientist*, vol. 19 (1976), p. 741.

2. This section draws from several of Tuchman's works. They include "Making News by Doing Work: Routinizing the Unexpected," *American Journal of Sociology*, vol. 79 (July 1971), pp. 110–131; "Objectivity as Strategic Ritual," *American Journal of Sociology*, vol. 77 (1972), pp. 660–679; "The Exception Proves the Rule: The Study of Routine News Practices," in Paul Hirsch, Peter Miller, and F. Gerald Kline, eds., *Strategies for Communication Research* (Beverly Hills: Sage, 1977); and *Making News: A Study in the Construction of Reality* (New York: Basic Books, 1978).

3. Quoted in Tuchman, "Making News by Doing Work," p. 111.

4. Tuchman, *Making News*, p. 57.

5. Tuchman, *Making News*, pp. 57–58.

6. See Lewis Coser, Charles Kadushin, and Walter Powell, *Books: The Culture and Commerce of Publishing* (New York: Basic Books, 1982), pp. 57–59, 208–209, 302–307, and *passim*.

7. See Joseph Turow, "Unconventional Programs on Commercial Television," in James Ettema and D. Charles Whitney, eds., *Individuals in Mass Media Organizations* (Beverly Hills: Sage, 1983), p. 112.

8. See R. Serge Denisoff, *Solid Gold* (New Brunswick, New Jersey: Transaction Press, 1974), pp. 154–55; Charlie Gillett, *Sounds of the City* (New York: Outerbridge and Diestfrey, 1969); and Charlie Gillett, *Making Tracks* (New York: Dutton, 1974).

9. Ann Orlov, "Demythologizing Scholarly Publishing," in Phillip Altbach and Sheila McVey, eds., *Perspectives on Publishing, Annals of the American Academy of Political and Social Sciences*, vol. 421, (September 1975).

10. Coser et. al., pp. 302–307.

11. Coser et. al., p. 353.

12. Coser et. al., p. 352.

13. Joseph Turow, *Getting Books to Children* (Chicago: American Library Association, 1978), p. 98.

14. Coser et. al., p. 338.

15. This kind of machine-based testing has its most important origin in the "program analyzer" developd for CBS Radio by Paul Lazarsfeld and Frank Stanton in the 1930s. Some movie companies later used a related method, the Cirlin Reactograph. For an interesting view of these techniques contemporary with their use, see Franklin Fearing, ed., *Mass Media: Content, Function, and Measurement*, a special issue of *The Journal of Social Issues*, vol. 3 (1947).

16. Michael Gross, "The Hits Just Keep Coming," in Robert Atwan, Barry Orton, and William Versterman, *Mass Media: Industries and Issues*, 1st ed. (New York: Random House, 1978).

17. One example is Ron Powers, *The News Business as Show Business* (New York: St. Martin's Press, 1977).

18. Susan White, "Indianapolis' First Family," *Indianapolis Magazine*, April, 1982, pp. 52–57.

19. Quoted in *TV Guide*, June 12, 1982, p. A-1 (Indianapolisn Edition).

20. Considerations of company morale can sometimes influence the material produced. Coser, Kadushin, and Powell found this in their study of adult trade book publishing and I noted it in studying mass market children's book publishing. In each case, the influence was not very strong. See Turow, *Getting Books to Children*, p. 76.

21. Bruce Felton and Mark Fowler, *Felton and Fowler's Best, Worst, and Most Unusual* (New York: Crowell, 1975), p. viii.

22. A good example of a star autobiography is *June Allyson* by June Allyson with Frances Spatz Leighton (New York: Putnam, 1982). An autobiography that advertises its frankness but seems to have be mostly fiction is Errol Flynn, *My Wicked, Wicked Ways* (New York: Putnam, 1959). See Charles Higham, *Errol Flynn: The Untold Story* (New York: Longman, Inc., 1978), p. 1.

23. John Cawelti, *Six Gun Mystique* (Bowling Green, Ohio: Popular Press, 1975), p. 35.

24. Cawelti, pp. 46–47.

25. Cawelti, pp. 34–35.

26. Harry Steinberg, "The Porn Brokers," *New York Times Book Review*, November 28, 1976, p. 55.

27. Russell Nye, *The Unembarrassed Muse* (New York: Dial Press, 1970), p. 312.

28. See Nicholar Tawa, "The Ways of Love in the Mid-Nineteenth Century American Song," *Journal of Popular Culture*, vol. 10 (Full 1976), pp. 337–351.

29. Denisoff, *Solid Gold*, p. 167.

30. Denisoff, *Solid Gold*, p. 167.

31. Clive Davis and James Willwerth, *Clive* (New York: Ballantine, 1974), pp. 218–219.

32. Horace Newcomb and Robert Alley, "The Producer as Artist: Commercial Television," in Ettema and Whitney, eds., pp. 91–107.

33. For a discussion of Gary Marshall's approach to TV production, see Robert Pekurney, "Coping with Television Production," in Ettema and Whitney, eds., pp. 131–144.

34. Leonard Maltin, eds., *TV Movies* (New York, Signet, 1969), p. 165.

35. In the late 1970s, the networks also began to order fewer episodes of a series at a time to protect against the cost of failure.

36. Nye, parts 1, 2, 3, and 4.

37. Quoted in Quentin Reynolds, *The Fiction Factory* (New York: Random House, 1955), pp. 88–89.

38. Nye, passim; and Myron Matlaw, ed., *American Popular Entertainment*, (Westport, Connecticut: Greenwood Press, 1979).

39. For an elaboration of this idea, see Joseph Turow, "Advising and Ordering on Television Dramas: The Display of Knowledge According to Male-Female Stereotypes," M. A. Thesis, Annenberg School of Communications, 1973.

40. On indignation over Arab stereotypes, see Jack G. Shaheen, "The Arab Sterotype on Television," *The Link* (published by Americans for Middle East Understanding), vol. 13 (April/May 1980), p. 1–14.

41. See Joseph Turow, *Entertainment, Education, and the Hard Sell: Three Decades of Network Children's Television* (New York: Praeger, 1981), pp. 119–123.

42. Amy Leifer, Neal J. Gordon, and S. B. Graves, "Children's Television: More Than Mere Entertainment," *Harvard Educational Review*, vol. 44 (May 1974).

43. The following discussion is drawn from Joseph Turow, "Casting for Television: The Anatomy of Social Typing," *Journal of Communication*, vol. 28 (Autumn 1978), pp. 18–24.

44. See "Love Boat," *TV Guide*, June 5, 1982, pp. 28–32.

45, For an overview of the issues, see Richard P. Adler, ed., *All in the Family: A Critical Appraisal* (New York: Praeger, 1979).

46. Adler ed., p. 93.

47. Daniel Marquis, "The Anatomy of Successful Innovation," in R. Rothberg, ed., *Corporate Strategy and Product Innovation* (New York: The Free Press, 1976).

48. C. Johnson, "Dying is Not an Option," *Innovation*, vol. 18 (1970), pp. 40–45.

49. Everett Rogers and R. Rogers, *Communication in Organizations* (New York: The Free Press, 1976), p. 144.

50. Charles Perrow, *Complex Organizations* (Glenview, Illinois: Scott, Foresman, 1980); and A. Downs, *Inside Bureaucracy* (Boston: Little, Brown, 1967).

51. Marquis, p. 15.

52. The following material draws on Joseph Turow, "Unconventional Programs on Commercial Television," pp. 119–127.

53. For an example regarding Disney and the genesis of the unconventional movie, *Tron*, see *Time*, July 5, 1982, pp. 64–65.

Six

The Struggle over the Big Picture

The preceding chapters have probed the many forces that guide the creation of mass media material. They have charted how interorganizational and intraorganizational struggles over society's resources, broadly understood, play critical roles in shaping images of society and its values. And, they have explored how activities within production organizations tie into events in the organization's environment to create continuity amid change in media culture, and change amid continuity. As we have seen, a wide spectrum of considerations weave the tightrope creators walk between different levels of novelty and repetition.

What remains to be done at this point is to address the issue of new media. It is difficult to discuss mass media in the late twentieth century without being drawn toward speculations about what people variously call the "new," "emerging," or "developing" technologies, referring to a gamut from cable television to satellites to videocassette records to videodiscs to video games and much beyond. Here, the speculations will concern a small, though crucial, slice of this subject. At issue is whether the most mainstream aspects of media culture—those patterns of messages shared by millions of people—will fade away as the years pass.

Certainly, there is support for this view. It received early systematic expression in a *Public Opinion Quarterly* article by Richard Maisel called "The Decline of Mass Media."[1] In 1973, Maisel pointed to the higher growth rate of "specialized" media as compared to "mass" media. For example, he noted the increase of narrow-interest periodicals over large circulation magazines, of suburban newspapers over central city papers, and of educational broadcasting over commercial broadcasting. Drawing upon a three stage theory of social development that saw the United States entering a "post-industrial" phase, Maisel argued that mass media would stop growing and specialized media would accelerate rapidly as the main media told of a highly "differentiated culture."[2]

The idea of a highly differentiated culture accelerated by specialized media has taken hold among many forecasters of the late twentieth century media scene. The forecasters disagree, though, about the desirability of such a society. Some writers have argued that information banks, home video equipment, satellite dishes, hundreds of cable channels, and the interaction of all these through home computers will liberate individuals to pursue their own special interests and allow mass media producers to target messages especially designed for them. Others fear that this kind of self-fulfillment will lead to unhealthy divisions in society. Some raise the possibility that the major fruits of the new communication technologies—economic and social knowledge and power—will be enjoyed by the wealthy and well educated, thus further broadening the historic knowledge and power gap between rich and poor. Some contend that the use of new technologies will push people into their own little worlds, where they will have little appreciation of other people's interests or concerns. For example, Stephen Effros, a former FCC attorney, predicts that "if my personal computer focuses on one area, and your personal computer focuses on something else, we will see what we want to see. We will know nothing about anything else."[3] George Gerbner voiced a broader concern regarding the decline of network television as cable signals divide the home viewing audience:

> Television is a mass ritual. It provides interaction for people who have little in common and has brought everyone into a huge mainstream. The mass ritual is a window on the world, and that is a need and a desire that the new machines won't satisfy. The big question is whether the new technologies will replace and improverish the mass ritual.[4]

Certainly, predictions regarding a differentiated society, particularly some of its more ominous aspects, should not be taken lightly. It does appear that the control of knowledge by some groups in comparison to others will accelerate as the educated extend their hold on very specialized conduits of information related to business and government. Less technical levels of public symbolizing, however, may very well camouflage these inequalities and continue to reinforce a view of a common society with commonly recognized legitimate institutions. That is, news and entertainment might still make up agendas that are shared by segments of society that cross knowledge and income gaps. The increased fractionalization of media channels should not blind us to forces already at work in the United States and elsewhere to move similar patterns of content across both entrenched and emerging media. Far from igniting the individualized, differentiated media culture that many envision, those forces hold a vested interest in carrying people and ideas across various media forms and maintaining the "mass ritual" Gerbner mentioned.

The process itself has certainly not originated with the late twentieth century's emerging media technologies. Recall from Chapter One that what we are talking about is linking pin activity. There we defined it as the movement of completed material or of people representing that material from production firms in one industry to production firms in another. And, we noted that it represents a key aspect in a media cross-fertilization process that ties together publics that might otherwise have little in common. What we did not note is that for production executives on both sides of the relationship participation by the production organization in linking pin activity is often desirable, even necessary. The reason is that the process represents a strategy through which executives can try to cope with those risks of failure described in Chapter Five. For executives in organizations accepting linking pin products, the cross-fertilization is an easy way to find creative elements quickly and efficiently, while also having some conception of the audience's previous interest in and recognition of these elements. For executives in organizations *offering* linking pin products, the process often brings two important benefits: (1) publicity for a company creation (and thus a possible boost to its success) and (2) substantial extra money to company coffers through the aggressive sale of various subsidiary rights to the material.

The risk reducing benefits at both ends of the linking pin relationship are reflected strongly in a fascinating full-page advertisement that appeared in a 1979 issue of *Advertising Age*.[5] The headline read "Our Salesman Have Door-to-Door Experience," and beneath it were pictures of four famous Saturday morning television cartoon characters from the highly successful Hanna-Barbera cartoon studio—Fred Flintstone, Yogi Bear, Barney Rubble, and Scooby Doo.

The ad extolled the tremendous ability of these characters to sell products and attract audiences in areas having nothing to do with cartoons. At the same time, it solicited more subsidiary rights business. Here are excerpts:

Fred, Barney, Yogi, and Scooby Doo are leaders of a team of more than 2,000 salesman who are familiar at doors throughout the world. They entertain millions of young people and most adults have grown up with their antics. The funtastic salesmen from Hanna Barbera are recognized instantly. Everywhere.

But they do more than entertain.... [They] work for a host of the world's greatest companies. The Flintstones sell cereal for General Foods and vitamins for Miles Laboratories. Character related collector cup and glass premium promotions worked for Procter & Gamble, Seven-Eleven Stores, and Kentucky Fried Chicken. Scooby Doo and his pals theme a string of Fun Factory Pizza Restaurants.... Yogi Bear sells Heinz Soup in England and ice cream in Australia.

Our globetrotting door-to-door salesmen [also] perform in Ice Capades shows and greet people at amusement parks, such as King's Island in Cincinnati, King's Dominion in Richmond, and the Blackpool Tower in England....

When you join our family, we become partners.... We develop ideas, match the right character with your product to make the program work best. Our creative services division even prepares the artwork you need....

Such use of mass media characters to adorn a wide variety of advertising and promotional material for products unrelated to the characters is quite common. Moreover, mass media production firms that license characters often involve themselves in even more intricate cross-fertilization activities. At the same time that they farm out their creations to help sell nonmedia goods, they also promote or circulate materials with those characters that are strictly media products, meant for various mass media industries. So, for example, Hanna-Barbera sells the Flintstone name for use by a vitamin firm, but it also carefully cultivates a more general Flintstone image through TV shows, comic magazines, and activity books. One belief underlying this two-track approach is that the characters will be especially credible and familiar to an audience (and thus attractive to merchandisers) if the producer spreads their images widely in "legitimate" media material at the same time that merchandisers use them for more obviously mercenary purposes.

As a related example, consider the activities of the Marvel Comics Group, creators of Spiderman, Incredible Hulk, and other superheroes. In a 1978 brochure soliciting children's advertisers for its comic magazines, the firm extolled the benefits of becoming identified with Marvel characters through regular space purchases.[6] Advertising widely in Marvel magazines, said the brochure, "generates *its own reinforcement* in other media ...at no costs to you. Since your ad appears in every Marvel magazine, every time *any* Marvel superhero crashes through into another medium, your message gets valuable recall." The brochure goes on to say that "as you've undoubtedly noticed, the crashes are getting bolder and more frequent." To illustrate, it cites the use of the production firm's characters in animated and "live action" TV series; in book publishing enterprises that reprint Marvel's "best" magazine issues and use the firm's characters for puzzles, activity books, novelizations, and comic paperbacks; in a daily newspaper strip featuring Spiderman; in a national fan club with "constant newsmedia coverage of all [its activities]"; and—"perhaps the most significant of all"—in a "variety of educational programs, constituting a mass market in itself."

A key point to underscore here is that moving with the characters across various media are perspectives on society and ideas about life. Particularly when the most pervasive mass media are involved, creators are likely to draw on formulas, or at least on settings and situations, that hold records of success and virtually ensure acceptability in a wide range of outlets and industries. As a consequence, the perspectives that underlie the material they create will likely fit neatly into the patterns of perspectives generated regularly by the mainstream media.

The same holds true for nonfiction material. The circulation of people and ideas within the across various mass media industries is an aspect of cultural life that has hardly been examined systematically. Fact is, though, that book publishers, movie companies, magazine publishers, television producers, and newspaper publishers follow each other in highlighting events and lifestyles. They also play an important role in providing creative fodder for one another. In doing so, they move ideas about "what is, what is important, and what is related to what" to various audiences that often cumulatively represent huge segments of the population. Recall, for example, the blizzard coverage in 1982 on the war between Israel and the PLO in Lebanon, and on the birth of a boy to Diana and Prince Charles of England. Recall, too, how difficult it was in the summer of 1982 to browse through mainstream magazines, newspapers, television, or radio without becoming aware of the import of Steven Spielberg's two new movies, *ET* and *Poltergeist*. But even if the specific subjects media carry are not the same, the similaritiy with which creators approach the world can still yield similar perspectives. When local television stations across the country daily fill their 7:25 AM newscasts with tales of overnight murders, robberies, and accidents, the general knowledge and world view that can be gleaned from those patterns might be the same, even though individual stories might not be.

Much of the material that does cross media boundaries moves in one way or another through the raw materials news industry mentioned in Chapter One. Recall that the industry—led in the United States by the Associated Press and United Press International—generates thousands of nonfiction stories that are sold as building blocks for newspapers, radio and TV newscasts, magazines, even books. The industry relies on a small army of full-time reporters and stringers who scan the world for news. As part of that process, they routinely plumb specialized trade and intellectual journals, from *Foreign Affairs* to the *British Medical Journal* to *The Annals of the American Academy of Political and Social Science* for items of interest to media selectors with broader audiences. It is in these very specialized publications that intellectual and scientific leaders set forth ideas that news selectors might consider both novel and interesting to a broader populace. Often it is the raw material news industry that relays these notions to the larger world. Idea-hungry hard and soft news producers needing to fill TV time or periodical space often turn to AP, UPI, Reuters, or other "wholesale" services for story suggestions, or even finished products.

The new media are already deeply involved in this process. For example, some of the first services widely available on cable systems were news-weather-time channels that used AP or Reuters tickers. The raw materials news industry also provides an important base for Ted Turner's Cable News network. Often, though, the industry's influence in spreading people and ideas is a lot more complex and indirect than that. The process cries out to be studied. One overall point seems secure, however. Through multiple and circular routes, mass media products reaching small audiences often spark similar creations from other producers aiming at other outlets. As a result, the public for those ideas sometimes snowballs to very large proportions.

Another major industry that works closely with various mass media sectors to snowball people and ideas across the public consciousness is the public relations industry. Public relations is a multilayered and many-faceted business. Generally, though, the aim of a PR campaign is to provide maximum favorable exposure for a client or client's product without turning to advertising. It follows that public relations agencies hold a very strong interest in trying to develop perspectives about their clients that will intrigue selectors in various media sectors. Creators need ideas, public relations people offer ideas, and the result is often a story that makes both happy. The political press releases that reporters are taught to read suspiciously and the "manufactured" political candidates that writers have exposed as public relations con jobs in such books as *The Selling of a President* are just windswept tips of a generally calm iceberg. Public relations practitioners are routinely and deeply involved in instigating stories at virtually every level of mass media. They deal with subjects as diverse as pharmaceuticals, oil, diamonds, hamburgers, moving to a new town, and dating. In fact, according to one well-known press agent, "If it were not for the combined efforts of publicists, press representatives, public relations people, and lowly space grabbers, there would be a lot of dull, perhaps unfilled air time on radio and television, and certainly a tremendous amount of white space among the print outlets."[7]

A great deal of media material originating from public relations agencies appears in the form of what journalists term soft news or features as opposed to hard news. To journalists, hard news consists of national, international, and local affairs of government as well as other nonfiction stories (such as recent crimes) that they consider immediately important. Soft news, by contrast, consists of noncriminal tales of ordinary people, descriptions of lifestyles, and observations about the arts; also, soft news typically does not have the urgent quality of hard news. Of course, soft news, whether conveyed through a recited story, an interview, a film, or a tape, presents agendas about life's activities and meanings that may carry profound implications. Nevertheless, journalists tend to give soft news a good deal lower priority than hard news. For example, when I explored the way local TV journalists produced soft news in a moderately large United States city, I found that they considered hard news the "real" news.[8] They felt it was the standard by which their stations and others judged their news departments. They also felt it related most to the area of life about which they held a responsibility to keep the public informed. They acknowledged features as pieces that serve the function of luring viewers because of their interesting bits of knowledge and their helping to fill up time in the newscasts. A news assignment editor expressed the feeling, which I heard from members of local TV talk shows as well, that "straight news" is often so negative that material must be brought in that "brightens up the world." A good soft news story was generally thought to be one that is visually interesting with an upbeat, positive approach to life.

Public relations practitioners know all this. Over the years they have developed approaches to plugging their clients that are attractive to a wide variety of media selectors. One important principle of recent years is the soft sell. Broadcast and print creators do not want to appear publicly like simple ringleaders for an endless stream of people who zealously plug their products. Consequently, public relations practitioners vie aggressively with one another to develop angles that tie the person or item they are plugging into an established or developing social trend, an aspect of a person's life that the selectors might relate to, or a lifestyle the selectors might find interesting or helpful for the audience. Donald Softness, head of a major public relations agency, put the point this way: "Today's sophisticated marketing oriented public relations firms rarely take a product and publicize it, per se. Instead, we take a facet of the product, or build a concept around the product or its use, or create a repositioning of the product, and then publicize the new concept or aspect, and not the product itself."[9]

The next step is to move the idea around the country through a gamut of channels. An entire support system has developed within the public relations industry to keep PR practitioners aware of new and established media outlets, of the people to contact in those outlets, of the kinds of material they like, and of the "lead time" they require to arrange for the idea's exposure. Large scale public relations campaigns often require the kind of close planning one associates with military campaigns. The territory is certainly very broad. For example, in 1977 Betsy Nolan listed a mind-boggling series of cautions and a list of preparations that must be undertaken in advance of a book author's publicity tour. In the process, she described the media that ought to be contacted:

> "Key" media in a multi-city tour include: major metropolitan area newspapers; mass-circulation magazines; and network, syndicated, and a few important local TV and radio interview shows....
>
> Other media in tour cities should receive a [press] release, a printed cover note giving author availability dates, and a reply (it doesn't need to be postpaid) reading something like "For a copy of (book title), just fill in your name...and return this card to us."
>
> A similar package can go to radio and print media in cities where the author will *not* tour. Instead of an "availability dates" note, attach a note offering to set up a telephone interview. Or you can prepare a canned feature story and send it to newspapers on an "exclusive to you in your city" basis.[10]

Sometimes, if the project is big enough and the client wealthy enough, such tours will not be necessary. The press can be brought to the client. So, for example, the television networks hold press junkets for print media representatives at the start of their major seasons. Interesting stories about the stars' lives and the shows' histories are presented to give the reporters a variety of soft sell angles. Major movie companies follow this practice as well. For example, in May, 1982, just at the point that *ET* and *Poltergeist* was released across the United States, *Time Magazine* highlighted producer/director Steven Spielberg's life and previous successes in a seven-page article. *Time* noted that "a frightening wave of publicity is building" for the films, not admitting its own complicity. "At one point, by actual count, Spielberg had filmed thirty-six separate distinct eight-minute taped question-and-answer sessions [with media representatives] without pausing for a cup of tea."[11]

The most developed of the new media, cable television, seems ripe for becoming an active public relations outlet. From a vantage of the early 1980s, it seems that much long-term interest of cable programmers lies in advertiser-sponsored *narrowcasting*. That means aiming material at specialized audiences. To public relations practitioners, the most attractive narrowcast programs so far are undoubtedly magazine and talk shows aimed at women, sport fans, business people, and high culture enthusiasts. One case in point is the women's cable service, Daytime, initiated by Hearst/ABC Video in 1982. The daily service consists of several segments built around several general themes and held together by a host.[12] Other examples that use a similar format are certain ABC ARTS channel programs which often highlight famous artists in their surroundings; a program on USA Cable called "The *Better Homes and Gardens* Great Idea

Notebook"; a "Scholastic Sports Academy" series also on the USA network; and a series on consumerism and finance coproduced by Home Box Office and *Money, Ms.* and *Consumer Reports* magazines.[13] These kinds of programs, like talk and magazine shows on broadcast TV, are tailor-made for public relations firms wanting to move people and ideas in front of certain publics through as many channels as possible. Quite possibly, too, they represent merely the most obvious way that public relations practitioners can take advantage of what one PR writer called "the new multimedia environment."[14]

The mention of ABC, Hearst, *Money Magazine*, and Home Box Office in this very brief discussion of cable television points to powerful forces other than the public relations industry or the raw materials news industry that have vested interests in cross-fertilizing mass media. Those forces are corporations with financial holdings in a variety of mass media industries. Such companies became increasingly common in the 1960s and 1970s, as entertainment conglomerates outdid one another in reaching across mass media boundaries to acquire or start a clutch of subsidiaries. In the list of 100 leading media companies generated annually by *Advertising Age*, it is rare indeed to find a firm that does not hold properties across two or three industries.[15]

Take ABC as an example. Its name—American Broadcasting Companies—belies the breadth of its activities. In 1982, it owned one television network, six radio networks, and several radio and TV stations. ABC also owned five magazine publishing companies with forty-three magazines ranging from *Los Angeles* to *Infosystems*, a motion picture production firm, a market research firm, a marketing database company, and a home video (i.e., cable, videodisc, and videocassette) programming firm. Hearst, too, is a giant media conglomerate. In 1982, it owned fifteen daily newspapers, twenty-eight weeklies, at least twenty-five magazines (including *Cosmopolitan* and *Good Housekeeping*), five television stations, five radio stations, several book publishing companies, a few magazine and newspaper distribution firms, an advertising service, a paper company, and more. *Money Magazine* and Home Box Office are owned by Time, Incorporated. In addition to these holdings, the corporation in 1982 gathered under its umbrella twenty-eight nondaily newspapers, seven magazines, one television station, one of the largest cable TV operations in the country, a one-third ownership (with MCA and Paramount) in the USA cable network, two book publishing companies, a marketing firm, the Book of the Month Club, and more.[16]

Smaller companies have joined the cross-media fray as well, whether through the starting of new subsidiaries or through alliances with other firms in new ventures. In the home video area, even the richest companies are joining with others in some high cost ventures. ABC, for example, has linked up with ESPN Cable and Getty Oil for a sports pay cable service and with Hearst for the ARTS and Daytime operations. In fact, a multitude of movie- and TV-related firms have begun to take advantage of the programming, distribution, or cash flow strengths of other firms to try to move strongly into emerging media industries. A *Wall Street Journal* article, surveying the situation, noted that one big reason for the cooperative ventures is the firms' uncertainty about the shape that the home TV market will take, or how soon it will take shape. "Only one thing is certain: Big money will be required to produce the programming demanded in the future. Other important questions, such as whether cable television or direct satellite broadcasters will become the dominant retailers of programming, remain unanswered."[17]

One reason so many firms have moved into a variety of traditional and emerging media sectors is related to the potential of the parent company to act as a linking pin among its various operations. The "buy everything in sight" perspective of the 1960s gave way in the 1970s and early 1980s to cautious acquisitions of companies that fit well with the overall perceived markets of the conglomerates. Acquisitive firms do not see their new subsidiaries as companies that can go their own ways. For one thing, they see them as vehicles to help smooth the high and low earning periods that occur often in mass media industries. The hope is that when one sector's profits are down, another's will be up. Beyond that, however, corporate executives see individual companies interlocking with other interests, products, and services of the firm so that all media opportunities are covered. Consider, for example, the following comments by Conrad Judson, corporate planning vice-president for Warner Communications, Incorporated (WCI). His remarks appeared in a 1982 issue of the Atari, Incorporated, employee bulletin. Warner owns Atari, a home and arcade video game and computer manufacturer and until late 1982 the fastest growing company in United States history.[18] Judson addressed himself to Atari's role in the WCI conglomorate:

> The challenge...is to marry the need for strategic planning with the "hit" business that WCI companies are famous for: hit movies, hit records, hit video games.... WCI is already in an enviable position. It is involved in publishing, cable transmission, film, TV programming, and video production ...all of which will make Warner one of the giants of the new home electronics age....

After Judson prognosticated about the interconnection of a multitude of media in the home, the editor concluded with a key question and an intriguing answer: "And how does Atari fit into this vision of the future? You'll have to use your imagination because that's 'classified' information."[19]

Much cross-fertilization between entertainment conglomerate subsidiaries is, however, currently visible and might well imply future directions. For example, Warner's movie subsidiary in 1982 was working actively with Atari to come up with video games based around the themes and special effects of its hit movies. In the same year, WCI continued to reap a cross-fertilization bonanza in linking its film company with its DC Comics subsidiary to create movies based on the Superman comic magazine hero. And the company was drawing upon the expertise of its Warner-Electra-Asylum-Nonesuch record subsidiaries to aid in its video music channel for cable, MTV.[20]

Many other companies have moved in similarly very visible directions. Many are also pursuing roads currently not so popular with consumers in the hope that in the future they will bear lucrative fruit. So, for example, a few book publishers are developing database-published products and seriously entering the database publishing business. In 1982, Harfax Database Publishing, owned by Harper and Row, offered a database containing sources of data on sixty industries through Bibliographic Retrieval Systems (BRS), an electronic database "distributor." R. R. Bowker (owned by Xerox) put its *Books in Print* and other references on line, also through BRS. Other publishers, such as Random House (owned by S. I. Newhouse Newspapers), Houghton Mifflin, and McGraw-Hill were beginning database publishing with videodisc products as spinoffs from existing databases.[21]

Conglomerate-orchestrated linking pin activities have intensified the battle for control over the major and minor roads to consumer eyes and ears. Smaller companies, with fewer resources, have been elbowed out of the way or gobbled up by expanding giants. The battle is fought not only through cross-fertilization of content, but through cross-fertilization of creators. As a Time, Incorporated executive pointed out, "The editorial resources of Time are not only the magazines it publishes, but the people who write them."[22] He was referring to the human resources the corporation could draw upon when it tested a teletext database operation on several of its ATC cable systems. Another Time, Inc. officer reflected the same perspective when discussing the way Home Box Office produces documentaries. Working for a company that owns magazines, she said with a bit of understatement, is "great for research."[23]

The many ramifications that these, and all, linking pin activities hold for the production of mass media culture have hardly been studied systematically. One way to slice into this situation is to take the resource dependence route this book has charted. Questions about the organizations in mass media industries and their interconnections; about the people who are part of those organizations; about the development and interconnection of artistic communities; about the perpetuation of formulas, stereotypes, and other patterns of content; and about the ability of material that is nonmainstream to survive and grow—these and other subjects this book has broached cry out for more study.

At the base of all of them lies a profound issue: the relationship between social power and power over knowledge. What is the most democratic distribution of power possible over the production, distribution and exhibition of symbols? How can that be achieved most effectively? There is much to understand and do in this complex area, and researchers have only just started. The production of mass media culture promises to be a fascinating and important area of inquiry for many years to come.

REFERENCES

1. Richard Maisel, "The Decline of Mass Media," *Public Opinon Quarterly*, vol. 37 (Summer 1973), pp. 159–170.

2. Maisel, p. 00.

3. Quoted in Martin Koughan, "The State of the Revolution, 1982," *Channels*, vol. 1 (December, 1981–January, 1982), p. 70.

4. Quoted in Kougan, p. 70.

5. *Advertising Age*, 1979.

6. Marvel Advertising Brochure, "Long Ago, in a Nearby Galaxy" (New York: Marvel Comics Group, 1979).

7. Gary Stevens, "Four Outstanding Moments in the History of Press Agentry," in Gary Wagner, ed., *Publicity Forum* (New York: Richard Weiner, 1977), p. 3.

8. Joseph Turow, "Local TV: Producing Soft News," *Journal of Communication*, vol. 33 (Spring, 1983), pp. 111–123.

9. Donald Softness, "The Emerging Marketing Challenge of Product PR in an Advertising World," in Gary Wagner, ed., p. 128.

10. Betsy Nolan, "Book Publicity," in Gary Wagner, ed., p. 67.

11. *Time*, May 30, 1982, p. 59.

12. *Advertising Age*, October 19, 1981, p. 81.

13. *Advertising Age*, October 19, 1981, p. 81.

14. Fred Schmidt, "The New Multimedia Environment," *Public Relations Journal*, vol. 34 (September 1978), p. 16.

15. See, for example, *Advertising Age*, June 28, 1982, pp. M1–M80.

16. *Advertising Age*, June 28, 1982, p. M10, M43, M71.

17. Stephen J. Sansweet, "Movie, TV Firms Building Alliances to Take Advantages of Home Video," *Wall Street Journal*, March 26, 1982, p. 41.

18. Terrance McGarry, "Movie, Record Industries Joining the Pack as Video Business Gobbles up Customers," UPI dispatch in *Indianapolis Star*, July 18, 1982, p. C-1.

19. Quoted in "Corporate Planning," *Atari*, vol. 2, No. 1, 1982, pp. 2–3.

20. *Advertising Age*, October 19, 1981, p. 76. See also Jim McCullaugh and Laura Foti, "Music's Role Upbeat in Cable TV's Future," *Billboard*, May 1, 1982, p. 1; and "Cornyn Affirms WCI's Interest in Potential of Musical Videos," *Variety*, March 17, 1982, p. 149.

21. Robyn Shotwell, "Getting into Database Publishing," *Publishers Weekly*,

September 11, 1981, pp. 45–46. For a view of the way newspaper publishers are crossing media, see "Protecting the Franchise via Videotex," *Advertising Age*, May 3, 1982, p. 80.

22. Quoted in Steve Knoll, "Time Inc. Teletext Test Will be Biggest to Date," *Variety*, August 8, 1981, p. 37.

23. *Variety*, May 5, 1982, p. 116.

Selected Bibliography

Adler, Richard P. *All in the Family: A Critical Appraisal*. New York: Praeger, 1979.

Aldrich, Howard. *Organizations and Environments*. Englewood Cliffs, N.J.: Prentice-Hall, 1979.

Altheide, David. "The Failure of Network News," *Washington Journalism Review*, 3 (May 1981): 28–29.

Altick, Richard. *The English Common Reader*. Chicago: University of Chicago Press, 1957.

Bagdikian, Ben. *The Information Machines*. New York: Harper & Row, 1971.

Baldwin, Thomas, and Colby Lewis. "Violence in Television: The Industry Looks at Itself." In *Television and Social Behavior*, vol. 1, edited by George Comstock and Eli Rubenstein. Washington, D.C.: United States Government Printing Office, 1972.

Bantz, C. R., K. S. McCorkle, and R. C. Bade. "The News Factory." *Communication Research* 7 (Winter 1980): 45–58.

Barber, J. D. "Characters in the Campaign: The Literary Problem." In *Race for the Presidency: The Media and the Nominating Process*, edited by J. D. Barber. Englewood Cliffs, N.J.: Prentice Hall, 1978.

Barnouw, Erik. *The Image Empire*. New York: Oxford University Press, 1970.

_____. *A Tower in Babel*. New York: Oxford University Press, 1968.

_____. *The Golden Web*. New York: Oxford University Press, 1968.

_____. *The Sponsor: Notes on a Modern Potentate*. New York: Oxford University Press, 1977.

Battestin, Martin. Introduction to *Joseph Andrews*, by Henry Fielding. Boston: Houghton Mifflin, 1961.

Bauer, Raymond. "The Obstinate Audience: The Influence Process from the Point of View of Social Communication." In *The Process and Effects of Mass Communication*, edited by Wilbur Schramm and Donald Roberts. Urbana: University of Illinois Press, 1971.

Becker, Lee, D. Charles Whitney, and E. Collins. "Public Understanding of How the News Operates." *Journalism Quarterly* 57 (Autumn 1979): 571–575.

Bedell, Sally. *Up the Tube*. New York: Viking, 1981.

Berkhofer, Robert F. *The White Man's Indian*. New York: Vintage, 1978.

Bogel, Donald. *Toms, Coons, Mulattoes, Mammies, and Bucks*. New York: Vintage, 1973.

Breed, Warren. "Social Control in the Newsroom." *Social Forces* 33 (May 1955): 109–116.

Brown, Les. *Television: The Business Behind the Box*. New York: Harcourt Brace Jovanouich, 1972.

Cantor, Muriel. *Prime Time Television*. Beverly Hills, Calif.: Sage Publications, 1980.

Cantor, Muriel. *The Hollywood TV Producer*. New York: Basic Books, 1971.

Caplette, Michelle. "Women in Book Publishing: A Qualified Success Story." In *Books: The Culture and Commerce of Publishing*, edited by Lewis Coser, Charles Kadushin, and Walter Powell. New York: Basic Books, 1981.

Cassata, Mary, and Molefi Asante. *Mass Communication*. New York: Macmillan, 1979.

Cawelti, John. *The Six Gun Mystique*. Bowling Green, Ohio: Bowling Green University Press, 1972.

Chase, Oscar G. "Broadcast Regulation and the First Amendment," In *Network Television and the Public Interest*, edited by Michael Botein and David M. Rice. Lexington, Mass.: Lexington Books, 1980.

Click, J. W., and Russell N. Baird. *Magazine Editing and Production*, 2d ed. Dubuque, Iowa: Wm. C. Brown, 1979.

Clift, Charles, and Archie Greer eds. *Broadcast Programming: The Current Perspective*. Washington, D.C.: University Press of America, 1979.

Cohen, Stanley, and Jack Young. *The Manufacture of News*. Beverly Hills, Calif.: Sage Publications, 1973.

Cole, Barry, and Mal Oettinger. *Reluctant Regulators*. Reading, Mass. Addison-Wesley, 1978.

Coser, Lewis, Charles Kadushin, and Walter Powell. *Books: The Culture and Commerce of Publishing*. New York: Basic Books, 1982.

Cox, Kenneth. "The Federal Communication Commission." *Boston College Industrial and Commercial Law Review* 11 (May 1970): 595–688.

Crouse, Timothy. *The Boys on the Bus*. New York: Random House, 1972.

Curran, James, Michael Gurvitch, and Janet Woollacott eds. *Mass Communication and Society*. London: Edward Arnold, 1977.

Davis, Clive. *Clive: Inside the Record Business*. New York: Ballantine, 1976.

De Sola Pool, Ithiel, and Irwin Shulman. "Newsmen's Fantasies, Audiences, and Newswriting," In *People, Society, and Mass Communications*, edited by Lewis Dexter and David M. White. New York: The Free Press, 1964.

DeFleur, Melvin, and Everette Dennis. *Understanding Mass Communication*. Boston: Houghton Mifflin, 1981.

Denisoff, R. Serge. *Solid Gold: The Popular Record Industry*. New Brunswick: N. J.: Transaction Books, 1974.

Dessauer, Jonn. *Book Publishing*. New York: R. R. Bowker, 1974.

DiMaggio, Paul, and Paul Hirsch. "Production Organizations in the Arts," *American Behavioral Scientist* 19 (August 1976): 735–752.

Donahue, George, Phillip Tichenor, and Clarice Olien. "Gatekeeping: Mass Media Systems and Information Control." In *Current Perspectives in Mass Communication Research*, edited by F. Gerald Kline and Phillip J. Tichenor. Beverly Hills, Calif.: Sage Publications, 1972.

Downs, A. *Inside Bureaucracy*. Boston: Little, Brown, 1967.

Duncan, Hugh Dalziel. "The Search for a Social Theory of Communication." In *Human Communication Theory*, edited by Frank Dance. New York: Holt, Rinehart, & Winston, 1967.

Dunning, John. *Tune in Yesterday*. Englewood Cliffs, N.J.: Prentice Hall, 1976.

Eastman, Susan Tyler, Sydney Head, and Lewis Klein. *Broadcast Programming: Strategies for Winning Television and Radio Audiences*. Belmont, Calif.: Wadsworth, 1981.

Emerson, Richard. "Power-Dependence Relations." *American Sociological Review*, 27 (February 1962): 31–40.

Emery, Edwin. *The Press and America*, 3d ed. Englewood Cliffs, N.J.: Prentice Hall, 1972.

Emery, Edwin, and Michael Emery. *The Press and America*, 4th ed. Englewood Cliffs, N.J.: Prentice Hall, 1978.

Ettema, James S., and D. Charles Whitney, eds. *Individuals in Mass Media Organizations*, Beverly Hills, Calif.: Sage Publications, 1982.

Evan, William, *Organization Theory*. New York: John Wiley, 1976.

Faulkner, Robert "Hollywood Studio Musicians: Making It in the Los Angeles Film and Recording Industry." In *American Music: From Storyville to Woodstock*, edited by Charles Nanry. East Brunswick, N.J.: Transaction Books, 1972.

Fearing, Franklin, ed. "Mass Media: Content, Function, and Measurement." *The Journal of Social Issues* 3 (Summer 1947): 1–60. (Special Issue)

Felton, Bruce, and Mark Fowler. *Felton and Fowler's Best, Worst, and Most Unusual*. New York: Crowell, 1975.

Fischer, J. L. "The Sociophysychological Analysis of Folktales," *Current Anthropology* 4 (June 1963): 235–272.

Fishman, Mark. *Manufacturing the News*. Austin: University of Texas Press, 1980.

Fletcher, Andrews. *Conversation Concerning a Right Regulation of Government for the Common Good of Mankind [1703]*. In *Famous Quotations*, 13th ed, edited by John Bartlett, New York: Little Brown, 1970.

Flynn, Errol. *My Wicked, Wicked Ways*. New York: Putnam, 1959.

Friedrich, Otto. *Decline and Fall*. New York: Harper & Row, 1970.

Fullerton, Ronald. "Creating a Mass Book Market in Germany: The Story of the 'Colporteur Novel' 1870–1890." *Journal of Social History* 10 (Spring 1976): 265–283.

Gans, Herbert. "Letters to an Anchorman," *Journal of Communication* 27 (Summer 1977): 86–91.

———. *Deciding What's News.* New York: Vintage, 1979.

Garay, Ronald. "Access: Evolution of the Citizen Agreement," *Journal of Broadcasting* 22 (Winter 1978): 103.

Gelatt, Ronald. *The Fabulous Phonograph.* Philadelphia: J. B. Lippincott, 1955.

Geller, Henry. "Law Review: Putting the Lock on Cable," *Channels* 1 (December 1981–January 1982): 61–62.

Gerbner, George. "The Social Role of the Confession Magazine." *Social Problems*, 6 (Summer 1958): 29–40.

———. "Institutional Pressures Upon Mass Communicators." *The Sociological Review Monograph* 13 (1969): 205–248.

———. "Communication and Social Environment." *Scientific American*, 227 (September 1972): 153–160.

———. "Teacher Image in Mass Culture: Symbolic Functions in the 'Hidden Curriculum.' " In *Media and Symbols, Part I,* edited by David Olsen. Chicago: National Society for the Study of Education, 1974.

Gerbner, George, Larry Gross, Michael Morgan, and Nancy Signorielli. "The 'Mainstreaming' of America: Violence Profile No. 11." *Journal of Communication* 30 (Summer 1980): 10–29.

Giddens, Anthony. *The Class Structure of Advanced Societies.* London: Hutchinson, 1973.

Gilett, Charlie. *Sounds of the City.* New York: Outerbridge and Diestfrey, 1969.

———. *Making Tracks: Atlantic Records and the Growth of a Multi-Billion Dollar Industry.* New York: Dutton, 1974.

Gitlin, Todd, *The Whole World is Watching.* Berkeley: University of California Press, 1980.

Goldstein, Paul. *Changing the American Schoolbook.* Lexington, Mass.: D.C. Heath, 1978.

Gross, Michael. "The Hits Just Keep Coming," In *American Mass Media,* edited by Robert Atwan, Barry Orton, and William Vesterman. New York: Random House, 1978.

Gurevitch, Michael, Tony Bennett, James Curran, and Janet Woollacott, eds. *Culture, Society and the Media.* London: Methuen, 1982.

Hannan, Michael, and John Freeman. "The Population Ecology of Organizations." *American Journal of Sociology* 82 (March 1977): 926–964.

Harmon, Jim. *The Great Radio Heroes.* New York: Signet, 1967.

Haskel, Molly. *From Reverance to Rape: The Treatment of Women in the Movies.* New York: Holt, Rinehart, & Winston, 1974.

Heston, Charlton. "Actors as Union Men." In *The Movie Business,* edited by A. William Bleum and Jason Squire. New York: Hastings House, 1972.

Hirsch, Paul. "Processing Fads and Fashions." *American Journal of Sociology* 77 (January 1972): 639–659.

Hirsch, Paul, Peter Miller, and F. Gerald Kline, eds. *Strategies for Communication Research.* Beverly Hills, Calif.: Sage Publications, 1977.

Hynds, Ernest. *American Newspapers in the 1980s*. New York: Hastings House, 1975.

Jacobs, Lewis. *The Rise of the American Film*. New York: Teacher's College Press, 1968.

Jameson, Frederick. *The Political Unconscious*. Ithaca: Cornell University Press, 1982.

Janowitz, Morris. *The Community Press in an Urban Setting*. New York: The Free Press, 1952.

Johnson, C. "Dying is Not an Option." *Innovation* 18 (1970): 40–45.

Johnstone, John W. C., Edward Slawski, and William Bowman. *The News People*. Urbana: University of Illinois Press, 1976.

Jowett, Garth. *Film: The Democratic Art*. New York: Little Brown, 1976.

Jowett, Garth, and James Linton. *Movies as Mass Communication*. Beverly Hills, Calif.: Sage Publications, 1980.

Kaatz, Ronald. *CABLE: An Advertiser's Guide to the New Electronic Media*. Chicago: Crain Books, 1982.

Katz, Daniel, and Robert Kahn. *The Social Psychology of Organizing*. New York: John Wiley, 1966.

Kluckhohn, Clyde. "The Study of Culture." In *The Policy Sciences*, edited by D. Lerner and H. Lasswell. Stanford, Calif.: Standford University Press, 1951.

Knight, Arthur. *The Liveliest Art*. New York: Signet, 1958.

Koughan, Martin. "The State of the Revolution, 1982." *Channels* 1 (December 1981–January 1982): 23–27.

Krugman, Dean, and Leonard Reid. "The 'Public Interest' as Defined by FCC Policy Makers." *Journal of Broadcasting* 24 (Summer 1980): 381–399.

Leifer, Amy, Neal J. Gordon, and S. B. Graves. "Children's Television: More than Mere Entertainment." *Harvard Educational Review* 44 (May 1974): 213–244.

Leroy, David, and Wenmouth Williams, "Citizen Feedback: A Review of the Literature." Tallahassee: University of Florida Department of Communications, 1974.

Less, David, and Stan Berkowitz. *The Movie Business*. New York: Vintage, 1981.

Lewis, Felice Flannery. *Literature, Obscenity and Law*. Carbondale: Southern Illinois University Press, 1976.

Lieberman, Jethro K. *Free Speech, Free Press, and the Law*. New York: Lothrop, 1980.

Lucoff, Manny. "The Rise and Fall of the Third Rewrite." *Journal of Communication* 30 (Summer 1980): 47–53.

MacNeil, Robert. *The People Machine: The Influence of Television on American Politics*. New York: Harper & Row, 1968.

Maisel, Richard. "The Decline of Mass Media." *Public Opinon Quarterly* 37 (Summer 1973): 159–170.

Maltin, Leonard ed. *TV Movies*. New York: Signet, 1969.

———. *Of Mice and Magic*. New York: New American Library, 1980.

March, John, and Herbert Simon. *Organizations*. New York: John Wiley, 1958.

Marquis, D. "The Anatomy of Successful Innovation." In *Corporate Strategy and Product Innovation*, edited by R. Rothberg. New York: The Free Press, 1976.

McGuire, Bernadette, and David Leroy. "Audience Mail: Letters to a Broadcaster." *Journal of Communication* 27 (Summer 1977): 79–85.

McQuail, Dennis "Uncertainty about the Audience and the Organization of Mass Communication." *The Sociological Review Monograph* 13 (1968): 75–84.

Miller, Randall M., ed. *Ethnic Images in American Film and Television*. Philadelphia: The Balch Institute, 1978.

Mintz, Jerome. *Legends of the Hassidim*. Bloomington: Indiana University Press, 1968.

Mogel, Leonard, *The Magazine*. Englewood Cliffs, N.J.: Prentice Hall, 1979.

Molotch, Harvey, and Marilyn Lester. "Accidents, Scandals. and Routines: Resources for Insurgent Methodology." *The Insurgent Sociologist* 3 (Summer 1973): 1–11.

Molotch, Harvey, and Marilyn Lester. "Accidental News: The Great Oil Spill." *American Journal of Sociology*. 81 (September 1975): 235–260.

Montgomery, Kathryn. "Gay Activists and the Networks." *Journal of Communication* 31 (Summer 1981): 49–57.

Nadel, Mark. *The Politics of Consumer Protection*. New York: Bobbs Merrill, 1975.

Newcomb, Horace, and Robert Alley. "The Producer as Artists: Commercial Television." In *Individuals in Mass Media Organizations*, edited by J. Ettema and D. C. Whitney. Beverly Hills, Calif. Sage Publications, 1982.

Nye, Russell. *The Unembarrassed Muse*. New York: Dial Press, 1970.

Olien, Clarice, George Donahue, and Philip Tichenor. "The Community Editor's Power and the Reporting of Conflict." *Journalism Quarterly* 45 (Summer 1968): 243–252.

Orlov, Ann. "Demythologizing Scholarly Publishing." In Phillip Altbach and Shelia McVey (eds.), *Prespectives on Publishing, Annals of the American Academy of Political and Social Sciences*, Vol. 421, (September, 1975).

Page, Ann, and Donald Clelland. "The Kanawha County Textbook Controversy: A Study of the Politics of Life Style Concern." *Social Forces* 57 (September 1978): 268–278.

Pekurney, Robert. "Coping with Television Production." In *Individuals in Mass Media Organizations*, edited by Ettema and D. Whitney. Beverly Hills, Calif.: Sage Publications, 1982.

Pember, Don R. *Mass Media Law*. Dubuque, Iowa: William C. Brown, 1977.

Pennybacker, John "The Format Change Issue: *FCC* vs. *U.S. Court of Appeals*," *Journal of Broadcasting* 22 (Fall 1978): 411–428.

Perrow, C. *Complex Organizations*. Glenview, Ill.: Scott, Foresman, 1980.

Peterson, Richard, ed. *The Production of Culture*. Beverly Hills, Calif.: Sage Publications, 1976.

Peterson, Richard, and Charles Berger. "Cycles in Symbol Production: The Case of Popular Music." *American Sociological Review* 40 (April 1975): 158–173.

Peterson, Richard, and Howard White. "Elements of a Simplex Structure." *Urban Life* 10 (April 1980): 3–24.

Powers, Ron. *The News Business as Show Business*. New York: St. Martin's Press, 1977.

Reynolds, Quentin. *The Fiction Factory*. New York: Random House, 1955.

Riley, John, and Matilda Riley. "Mass Communication and the Social System." In *Sociology Today*, edited by Robert Merton, Leonard Broom, and L. S. Contrell, Jr. New York: Basic Books, 1959.

Rogers, E., and R. Rogers. *Communication in Organizations*. New York: The Free Press, 1976.

Sansweet, Stephen J. "Movie, TV Firms Building Alliances To Take Advantages of Home Video." *Wall Street Journal*, March 26, 1982.

Schiller, Dan. *Objectivity and the News: The Public and the Rise of Commercial Journalism*. Philadelphia: University of Pennsylvania Press, 1981.

Schlessinger, Philip. *Putting Reality Together*. London: Constable, 1978.

Schmidt, Fred. "The New Multimedia Environment." *Public Relations Journal* 34 (September 1978): 16–19.

Schudson, Michael. *Discovering the News: A Social History of American Newspapers*. New York: Basic Books, 1978.

Schwarzlose, Richard. *The American Wire Services*. New York: Arno Press, 1979.

Shaheen, Jack G. "The Arab Sterotype on Television." *The Link* 13 (April/May 1980): 1–14.

Shankman, Arnold. "Black Pride and Protest: The Amos 'n' Andy Crusade of 1931." *Journal of Popular Culture* 12 (Fall 1979): 236–253.

Siegel, Kalman. *Talking Back to the New York Times*. New York: Quadrangle Books, 1974.

Sklar, Robert. *Movie-Made America*. New York: Random House, 1975.

Smelser, Neil. *Theory of Collective Behavior*. New York: The Free Press, 1962.

Spencer, L., and A. Dale. "Integration and Regulation in Organizations: A Contextual Approach." *The Sociological Review* 27 (Winter 1980): 679–702.

Stedman, Raymond. *The Serials*. Norman: University of Oklahoma Press, 1977.

Steinberg, Harry. "The Porn Brokers." *New York Times Book Review*, 28 November 1976.

Sterling, Christopher. "Cable and Pay Television." In *Who Owns the Media*, edited by Benjamin M. Compaine White Plains, New York: Knowledge Industry Publications, 1979.

Sterling, Christopher, and Timothy Haight. *The Mass Media: Aspen Guide to Communication Industry Trends*. New York: Praeger, 1978.

Stevens, Gary. "Four Outstanding Moments in the History of Press Agentry." In *Publicity Forum*, edited by Gary Wagner. New York: Richard Weiner, 1977.

Stinchcombe, Arthur. "Bureaucratic and Craft Administration of Production: A Comparative Study." *Administrative Science* 4 (Winter 1959): 168–187.

Stokes, Geoffrey. *Starmaking Machinery*. New York: Vintage, 1976.

Tawa, Nicholas. "The Ways of Love in the Mid-Nineteenth Century American Song," *Journal of Popular Culture* 10 (Fall 1976): 337–351.

Tebbel, John. *A History of Book Publishing in America*, vol. 1. New York: Bowker, 1972.

Tebbel, John. *The Media in America*. New York: Crowell, 1974.

Thompson, Stith. *The Folktale*. New York: Holt, Rinehart & Winston, 1946.

Tichenor, Phillip, George Donahue, and Clarise Olien. *Community Conflict and the Press*. Beverly Hills, Calif.: Sage Publications, 1980.

Tuchman, Gaye. "Objectivity as Strategic Ritual." American Journal of Sociology 77 (January 1972): 660–679.

_____. "Making News by Doing Work: Routinizing the Unexpected." *American Journal of Sociology* 79 (July 1973): 110–131.

_____. *Making News: A Study in the Construction of Reality*. New York: Free

Press, 1978.

Tuchman, Gaye, Arlene Kaplan Daniels, and James Benet, eds. *Hearth and Home: Images of Women in the Mass Media.* New York: Oxford University Press, 1978.

Tunstall, Jeremy. *Journalists at Work.* London: Constable, 1971.

Turow, Joseph. "Talk Show Radio and Interpersonal Communication." *Journal of Broadcasting* 18 (Spring 1974): 171–179.

————. "Another View of Citizen Feedback to the Mass Media." *Public Opinions Quarterly* 41 (Winter 1977–78): 534–543.

————. "Casting For Television: The Anatomy of Social Typing." *Journal of Communication* 28 (Autumn 1978): 18–24.

————. *Getting Books to Children.* Chicago: American Library Association, 1979.

————. *Entertainment, Education, and the Hard Sell: Three Decades of Network Children's Television.* New York: Praeger, 1981.

————. "The Role of 'The Audience' in Publishing Children's Books." *Journal of Popular Culture* 16 (Fall 1982): 90–99.

————. "Unconventional Programs on Commercial Network Television." In *Mass Communicators in Context*, edited by D. Charles Whitney and James Ettema. Beverly Hills, Calif.: Sage Publications, 1982.

————. "Local TV: Producing Soft News." *Journal of Communication* 33 (Spring 1983): 111–123.

Wasko, Janet. *Movies and Money.* Norwood. N.J.: Ablex, 1982.

Weick, Karl. *The Social Psychology of Organizing.* Reading, Pa.: Addison-Wesley, 1979.

Welles, Chris. "The Numbers Magazines Live By." In *American Mass Media*, edited by Barry Orton and William Vesterman. New York: Random House, 1978.

Whiteside, Thomas. *The Blockbuster Complex.* Middletown, Conn.: Wesleyan University Press, 1981.

Willhelm, Sidney, and Gideon Sjoberg. "The Social Characteristics of Entertainers." *Social Forces* 37 (October 1958): 71–76.

Williams, Raymond. *Marxism and Literature* New York: Oxford University Press, 1977.

Woll, Allen L. "Hollywood's Good Neighbor Policy: The Latin Image in American Film, 1939–1946." *Journal of Popular Film* 3 (1974): 278–293.

Woods, L. E. "For Sex: See Librarian." *Library Journal* 103 (September 1978): 1561–1566.

Yuchtman, Ephraim, and Stanley Seashore. "A System Resource Approach to Organizational Effectiveness." *American Sociological Review* 32 (December 1967): 891–903.

L. A. Zurcher, G. K. Kirkpatrick, R. G. Cushing, and C. K. Bowman, "The Anti-Pronography Crusade: A Symbolic Crusade." *Social Problems* 19 (Fall 1971): 217–237.

Index